Unfold your wings

and watch life take off

Sketches by the author
Wallace Huey

A Life Discovered Publishing
www.alifediscovered.org

A Life Discovered Publishing
www.alifediscovered.org

Copyright © 2004 by Wallace Huey

Edited by Mary Winifred Hood
Cover design by g2 design
Text design by Jeff Schwaner

Wallace Huey has asserted his moral right to be identi-
fied as the author of this work in accordance with the
Copyright, Design and Patents Act 1988.

First published in Ireland in 2005.
ISBN 1-59457-582-7
Printed by Booksurge at different locations worldwide.
Printed on opaque acid free paper.

Distributed worldwide to the trade by:
www.booksurgedirect.com
RR Bowker's www.booksinprint.com
www.globalbooksinprint.com
www.whitaker.co.uk for UK orders
Baker and Taylor www.btol.com for USA orders

31/03/05.

This book is dedicated to all who are searching
for that elusive connection that will make their
life abundant and whole.

To you I offer the hand of friendship.

—Wallace Huey

To Mainud
with Love
Wallace.

Contents

Part 3
Your Healing—Autumn Reflections   157

Part 4
Your Rewards—Winter Tales   241

The Myth Of The Sacred Swan   243

Acknowledgements

I always considered writing to be a solitary affair. However, once I began Unfold Your Wings and Watch Life Take Off I realised as it progressed that I needed to share my work with people close to me. As a result, Unfold Your Wings and Watch Life Take Off is very much a group effort. Without the help of many friends, relatives and some friends I have yet to meet, who offered support, this book would not have been possible.

As this book and its associated website have progressed, I have received unwavering support from my wife Carolyn. Her devotion has helped keep me motivated and focused, her patience has been unwavering and her amazing creativity has helped my project become practical.

In the compilation of this book thanks are due to Paul Herd for being my confidant while writing was in progress. I am deeply grateful to my mother for her patient editing skills and words of advice once the first draft was complete, for her committed support throughout development and for help in editing the final draft. To Andrew McKibben and Pat Kerr for their advice and feedback on the first draft.

I would like to thank the many readers who helped develop the second draft, including Maggie Burch, Yvonne Blyth, Susan Cunningham, Dr. Joe Gaston and Alf Armstrong, with special thanks to Mark Murray for his perceptive observations. Further thanks are due to Niall Hickey, Mary Burke, Caroline Huey and Cecil Kavanagh who made many perceptive comments on the third draft. I would like to thank Michael Bell for the patient proof reading skills he applied to the fourth draft.

Finally I would like to thank other members of my family and many other people whose helpful comments and support have made this book possible.

A Letter To The Reader

www.alifediscovered.org
Dear Reader,

As I sit looking out of my office at the sun setting outside and my book almost complete, I feel drawn to reflect on why I have written Unfold Your Wings and Watch Life Take Off. It has been written because I want to share myself with you. Writing it has, on occasion, moved me to tears and opened up new levels of joy, peace and understanding. As a result the book has unfolded and evolved in its own time.

Writing Unfold Your Wings and Watch Life Take Off has helped me become clear about my inner guidance. Searching through my memory for examples to illustrate the points in the book has helped me come to terms with my past. With my past resolved and my inner guidance clear, I now feel ready to start my new life as a guide and coach to others.

I invite you to discover your inner guidance. There is no greater discovery. This calling, which resides in your heart, will change your life. If followed it will open up your potential, heal your wounded heart and bring you abundant rewards. Eventually, if followed most sincerely, you will discover your life's mission and your connection to all that was, is now and forever will be.

Yours sincerely,
Wallace Huey

A Swan on Hillsborough Lake

Deep within your heart is a calling.

It is very gentle
It is very loving.
It is very persistent.

Would you like to discover
Its purpose?

Introduction

It was a dry sunny day and our family was heading to the beach to have some fun. As we drove toward the Mourne Mountains we passed by a lake and I cried out,

"Please Mum, stop!"

I was only 8 years old and I had recognised something. We all climbed out of the car and stood on the lakeshore to see why I had stopped the car so abruptly. There in the distance, a swan floated on the shimmering lake; it was my first glimpse of a swan. I was captivated and wanted to get closer, but couldn't. Eventually the rest of the family became restless. We climbed back into the car and headed for the beach.

At school I was inattentive, dreamy and hyperactive. I had little inclination to study or do well in exams. Then, as I was about to embark on studies that would prepare me for university, I felt this strong urge to make something of my life. I resolved to be somebody— to achieve something—and became determined to qualify as an architect. I did not know it then, but this was the first early stirring of my inner call. I was expressing it in crude and discordant ways, but it was there. This deeply felt inner guidance was to carry me through university, and out into the world. As I stood on the steps of our home ready to start life as an independent adult at university, I turned to my mother and said with conviction, "I mean to reach the top."

I didn't.

Twenty-seven years later I found myself walking on the banks of Hillsborough Lake near my home. There on the lake was a solitary pure white swan. I was captivated. Recalling the event from my youth I felt drawn to remain with the swan all day. I was fascinated by her silence and beauty and the way she gracefully turned her head to watch everything that was happening. I could sense her power as I watched her unfolding and flapping her wings, while floating on the still, clear water. I wondered what it would be like to fly like a swan. She evoked something...or someone. That day was spent in silent communion. It was a day of profound inner peace.

What had happened in the intervening twenty-seven years to change me from restless, arrogant young man to a serene and peaceful adult?

That is the secret told within these pages.

The Radiant Swan Within

Being still I wait
For the swan on a forest lake at sunrise,
Whenever I need to be supported, loved and cared for.
Whenever I need a passage
Through the mists of my confusion and loneliness,

The call is always there.

No-friend ever loved me thus.
The call helps me glide serenely through life.
Its feather soft touch and serene presence,
Helping spread my wings to fly home,
Home to wholeness, home to peace, home to love.

I can glide on the still waters of eternity.
I can fly up to Heaven's gates and behold the wonders of earth.

Part 1

Your Calling

Your Calling introduces a vast untapped power ready to support and guide you. This power is your inner guidance.

"If today you hear his voice, harden not your hearts..."
—Psalm 95

Dawn

To the east a pink hue touches the horizon.

Mist hovers mysteriously over the still lake. Specks of grass float past with silken smoothness. A rich cacophony of birdsong fills the air.

A solitary, pure white swan glides gracefully over still water. She reaches upward to flap her majestic wings and settle once more into icy coldness. The swan turns and glides silently across the lake into mist, causing small ripples to fan outward on either side until they reach the bank.

Some ducks twist and turn playfully on the water's gently rippled surface. Other ducks glide in and out of a nearby reed bed.

Tiny white crystals of frost sit on long blades of grass that grow on the lakeshore.

An early morning group runs past. They are intent on arriving.

The sky is filled with powder blue light and half-light. In part of the sky the powder blue is masked by high cirrus cloud. Seagulls fly past, sometimes flapping, sometimes gliding, in the vast all encompassing space.

The swan is still now. She turns her small head in quick alert movements…watching.

Peace penetrates, like a silent blessing.

It is dawn.

Spring Reflections

Golden sun radiates soft light from a clear blue sky. The ground is clothed in a blanket of pure white snow that unites path and woodland. Behind bushes, a small delicate pagoda—its roof covered in a thick blanket of snow— protects wooden seats beneath. Then from inside the pagoda, a hypodermic needle is thrown over the bush, staining the pure, unsullied snow blood red.

Your Calling Is Inside

We live in a harsh, cruel world—a world of war, famine, poverty, environmental degradation, drug addiction and abuse of every kind. At a personal level our jobs are becoming ever more demanding, our marriages are under pressure, and we are fearful of the future society we are creating for our children.

In our unease we turn to advertised products, entertainment, self-help books, and gurus of every kind to fill the void and give direction and hope to our fractured lives—but it isn't working.

The call is inside.

The world is suffering because people are not listening to their calling. What is this calling? It is the call to love and to care and it comes from the heart. It is inside every one of us and it is inside you.

Envoi

Throughout the ages, down through the aeons of time,
Across the mists of space, the call has sounded.
The call speaks.
It speaks to the trees. It speaks to the stars.
It speaks to the clouds.
It speaks to the animals and it speaks to us.
For man is unique in nature's kingdom.
The call speaks to us personally
In the quiet whisperings of our heart.

The call is inside.

It is as precious as sunlight, as soft as a bird's feather,
And as loving as your mother's first kiss.
Please wake-up. Wake up to your true inheritance.
Wake up to your bountiful inner gift.

Green grass is emerging through pockmarks in the dank, sullied snow.
City streets are awash with ice-cold water and slush. Drops of rain wriggle
down the window pane as the wind howls and roars. Outside trees buckle
and flex in the chaos of the equinoxal gale.

Your Calling Can Be Hard To Hear
(amid all the hurly burley that goes on in your head)

Our calling can be hard to hear among the many thoughts and images
whirling in our minds. Inner guidance is not intellectual. It is not a
clever argument or astute questioning (although it may respond to astute
questioning from time to time). The call is from our whole being. Inner
guidance therefore is a feeling, an image or a thought, the slightest hint
of a direction or a suggestion. The call needs to be sensed, rather like
tuning our radio to a station that is difficult to receive. There can be lots
of crackle and interference.

How do we know the impressions we are receiving are from our being
and are guided from within? We know, because senses and directions
given to us from this source are suffused with peace and help us to grow
spiritually. With peace as our guide, we can be assured that these gentle
promptings will be both in our own highest interests as well as in the
highest interests of all those involved.

How can we best develop our ability to receive these gentle promptings? We need to cultivate silence, silence and still more silence. It is
nearly impossible to tune in to our being amid all the frantic activity that
passes for modern life—so to listen to inner guidance we need to cultivate periods of both outer and inner quiet. These periods will reveal the
gentle inner promptings of our heart.

This does not mean we have to become monks or hermits, although
sometimes we may wish to. What we need are some periods, however
infrequent, to stop and listen. Inner guidance is always there. It is our
best friend. I have made it my own life's purpose to fall in love with the
call. In time you may wish to do the same.

I remember the first time I consciously listened to my inner guidance—I was a 23-year-old architecture student in the fourth year of my
course at university. We had been given a very tough problem for archi-

tectural students to solve. Working in teams of four, we had been asked to design a complete extension to a city in England. This was a real project. We were being asked to use this project as a design exercise that would teach us town-planning skills.

In those days I was a rather supercilious young man and imagined I was a cut above the rest in terms of my design talents, since I thought I was a prize well worth having. I decided to hang back when the teams were being selected and wait for a team to pick me. I was asked to join a team of very good designers. I thought my number had come up! Now I was going to show them what I could do.

We had only ten weeks to complete the task including the design drawings, so there was no time for hanging around. I was sure I could lead the team well enough for us to get an A grade. I was proud of my abilities. At the first team meeting we set to work, but soon sensed that something was going seriously wrong. All four team members were headstrong—each one of us had great confidence in his own opinion and each was sure of he was right. As our opinions were often pulling in opposite directions, we fought and squabbled continually about whose ideas were best. I considered myself the best designer and of course preferred my ideas.

The result was a mixture of bitterness, recrimination and animosity. My dream of getting an A grade was turning into a shambles. At lunch-time one day I confided our group's problem to one of my close friends who was an architecture student in the same year doing the same project in another group. He admitted that his group had exactly the same problem. Interestingly I discovered that members of every design group were being antagonistic.

Time was running out. We began to get desperate. There were two weeks left to work on the project and we still had not produced a single design drawing. The closer we came to the deadline the harder we fought one another. I could feel the spectre of failure looming over the horizon. One morning I awoke and could not face going in to do battle yet another day.

I walked across my student bedroom. The late November frost was on the grass outside and cars were speeding by on the busy main road. Gazing absentmindedly at the early morning sun, as it hovered motionless above an indented red brick skyline, I admitted I was a beaten man and did not know how to solve the design problem with my team. I admitted I needed help. Falling silent, I began to listen to my feelings inside and began to sense what I needed to do.

My inner guidance revealed that I was worn out and I felt drawn to take care of myself. I knew I needed a break. Thoughts that were not my calling—thoughts motivated by fear—told me that if I took a break at this late stage in the project, the other members of my team would be very angry. I decided not to listen to these thoughts but instead listened to my inner guidance, which I knew was suffused in peace and had my best interests at heart. I took the break I needed.

That afternoon I wandered through the university campus. I was lost, simply walking, did not know why I was wandering. My intuition was suggesting that I walk around the campus and I was following its gentle inner promptings. I ambled through the science area, along the majestic paved pedestrian plaza, past the science library, up the grassy hill with its leafless birch trees towards the student's union.

Following the path behind the student's union, I wandered into the main university library, not really knowing why I was there, and stopped—transfixed. A book title simply jumped out at me. It was Carl Rogers' book On Becoming a Person.

I took the book down from the shelf and studied it. It contained information on interpersonal communication that helped me understand how to bring unity to our divided group. I took the book back to my bedroom and read it cover to cover in three days and found it contained exactly what I needed to know to have our team work together in harmony. I realized we were all working for our own ends and that we were not pulling together as a team because no one was working for the group. We were all being extraordinarily self-concerned.

After reading the book I resolved to return to my group armed with a new understanding and a bit more humility about the best role I could play in the creative process. I resolved to be the one person in the group who would work for the group and became committed to creating ideas that would link together other ideas put forward by group members.

Having been away for two days, I walked into the group meeting, to receive a barrage of abuse. I was accused of being a lazy layabout and was threatened with expulsion. I said nothing. In time the abuse ceased and we began work. As conflicts arose I acted as the peacemaker by creating linkages between different ideas. Immediately the atmosphere changed. The creativity began to flow. We had produced our first drawing by lunchtime. We all sensed something important was happening.

Over the course of the next two weeks an abundance of elegant drawings were mounted around the walls of our room. My friend walked in one day by mistake. He must have sensed the atmosphere of harmony and abundant creativity, because at lunchtime he asked me how our group was doing so well when all the others were in chaos. I tried to explain.

When the projects were handed in and assessed, our group came top of the class with the A grade I had always wanted, but achieved by a totally unforeseen approach. I was a changed person. Ever since then, I have always been able to bring harmony and unity to any group of people with whom I have been involved. All this happened because I listened to my inner guidance. This is the power of the inner call.

 UNFOLDING
YOUR WINGS

Next time you are discussing a difficult problem with a group of people, try being the facilitator. Give up your own particular viewpoint and focus instead on finding the viewpoint that unites all those present by becoming detached from the passions of the various arguments put forward. From this place of inner calm listen within for ideas you can contribute that knit together other people's disparate ideas. You may be surprised at the influence you wield when you start working for everyone else!

The above true story has all the ingredients for learning to hear inner guidance. There was an admission of my own inadequacy to deal with the situation. I became silent outwardly and inwardly. In that silence I listened for the gentle promptings from my being, like a beautiful radiant swan deep within. Finally I was able to discriminate between the gentle promptings suffused in peace given to me intuitively, and other unhealthy thoughts and feelings suffused in fear.

Envoi

I am so busy.
I am so concerned to achieve.
I am so pre-occupied.
I am so stressed.

No wonder I am deaf to the call.

You are always there, but I do not hear you.
But I can learn.

I can learn to be less busy.
I can learn to give up striving.
I can learn not to be so pre-occupied.
I can learn to relax.

I can learn to seek help from my calling.

When my mind is still I will hear.
When I take time to listen I will hear.
When I admit I need help I will hear.

There is no problem my calling cannot solve.
There is no confusion my calling cannot clarify.
There is no answer my calling cannot find.

I practice.
Being still, I learn to listen.

A mild gentle breeze moves through the park. People smoothly skirt the open tree-bound grass. An elderly couple ambles, allowing awareness. Points of tree-top melody sing out across open space. Light hangs on to the day. Gentleness, birdsong, lingering light, and a subtle pervasive awakening announce spring.

Your Calling Will Direct, Heal And Transform Your Life

Opening up to our calling is like the awakening of spring, it happens so gradually we are barely aware of it. All that is needed is for us to gently turn inward to hear our direction and guidance. People ask me, "How can I hear my calling?"

Our guidance comes from our heart and can be sensed when we are quiet and still. As we learn to tune in to our heart we become more aware of messages we receive from our whole being. Instead of striving to meet fixed deadlines, we learn just to be—and to trust. Guidance is formed from feelings, images and thoughts that arise within while in this state of being. Working together, these feelings, images and thoughts guide our actions and decisions. Giving rise to a range of inner faculties they direct, heal and transform our lives. These inner faculties include:

Intuition
An inner knowing and thought arises from this, sometimes expressed as "a gut feeling," "a feeling in my bones," "following my nose" or "a feeling in my waters."

Insight
A breakthrough in understanding, received from perception of the wholeness of life.

Dream
An aspiration we hold for our lives.

Creativity
A breakthrough in expression achieved by leaps of the imagination.

Conscience
A discomfort caused by misguided action.

Night-time Dream
A symbolic image or story, received while sleeping, which can support, or warn against a course of action.

Supernatural Guidance
A direct communication received from beings in the spiritual realm.

Taken together, these faculties represent the Spirit within Man, and lead us to discover our true selves—the Christ Within. These inner faculties have both masculine and feminine characteristics. We may feel guidance towards being determined and single minded—a masculine characteristic, while at the same time displaying flexibility and sensitivity—a feminine characteristic. These inner faculties are illustrated in this book, through my own life story.

Envoi

The call is so gentle.
The call is so soft.
The call is so determined.

The call is a feeling, an image or a thought.

Deep inside, I sense my calling.
Listen, and I find her there.
All I need to hear is silence.

My calling hints.
He hints at finding new directions for my life.
She hints at building true friendships.
It hints at being of service to others.
I nurture these hints, these subtle promptings.

As I nurture them, they grow.
They grow into actions.
These are the actions that will make us whole.
These are the actions that will transform the world.

A patch of light from the setting sun brightens the circular flowerbed. Small colourful flowers of yellow, violet, white and lavender sparkle in the sun's low slanting gentle rays. In this patch of sunlight a few tiny flies dart and hover above the flowers. A magpie pecks persistently on the nearby grass as petals dance in the gentle breeze.

Your Calling Can Be Checked

Our guidance is usually very gentle. We sense its presence through our feelings, images and thoughts. People often ask me, "How do I know if the feelings, images and thoughts I am having are from the call?" There are five ways we can tell if they are coming from inner guidance. I would like to share with you a major decision I made a few years ago and then use this as an example to illustrate how we can know if we are being guided from within.

When my wife Carolyn and I were courting, I lived in Belfast and she lived in Dublin 100 miles away. Since we were seriously exploring making a life together, we had to agree where to live. Was it to be Dublin or Belfast or somewhere else? This was not an easy decision as we had lives rooted in our respective cities. In our discussions about bringing our lives together we were both prepared to make compromises. I reflected privately on this question about where we should live, and sensed that it was right for me to move to Dublin. By offering to move to Dublin I felt I was offering a gift that would bring us closer together.

One summer's day, as we lay in long grass looking out across open fields on the edge of a hilltop wood, I offered to move to Dublin. I made the offer with the reservations that I would try living in Dublin with Carolyn for periods to see if I liked it, and that we would discuss the possibility of living in the countryside some day. My partner was overcome with emotion and shed a few tears. We realised that my decision was taking us closer to marriage and a shared life.

In making this decision I was guided by my insight, which revealed that it was better for the relationship if I moved from Belfast to Dublin, by my dreams which imagined a new attractive life together in Dublin, by my conscience which sent feelings of discomfort about asking Carolyn to move to Belfast, and by my intuition because I felt in my bones that

I wanted to move to Dublin. But how could I be sure this decision was guided from within and was the right decision?

UNFOLDING YOUR WINGS

If you are in doubt about your inner guidance on a particular issue, try moving in the direction you are considering in small steps. You can imagine making the decision and see how you feel, or you can make the decision provisionally or else with reservations. As you progress toward your goal, use the guidelines below to notice whether your guidance is supporting this new direction, or seeking to move you back to your original path or onto a new path.

Firstly, I felt enthusiastic at the prospect of living with Carolyn on a try-it-and-see basis in Dublin. There was a natural inner energy supporting this move. I could release the energy of this enthusiasm to sort out the many tasks that would need to be addressed before I could make life in Dublin with Carolyn a reality.

Secondly, as I imagined a life in Dublin with Carolyn, I felt at peace. Of course there were complications and some anxieties in making this decision. I would have to sell my house, leave my parents and two sisters and the many friends I had made over the years in Belfast. Although I knew I could take my Internet project with me, I would have to find work in Dublin. Despite all these complexities, I felt a deep inner peace when I considered making this decision.

Thirdly, I just knew it felt right for me to explore living in Dublin. There was an inner "knowingness" that persisted. I had the feeling that, whether or not it would work out for us in Dublin, I was taking the right course of action.

Fourthly, by moving to Dublin and creating a life with Carolyn, I would have to make many new friends, find work and carve out a life for myself in a strange city. As I contemplated making this move, I felt I had the persistence to see the adventure through because I had the patience to focus on building a new life by overcoming every obstacle one step at a time.

These are the four ways I used to know if my decisions and actions are guided from within. The decision or action is surrounded by feelings of enthusiasm, peace, knowingness, and patience.

Of course, before making a major decision I may wish to share the background to my decision with business colleagues or close friends and family. When I shared my wish to move to Dublin, and the background to this decision, with close friends and family members, they had some reservations as I had, but could see the value of making this move. Had they been dubious, I would have discussed matters extensively with them to discover the nature of their objections, before coming to my final decision.

Through sharing with people close to my heart who know me intimately I come to understand the nature of my decision, but I always rely on my inner guidance to make the decision, and do not follow others' opinions. Tuning into my inner guidance empowers me to act in a truly free and independent manner while taking into account the perspectives that other people offer.

Where we need the cooperation of others to fulfil a goal, for example within a marriage, or on a committee, we need to keep communication open and free-flowing by encouraging each person to freely share what is in their heart, until consensus about the way forward is reached, (see Your Healing From A Broken Relationship page 214).

Envoi

I listen.
I hear my calling.
But I doubt.
Is it really you?
Are these feelings, images and thoughts
Really from the Source of Life?
Can it be this simple to know my guide?

I listen to these gentle inner promptings.

Feelings of enthusiasm mean you are near.
Feelings of peace suggest you are with me.
Feelings of knowingness reveal your presence.
Feelings of patience have you by my side.

You are my loyal friend and ally.
To you I entrust my life.

The long straight path narrows and turns to skirt a mass of small elegant trees. These trees offer shade to the soil beneath. Shaded earth responds with small clumps of green-leafed plants bedecked with masses of tiny white flowers. Cascading leaves droop from the slender branches. On the outer edges of this copse, leaves dance to a passing breeze. Within all is still.

Your Calling Responds To Relaxation

Although the outer fringes of our lives may be a flurry of activity, by nurturing stillness within, we open to our inner guidance. At this still centre our loving nature is revealed. We are able to tune in to feelings and follow leads that come from our heart. The feelings we receive from the call come from The Source which is both personal and universal. This is marvellous news, as it means we can request guidance and develop our understanding.

So how can we use this guidance to bring love, creativity and healing into our lives? We can choose to nurture these inner promptings by drawing on the calming effect of relaxation, questions and contemplation.

TAKING FLIGHT
A Simple Relaxation Exercise

Why not try this the next time you are really frazzled? Find a quiet space where you are undisturbed. Sit in a comfortable chair and gently hold an existing problem from your life. Hold it so gently that you forget it is there. Just sit for a while and absorb the sounds in and around the room. Relax a little.

To deepen your relaxation start from your toes and systematically tense and release each set of muscles in your body. Starting with your toes, pull them in and tense the muscles in your left foot. Hold the tension for five to ten seconds. Let them relax. Do the same with your right foot. Next, tense the muscles in your lower left leg for five to ten seconds and then let them relax. Follow this with the right leg. Continue tensing and releasing each set of muscles, working your way up through your body. End with the muscles in your face.

Once all your muscles are relaxed become aware of your breathing. Notice your stomach and chest rise and fall with each breath. Stay alert and gradually slow your breathing and breathe naturally and deeply. Practising the above will help you to become more relaxed about life. You can enjoy being, instead of doing. We are human beings after all, not human doings!

While you are sitting quietly, do not be surprised if you become aware of gentle, loving feelings and notice ideas that form around these feelings in response to the problem you are gently holding. This is your inner guidance speaking to you! I am sure the ideas you receive from this source will be more relevant to the problems in your daily life and of a much higher quality than your normal frantic ideas. Such ideas don't just help you to cope, they help you to grow.

When we take the time to relax, we are more intuitive. Although on rare occasions our calling can speak with loud obvious thoughts, for the most part it speaks to us with quiet gentle promptings. That explains why we do not often hear our inner guidance. Our minds are simply too busy to notice. A busy mind cuts us off from our loving feelings and from the information being sent to us intuitively.

In today's frantic world, when people have problems they rush around and become increasingly stressed as they try to deal with and solve their many concerns. If only they knew that there is an inexhaustible source of knowledge, wisdom and understanding inside. By taking the time to relax we learn to hear inner guidance.

Envoi

Can I really relax?
Sitting comfortably I relax my body,
And I slow my breathing.

Slowly, slowly my mind quietens,
Slowly, slowly I begin to relax,

Slowly, slowly I become aware of my feelings.
In quiet and stillness the call speaks to me.

Branches of Scots Pines are swaying softly in the wind. The sky is milky blue interspersed with menacing grey cloud. The smell of impending rain hangs on the wind. A grey squirrel hops across the path, hesitates and climbs a hawthorn tree with reckless ease.

Your Calling Needs To Be Trusted

As we learn to tune into and trust our calling, we are able to live with reckless ease.   Learning to live with such grace needs finely tuned discrimination as to what is and is not inner guidance, gained from practice and experience. I have made many painful mistakes in learning to discern and then trust my calling. The temptation when I make a mistake is to close up and shrink from life. This is a perfectly natural reaction to failure, pain and stress. If we can learn to discriminate and trust inner guidance as a result of reflecting and learning from our mistakes, we will discover our potential, our lives will blossom and we will gain a quiet inner confidence.

When I was at architecture school I wanted to learn something significant from my time at university. My first two years at University were relatively uneventful. I had learned a little about design but had not learned much about life.

Then in my third year a new tutor joined the school. He was tall with a dignified look and fierce penetrating eyes that set him apart from the other tutors. I soon realised that he was a very able designer and an excellent tutor who had an awareness about life that others lacked. Through this awareness he seemed able to control what went on in the architecture school, even though he was neither a professor nor head of department. Over the next two years I came to admire him for his positive qualities, but chose to ignore the many small signals that suggested he had a darker side.

At the end of fourth year we were invited to choose a project for our design thesis. I had selected this teacher to be my personal tutor and had decided to design a crematorium. A short time into the yearlong project I called on my tutor for some help and guidance. When I told him about my wish to design a crematorium he said, "That's already been solved." He took down a book of designs and opened it at a crematorium explaining the significance of the symbolism as he did so. His explanation must have made a big impression because I left the room stunned. For the first time in my life the significance of death really hit home.

I wandered in a daze back to my flat where I proceeded to cry. I could not stop. The tears continued for three days. My flat mate had no idea what was happening to me, but I knew. I had accepted the inevitability of my own death. After this period of intense grieving I felt a new level of inner peace and contentment. I was amazed at my tutor's awareness and began to feel he was someone I could really trust.

When I visited him again he suggested that I do a cathedral as my design thesis instead of a crematorium. I was surprised. Did he really think that I, a mere architecture student, could design a cathedral? Then I made a big mistake. I decided to design the cathedral because my tutor felt it was a good idea. I trusted his judgement instead of my own gut feeling, which was suggesting I design a crematorium. I did not know it then, but I had just put myself in the power of a manipulative man.

I returned to my tutor and told him I had decided to design a cathedral. He was delighted.

"I have been interested in the cathedral as a design problem for a long time," he said. We started to meet regularly to advance the project. At the second of these meetings he began to stare at me intensely. Then to my surprise an energy wave came out of his forehead and went right through me. I felt as if the cobwebs were being cleaned out of my mind. When I objected to this treatment he said,

"Perhaps I should take the candle to you instead of the searchlight."

When I left the room I was full of energy and for the next few days could not settle to do my work. I felt compelled to visit his strange new home outside the city.

I visited him on Saturday. We worked together on putting the finishing touches to his unusual modern house. That evening we went for a drink, returning late in the evening. Around midnight his wife went upstairs to bed and I was left sitting beside this strange man with paranormal powers. He turned to me and made it obvious that he wanted some kind of intimate sexual contact. I refused to cooperate. He was annoyed and rose to go to bed asking, "You'll survive on your own?"

I spent a restless night in bed downstairs, had breakfast with the family in the morning and then left as soon as there was a bus back to my flat.

The following week I endeavoured to return to my studies but could not concentrate. How could I work on a cathedral design project with a tutor who wanted a homosexual relationship with me? How could I do the project without his help? I had only chosen it because he thought it was right for me. I was well into the final year and it was too late to change my project or tutor. If I failed this project, four years of study would be wasted. I was becoming very stressed because I was unable to see a way forward.

UNFOLDING YOUR WINGS

Remember to always follow inner guidance. It is good to listen to the views and perspectives of others around you. Being open to a variety of perspectives can help us understand our situation by stimulating insight. But if other people's advice runs counter to inner guidance it is best to have confidence in and be guided by your own intuition.

One afternoon I rang my mother in an agitated state of mind. The next day both my parents appeared at my door unexpectedly. They had sensed something was terribly wrong and had come from Ireland. I did not tell them what had happened, but did say that I could not cope with my studies. We decided to visit the tutor that evening.

At the meeting he denied suggesting I design a cathedral and we agreed that I should take a year away from university to recover. When we returned to my flat I still felt distressed and agitated. That night I awoke and as I opened my eyes saw a long dark tunnel with a light at the end. I rose from my bed and went out to the landing. I sat on the stairs in a completely disoriented state, not knowing who or where I was. Returning to bed I waited for daybreak.

The next morning I was still disorientated. My parents suggested I immediately return home with them to Belfast. I lay in the back of my father's estate car for the whole journey. Looking out the windows from my prone position at passing trees and clouds, I was unable to think or use my mind in any constructive way. On arrival in Belfast I had an emergency meeting with a psychiatrist, who immediately admitted me to a psychiatric hospital, where I was put on medication. I was not given the name of my condition because the doctors and my parents thought, in my fragile state, it would be too much of a shock. I had been diagnosed as having schizophrenia, a condition that was to haunt me for years.

Schizophrenia is a malfunction in brain chemistry triggered in some people by exposure to extreme levels of stress. The stress and pressure I experienced while in the company of this tutor had sparked the condition.

When I explained to the doctors my experience of the energy wave passing through me from the tutor's forehead, they considered it part of my breakdown and therefore a psychotic illusion. I am sure it was a real experience. It was different from any experience I have ever had. I have since read about the "third eye," an energy centre in the forehead that a few people have managed to activate, and now believe this was the source of the energy I experienced.

Once I recovered my mental faculties sufficiently to understand what had happened, I was very bitter and resentful. How dare that tutor prey on me! How dare he cause a devastating illness from which I would suffer for the rest of my life!

I felt my tutor had caused my breakdown and subsequent disability. As I reflected on the experience, I realised that I was the one who had chosen him as my tutor and I was the one who had chosen to become very stressed and feel trapped when he started to put pressure on me to do what he wanted. I had other options. I could have reported the tutor's inappropriate behaviour to my professor.

I eventually recovered well enough, with the help of the medication, to return to college. This time when it came to choosing my design thesis and tutor, I was more tuned in to my inner guidance and had learned through bitter experience to trust it more. I designed a crematorium and chose a gentle, caring, humble man as my tutor. These wise choices were instrumental in helping me pass my final year, even though I had a disability that made me vulnerable to stress. While there I avoided my old tutor.

My final year over, I left to enter the workplace, but I was not the person I had been. For the rest of my life I would have to learn, by trial and error, how to manage my medication and my stress levels so that I could lead a normal life. I could not escape the presence of my tutor. An invisible thread, woven from my bitterness and resentment, connected us. I was now a disabled person, and for a long time considered him to be the cause of this misfortune.

As time went by I managed to forgive my tutor. I saw him as he really was, a man with good qualities who was also selfish and misguided. I began to grow and mature as I understood the lessons in this misfortune. On reflection I realised that in choosing this tutor and deciding to design the cathedral, I was moving counter to my inner guidance. My maturity developed still further when I learned the spiritual lessons from living with disability.

Now, as I sit typing this, it is obvious that when misfortune befalls there are valuable spiritual lessons to be learned. Experiencing this setback and learning the lessons contained in it gave me much of the knowledge necessary to write this book. As I grew in wisdom I was able to find it in my heart to forgive my old tutor—the twisted cord of bitterness and resentment that had connected us all those years dissolved, and I was free.

UNFOLDING YOUR WINGS

When you experience suffering you will grow if you refuse to blame it on other people. Instead ask how you can improve your discernment. Improving your discernment will help you tune to inner guidance ever more precisely. As your ability to tune in improves you will discover that your guided life is providing protection from harm.

The great religions of the world, like Christianity, are in their essence about the spiritual journey and this inner call. This is the journey they teach, although it has somehow become lost in the mists of time. That is why Christianity places such a great emphasis on faith. What is meant is not blind faith, like the faith I had in my tutor, but faith in ourselves, in our inner guidance, intuitions, insights, dreams, creative ideas, conscience, in Christ Within and faith in a transcendent reality to which we can aspire.

So let us have faith. We can trust our guidance, the radiant inner swan that grants discernment, from all the hurly burley in our mind. Then we can choose to trust that guidance. We can test our intuitions, insights, dreams, creative ideas and conscience in the real world and see if they work. Ask yourself, is following my calling helping? Am I able to avoid harm? Am I becoming wiser, more loving and more peaceful? I invite you to experiment and find out.

Envoi

Although I have experienced suffering,
And my ability to trust has been shaken,
I realise that it is my lack of discernment
That has made me vulnerable.

Learning my lessons I become perceptive.
Learning my lessons I become wise.
Learning my lessons I become knowledgeable.
I am learning to tune to the inner call.

As I learn I grow
I grow in peace.
I grow in love.
I grow in wholeness.

And I discover I can trust anew with confidence.

Beside the curving path, a small grassy alcove shelters a diamond shaped bed. In the bed tall flowers grow, yellow and maroon. In the still air, hornets dart with quick alert movements between slender, colourful stems. Suddenly a butterfly appears, white wings picked out by strong sunlight as it flits playfully over this dense soft pond of colour. White wings pause on yellow, and flutter, disappearing behind a sheltering fir. The maroon and yellow flowers sway gently in a puff of wind. Who knows where the butterfly has gone?

Your Calling Responds To Questions

We can also develop our relationship with the call and receive more help, by learning to ask it questions. I practice asking direct questions relevant to my daily life. Questions like "Do people live on Mars?" are not likely to receive a meaningful response! It is also helpful to phrase the question well. "How can I apologise?" is not as good as, "How can I apologise to my boss for messing up the photocopier?" Be specific.

TAKING FLIGHT
An Exercise On Living With Questions

You will solve your problems more easily by not seeing them as big immovable objects. Learn instead how to stimulate inner guidance by holding problems in your life as questions. Living with questions frees you up and invites your inner call to speak. Always be ready to receive an answer. It can come at any time!

Do not hold the question in your mind. Hold it deep in your heart. To learn this, frame the question in your mind and then imagine it being taken down to your heart. Taking your question down to your heart will help prompt your guidance. Then listen for and nurture any feelings that emerge. Nurtured feelings turn into inspired thoughts!

At the present time I am considering moving 100 metres from my home where I have lived for the past 16 years, to a new apartment. I am gathering information and developing my feelings intuitively by living with the question, "How can I sell my own house, and is moving to the apartment right for me?"

As I wait for this question to be answered, I am also moving in the direction of selling my house and buying the apartment, without committing to either path until I know for sure that this is the right course of action.

Asking your inner guide questions can also be used along with relaxation, contemplation, talking and meditation. To do this, simply ask your question when your mind and heart are quiet while meditating, relaxing, contemplating or talking. Then leave it open to inner guidance to speak in its own time. Be ready to receive and then remember any new feelings, promptings or ideas. Remember, the call is always with us. Our guide is always there. This feeling gives profound security.

Envoi

I have a personal problem.
I ask a friend, but he knows not.
I ask my partner but she knows not.
I ask my parents but they know not.
I ask the call and it knows.

The answer comes, not with the
Booming voice of false authority,
But in a quiet inner knowing,
Formed in response to the question I hold deep in my heart.

Beneath giant trees grow shrubs. Beneath the shrubs grow leafy stalks. At the end of the stalks grow flowers. They hang like little lavender lanterns. Bees come here to play, each flower vibrating briefly when a bee lands. The tallest bells bob in the breeze as a puff of wind worms its way in from the west. The lanterns vary in shade from almost pure white to strong lavender. Sheltered from the wind, these delicate flowers sprinkle colour on dark green woodland. They quiver silently in the gentle breeze.

Your Calling Can Make You Quiver

Leading a guided life is challenging. At times we may quiver at the decisions we are being invited to make. We often wonder how to make difficult decisions, saying, "How do I know if the feelings, images and thoughts I am having are from my conscience?" We are confused between inner promptings coming from our conscience and feelings of guilt and fear based on our conditioning.

Some time ago I faced a difficult decision and was guided by my conscience. I had been receiving government disability benefit as I was living with schizophrenia, a handicap that prevented me working in a regular job. My disability was improving dramatically as I had been following my calling for years and was experiencing profound healing as a result. The government sent out a social worker to interview me and assess my current level of disability.

After interviewing me the social worker sent in her report. The authorities must have decided that I was now in much better health because they decided to take away two of the disability benefits that I was receiving. I now had only a very small amount on which to live, but was still unable to work in a regular job. I had only a small sum in the bank and became nervous about my financial situation. Then a family member put me in contact with a retired social worker who said she could help me have my benefits reinstated. I agreed to cooperate. We applied for and received the forms to re-apply for the two benefits. She helped me to fill in these forms in an exaggerated way.

When these forms were finished they were not an accurate representation of the truth. I was unhappy about the level of honesty in these forms and was reluctant to post them. I came under pressure from my family to do so and I relented. After posting the forms I very quickly felt a deep unease about what I had done. I could not settle. My sense of inner peace was disturbed. I felt this strong calling to cancel my application. This was my conscience at work.

I knew this was my conscience and not unmerited feelings of guilt, because I was also being guided by my insight. Through my insight I saw that extra benefits were offered to citizens who found domestic responsibilities troublesome and to people who had difficulty moving around outside the home. Although I had needed these benefits at one time, I was now well able to take care of myself and could move around freely. I saw, that because my health was improving, I no longer needed or deserved these extra benefits, and although I had less to live on, I would somehow be able to manage. I knew I had to trust my calling and that my financial future would be taken care of. Two days after posting the forms I wrote to the government department concerned and cancelled. As soon as I had posted the cancellation letter peace returned. This was another sign that my inner guidance was working through my conscience.

A few months later my mother had an interview with her financial advisors and decided as a result of their advice to give a sum of money to my four siblings and myself. I had trusted my calling and my financial needs for the coming year were met in an unexpected way.

With the help of our insight we can learn to discriminate feelings, images and thoughts coming from our conscience. Our insight will reveal which action is in the best interests of all concerned. In this case it was misguided to try and claim benefits that I could not secure without exaggerating the level of my disability. I could see that by doing this I was seeking to claim money from government funds that were not intended for me, and in doing so unjustly adding to the taxpayers' bill. I also became aware that I was ready for the challenge of greater self-reliance. My insight was revealing the best course of action for all concerned.

UNFOLDING
YOUR WINGS

Next time you feel your conscience and insight nudging you to take a certain action, why not experiment by taking the action inner guidance suggests? See if the result of your action works out for all concerned. Experiment on a small issue at first and as your confidence develops you can take actions your conscience prompts and your insight suggests on bigger issues as well. You will have more personal integrity because your intuitions, words and deeds will be one and the same. Consequently you will feel more at peace with yourself and the world.

If we have never sought to develop our insight then we may need to learn new skills of understanding to aid our discrimination. With a little practice, we can become certain when we are receiving feelings, images and thoughts from our conscience. When this happens our conscience becomes clear and can be trusted, even if we do quiver at some of the decisions we are being called to take!

Envoi

Some decisions are right,
But right decisions can be difficult.
How do I discriminate between right decisions
And decisions that are misguided?
My conscience and insight work together
To guide my actions.
These actions bring peace, harmony and justice
To a chaotic world.

The broad path reveals views of river and lawn. Further along overarching trees enclose, their cool embrace enveloping and sheltering. All around branches sing in the fresh spring breeze. This sheltered space, a place protected from wind and sun, has womb-like security.

Your Calling Responds To Contemplation

We can nurture security in our lives by taking time for contemplation. If we have a problem with a person or situation, we can learn to sense the answer. It is helpful to have a relaxed, undisturbed place for your contemplations. My favourite is a long walk up the river.

When I go upriver I walk along the Lagan Towpath. Before I enter the towpath I pass a small attractive shop. I usually go in and buy a few nice things to eat and drink. With my picnic complete I head up river to Moorlands Meadow, where I sit under a tree with my treat. After my picnic I lie with my back against the tree and contemplate the situation with which I am seeking guidance, by lovingly holding it in my awareness and allowing ideas, feelings and thoughts to form. Quite often I return from the walk with complete clarity about the way forward and the actions I need to take.

Through contemplation we are able to discern higher quality solutions and resolve dilemmas and problems. I recently visited the local DIY store to buy some shelves for my consulting room. In the store I was drawn to two different types of shelves. The first set of shelves was contained within a frame. These drew my eye because this frame would be able to hold my many books, without them sliding off the end of each shelf. The second set of shelves was more attractive with soft curves, but had an open-ended design, not apparently suitable for holding books in place. After standing in the shop contemplating this situation for an hour with my wife I received a wonderful insight. If I chose the attractive shelves and placed one above the other at just the right height, then the wooden brackets that supported the shelves would act as bookends. Now that I knew how to store my books securely I was happy to buy the more attractive shelves with confidence.

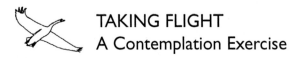

TAKING FLIGHT
A Contemplation Exercise

To contemplate a particular problem, lovingly and gently hold the situation in your awareness. Holding it in this way connects you to loving feelings in your heart. This helps you tune into your guidance. As you hold the situation, thoughts may form around the loving feelings created. This is your inner guidance at work. Watch the thoughts as they form and dissolve in your mind. Don't interfere. Simply observe. This is good for creative problem solving.

Quiet contemplation is particularly good for solving design or business related problems. Business managers please note, the typical business environment is very far removed from that best suited to quiet contemplation. Could this be one of the reasons so many executives suffer from stress? (See Your Calling Helps You Succeed At Work, page 73). We may have to contemplate a situation for a long time before it is resolved. This is often true with bigger decisions. When contemplating a major decision we need to be able to live with feelings of uncertainty and confusion for protracted periods. This can feel uncomfortable, but it is important not to try and relieve the discomfort by jumping at a decision before everything becomes clear.

I was considering how to design the website that accompanies this book. I designed three different design concepts, each one a development of the previous version. In my design work I would go through a period of intense creativity prior to forming each design idea, then see the flaws in my approach as I contemplated the solution. Seeing the flaws in my approach brought up feelings of uncertainty and confusion. I needed to be still and present for weeks, letting the confusion settle, before I felt drawn to embark on another period of creative exploration.

I was on holiday in Ballycastle when I suddenly received the idea of doing the home page as an illustration, using visual images from the Myth of the Sacred Swan, the mystical story at the end of this book. Soon after receiving inspiration, the fourth design concept fell into place.

I was completely happy with my fourth design and made the decision to place it on the internet.

Contemplation is also excellent for helping us resolve relationship problems. The key to successful relationships is to always act in loving ways. If we are holding negative feelings about our partner, this will separate us from our inner guidance and we may pursue misguided actions that we later regret. By lovingly holding the difficult situation I share with my partner quietly in my awareness, I am able to sense the best course of action, (see Your Healing From A Broken Relationship, page 214).

My wife and I were employing some men to cast a concrete step at our front door. Carolyn wanted a curving semi-circular step. I wanted a rectangular step with chamfered corners—this was because I wanted to tile the step myself at a later date and tiling a curving step was going to be very difficult. Carolyn and I discussed the problem and after taking time to contemplate our dilemma we received a wonderful insight. We decided to do a curving step. But instead of tiling the whole step at a later date, we bought a small number of small tiles that matched in with our front door, and asked the workmen to set them into the step in an attractive design when the concrete was still soft. The finished step looked wonderful. Through contemplation and discussion we had come to a decision where both our needs were met and we had created a better quality solution.

Envoi

When in disagreement with my partner,
I need the call to love and to care.

I hold my partner and her choices lovingly in my awareness.
I hold my partner and her choices privately in my awareness.
I hold my partner and her choices quietly in my awareness.

Slowly the call comes to me.
Slowly my thoughts change.

I see and understand her point of view.
She sees mine.
Then we receive a sudden insight and a breakthrough.
Where we felt confused, we now know clarity.
Where we felt separated, we now know marriage.

The water glistens in strong spring sunlight. A meadow of soft thick green, laced with spots of white, rests beside the stream. A hint of path slopes to visit flowing water between piles of neatly stacked brown logs. Large bubbles smoothly skirt small boulders, bump over rippling rapids and dissolve. A solitary bird calls out passionately from a nearby tree. From the dark depth of a deep pool small pieces of weed surface, and are carried effortlessly downstream.

Your Calling Transforms Fear Into Love

Thought emanating from fear is not inner guidance. Simply allow it to surface. Express it and it will leave us. We need to feel free to express our fears in any way our calling suggests. We can write down our fears and then burn them. Symbolizing our fears being consumed by fire in this way can rid us of them. We can confess our fears to a close friend who would understand. Fears can also be symbolized in drawings.

With high levels of fear we may wish to go into a forest and scream. I have done this myself and found it very therapeutic. Once I did a workshop in Scotland because, as a young man of 29, I was finding it difficult to make peace with my sexual desires. I received information about the workshop in Scotland and read it with interest and more than a little trepidation. In my quiet moments I felt called to attend this workshop. This desire came from my own need for healing, was suffused in peace and was intuitive. Thoughts emanating from fear that were not intuitive were telling me to run a million miles from such a workshop. I went to the workshop.

My insight was guiding me to be totally honest about my thoughts, feelings and inclinations around my sexual desires. I understood this was the only way I was going to receive healing. Being so honest about my sexual desires was going to be very difficult.

I flew from Belfast to Glasgow and then took the train all the way to a small village in northern Scotland where the workshop was to be held. I could feel the trepidation build with every mile the train travelled along its tracks. It was September, and the highlands of Scotland were extraordinarily beautiful.

I tried to distract my mind, which was doing somersaults, by gazing out the train window as we passed through the mountains and valleys. The mountains were covered in brown and purple heather. Occasionally dark clefts of bare rock broke through the heather carpet. Although I was suffering from nervousness, underneath I felt a strange almost transcendental calm. I knew I was taking the right course of action.

I arrived in the village in the afternoon. The warm welcome I received helped calm my frazzled nerves. I could sense I was in a healing place. I felt safe. The next day groups were formed to do the workshops. I happened to find myself in a group of five women! How could I confess my thoughts and feelings around my sexuality to five women? The fear and trepidation began to rise like never before. But beneath my fear the strange calm persisted. I realized there was no going back. It was all or nothing.

Over the next few days of the workshop I confessed some of my difficulties concerning my sexuality and my sexual desires. It was a difficult experience. One of the women, who was quite young, said some unpleasant things to me. The other women were so understanding and loving. At the end of the workshop I felt really healed.

On the last night each group was invited to do a short dramatic performance to convey the feelings the workshop had released. During the dramatic performance I rose from the floor and as I did gave a deep growling scream. The fear was starting to leave.

When I went home I could not settle. I felt this energy rising inside me. My intuition was prompting me to go into the woods and let it out. That is exactly what I did. I still remember standing in the woods at night howling for all I was worth. My sexual desires never troubled me to the same extent ever again. I had been released.

I have found that expressing fear helps it leave. This is necessary because our calling will lead us to activities and decisions that will bring our fears to the surface. In this way the call changes our fear into love. Ever since I have expressed and let go of these fears, I have had more loving and gentle feelings regarding my sexuality. As a result, since this workshop, I have been able to improve my relationships with women.

UNFOLDING YOUR WINGS

If you feel fear surfacing as a result of actions you want to take but are frightened of pursuing, try experimenting with letting the fear out. Find a private place where you can do this harmlessly. By expressing your fear in this way, you will find it easier to love yourself and to move your life forward.

We will learn the best and most appropriate ways to express our fears by listening to the feelings given by inner guidance. You might like to experiment by expressing your fear in different ways. (See Your Calling Is Elevated Through The Release Of Pain, page 66).

Envoi

Fear, you are an illusion.
Love, you are the only reality.
How can I know love when I am filled with fear?
When I am filled with fear, my reality is an illusion.
The call knows the cure.

With its gentle promptings my calling
Leads me right into the heart of fear.
If I never feel terror, I can never feel love.
Love rests on the other side of terror.
My journey to love is through terror.
The call...you are the signpost to my healing.
But am I a willing traveller?

The circular gazebo is surrounded with earthen beds of freshly pruned roses. Three gardeners stoop, bobbing up and down, moving from rose bush to rose bush, pruning. Only the gentle snip, snip of pruning scissors and bird-song break the quiet. An icy wind rustles tiny green leaves on the gazebo's climbing plants. The fresh, neatly prepared roses are waiting.

Your Calling Is Elevated Through Talking

We do not need to wait helplessly for our calling to reveal itself. We can prepare to receive inner guidance by elevating our heart through talking, meditation and the release of pain. As our heart is elevated and refined we become a clear conduit for guidance. Then The Great Universal Power is able and willing to express itself through us.

To converse is to communicate directly with the source of our calling—the Creator who is present everywhere. For talking to work, for it to be powerful, it must be simple and sincere. We can use conversation to help us become an open conduit for the call, and to ask for guidance on particular issues.

For talking to help us become an open conduit to our inner guide we need to ask the highest part of ourselves for changes and improvements in our character. We must ask for a pure heart. Conversation is very flexible. We can converse spontaneously in a corridor before an important meeting, while we are out walking our dog in the park, as a regular part of our life before going to bed or when we awaken. We need to make our conversation suit us. It is very important that when we talk we are sincere. Sincere conversation will reach the Source; insincere dialogue will fall well short.

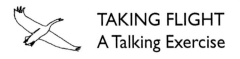

TAKING FLIGHT
A Talking Exercise

As you go about your daily life, try stopping occasionally to remember and talk to the most elevated part of yourself. Try trusting your calling. This will nurture a deep and profound security within.

If you are asking for a change in your character, you need to request help with all your needed changes and then do your best to implement these changes in your character as you go about your daily life. If you converse with sincerity you will notice that it will become much easier to bring about the changes you desire.

As your character improves and you attain higher levels of personal integrity you become increasingly sensitive to your calling. Improving your character refines your heart. A pure heart opens up a conduit to the inner call. With this clear channel you receive the grace and wisdom to lead an inspired life of worthwhile service.

When I ask for guidance (from what I have referred to as my inner swan) on a particular issue, I always request answers to problems that are either current or coming over the horizon. These are issues that are important to me in my life, are close to my heart and with which I want help from the call.

Before I wrote this book, I had withdrawn from the world. I was spending a lot of time peacefully in my own at home in Belfast. I was experiencing a level of contentment I had never known. After some time being peaceful at home, I felt I needed a project for my life in retreat. The peace surrounding this feeling suggested my inner guidance was at work. This was an issue that was coming over the horizon.

That night, before going to bed, I talked to the most elevated part of myself. I requested from my heart that I would receive a project that would help me reach people and touch their lives. The next day I was sitting quietly after a long period of meditation, when I sensed that I wanted to write. I fetched some paper and began to express the words and ideas that were arriving in my mind. This was the start of the book you are reading now. I know in writing this book, whenever I need help or inspiration, I can turn to my inner mentor. This gives me a great feeling of security. I also give thanks for the help and support I am receiving. That is the power of conversation when linked to inner guidance, the beautiful radiant swan within.

Envoi

I am alone.
I am lost.
I am confused.

Talking to the most elevated part of myself,
I tell of my confusion.
I cry out from my heart.
I feel loving feelings of connection.
I ask for help.
"Please bring me clarity that I may see the way forward.
Please give me the answers I need."

The morning stillness fills the room.
I sit quietly, listening to the ever-changing
Sounds of the city at daybreak.
When least expected, the answer comes.
I am not alone.
I am never alone.

A small flock of doves precision peck persistently. Their quick furtive movements are in sharp contrast to the stillness of the surrounding park. Jerkily they go about their gathering. One dove is still. He keeps lookout for his pecking companions. Someone passes. All doves stop and stand still. They are alert and ready. Strong sunlight bursts through cloud. One dove cautiously starts to peck. Gradually others join in. The single lookout continues cautiously.

Your Calling Speaks In Different Ways

Our calling is the optimum response. Guided actions seek out what we need to grow and are an inner response to changes within and to a changing environment. Therefore we need to be constantly on the lookout, ready to hear at any moment. Communications received may range from the soft and subtle, to the direct and overwhelming.

We need to be alert and ready to hear inner prompting because inner guidance usually communicates in soft and delicate ways. I was recently contemplating selling my house and moving to an apartment close by. This apartment was slightly farther upriver from my house and had almost exactly the same attractive river views. When I visited the apartment I felt that this could be my home. I was attracted by its tidy, clean appearance.

There would be many advantages in moving to the apartment. It would need less maintenance than my old terrace house and would be more secure, an advantage when I am away on long trips to Dublin. My mind was convinced of the benefits of the move, so I waited to see if my heart would engage and I would receive the call to move. I sensed that it was right for me to smarten up my existing home with a view to selling it. So I started to paint the outside of my house. This was an activity I was definitely being called to pursue.

I worked for eight weeks painting my house and throwing out a lot of rubbish that had collected over the years. As I did this I was still unsure what my calling was saying. After two months' work I had a clean, fresh home, but I still hesitated to place it on the open market and was not being drawn to place a bid for the apartment. Then I heard that the apartment had been let and I had missed my opportunity. I was not disappointed, as you might expect; I was delighted. I felt that I was making a new start in my fresh, tidy house.

A few weeks later I discovered that the prices for apartments were at an all time high and that a number of large new developments of apartments were coming on the market. As a consequence the prices people were asking for apartments were now somewhat inflated. I discovered it was wise to wait because prices would almost certainly fall. This was unknown to me when I was considering buying the apartment.

Using my insight I came to the conclusion that I was really being called to tidy up my life and make a clean, fresh start. This did not necessarily mean I had to move house. I continued to tidy up my life now that it was clear what I was being called to do.

Although our calling usually speaks in subtle ways, it can on occasion speak with loud unmistakable authority. This has happened to me a few times in my life. I have found definite, strong communication to be significant and life-changing. I have received this type of communication after periods of quiet withdrawal. That is how I received the inspiration to write this book and create A Life Discovered (www.alifediscovered.org), the book's supporting website.

UNFOLDING YOUR WINGS

If you would like to gain inspiration for the way forward in your life, consider a period of quiet withdrawal, meditation and contemplation. You could rent a cottage in the country for a week or two and take time to be alone. Do not be tempted to fill this retreat space with busy-ness. Instead, open up to your solitude. If you wish, engage in simple tasks, like gardening, for part of the day. Do not work at finding answers. Instead live with the questions that interest you and simply trust that insight, understanding and inspiration will emerge in their own time.

I was on retreat some months ago. Before I felt called to withdraw, I was struggling with how to write the last chapter of this book. I did not know how to communicate the rewards of living by your calling. I had already written the last chapter twice and scrapped it. Towards the end of my retreat I received powerful inspiration to write the last chapter as a myth set in ancient Celtic Ireland. Once I could see how to approach the final chapter, writing it was easy. When I asked a few friends to read the last chapter, they loved it.

I have had other powerful visions to do with my life while on retreat which are deeply meaningful, but at this point in time it feels right to keep them private. You do not need to be on retreat to experience a powerful calling. Mother Teresa received her calling to live and work among the world's poor while sitting on a train. If you nurture communication with the most elevated part of yourself and endeavour to refine your heart you can receive such life-changing inspiration at any time.

Envoi

I long to know my life's purpose.
By being still,
By listening within,
By learning to communicate with
The most elevated part of myself,
By developing my character,
By aligning my thoughts, words and deeds,
I am Being Prepared.

Then from nowhere I receive powerful inspiration.
I have discovered my life's purpose,
It is more than I could ever have hoped
And I am deeply grateful.

With you as my guide I can journey in harmony and in love.

You cost nothing and yet you bring great wealth.
You demand nothing and yet you attract my cooperation.
You need nothing and yet you give so much.

A thick tall hedge of tiny needle-like leaves, shelters the herbaceous border. Swirling puffs of wind enter between nearby trees and flow along the high hedge. Tall slender stems sense the wind's invisible dance, each red flower head rocking rhythmically to even the gentlest puff. Bees busily buzz between nearby stems of tiny lavender flowers. Each slender stem bends slightly and vibrates in response to the bees' gentle touch.

Your Calling Is Elevated Through Meditation

Meditation touches us in a deeply profound way. It is very effective in helping us purify our heart and sense our calling. Silence outwardly and inwardly helps open a conduit to inner guidance. This silence is the place from where all creativity, right action, clarity and inspired thought emanate. By meditating on our hearts, we become more sensitive to Being. Inner and outer quiet helps us know.

To be in silence is totally fulfilling.

Through meditation we develop a quiet mind. As our mind quietens we become much more aware of the world around us. We see buds form in spring, feel dusty earth beneath our feet in summer, smell fallen leaves in autumn and hear wind blowing through trees in winter, a state of being similar to that of children. We also become more aware of our inner world—our thoughts, feelings, moods, and emotions. Messages from our body are noticed more easily. Through meditation we come to realise that we are not our thoughts, feelings, emotions, moods or body. We discover that we are the one who watches our inner and outer world. The mind is transcended. We become aware. When we are aware we always know exactly what to do and how to behave. We lead a life guided from our silent inner essence.

To discover a degree of inner silence I invite you to try the simple heart meditation below. As you practice this technique begin initially by consciously focusing on the method. If your attention wavers or you become distracted, simply return to the technique. Meditation begins with attention to the method. After a period of practice you may no longer need to focus on the method. You may feel able to drop the method and be left with pure attention. At this point your meditation experience will feel effortless. This happens when our focus is unwavering.

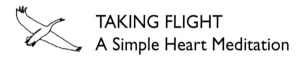

TAKING FLIGHT
A Simple Heart Meditation

To meditate on your heart, find a quiet place where you will be undisturbed and sit in a comfortable chair, fairly upright so you won't be tempted to fall asleep! Make sure your muscles are relaxed. Let your awareness centre on your heart. (This is located at the top of your rib cage, where the two wings of your rib cage meet, in the hollow at the centre of the chest.) Let your eyes rest gently. It is best if your eyes are held half open.

Breathe naturally and slowly through your nose, with your awareness centred on your heart. Withdraw awareness from your five senses. As you breathe in, feel that you are drawing in pure energy and as you breathe out, feel as if you are letting go of all restlessness. Now you are meditating. You should be experiencing a state of relaxed awareness. Stay in the meditation for five minutes then gradually and slowly return your awareness to the room.

You can practice this daily. In the morning before breakfast is a good time. Between 6am and 7am is the best time to have a deep meditation, because nature is still asleep and everything is quiet. You can gradually build up your commitment by adding a second meditation period in the day. Evening before tea, or just before going to bed are suitable times. You can gradually lengthen your meditation to 10, 20 and then 30 minutes.

Techniques you can add to improve your meditation:

Light A Candle

Before you start meditation light a candle and place it straight ahead of your sitting position. This creates atmosphere. I associate the candle flame with the light, wisdom and security brought to me through the inner call. Remembering the symbolism of the candle flame helps prepare me for meditation.

Wrap Yourself In A Shawl Or Blanket
This will help you feel comfortable and protected as you enter meditation. If you live in a cold climate it will also help keep you warm.

Feel Grateful And Joyful
Before you start meditating and while in your meditation try and feel an inner gratitude and inner joy. This is your true nature, even if you do not feel it much at present. Consciously feeling inner gratitude and joy while meditating will help you absorb the beneficial effects of your meditation.

Consciously Relax All Your Muscles
Start at the toes and one by one tighten and then relax each of your muscles finishing with your facial muscles. Do this before you start your meditation. This is very appropriate for people who come to their meditation in a tense agitated state. Practicing this will help you enter into meditation.

Let Your Eyelids Half-Close
While entering the meditation let your eyelids close slightly and hold them half-closed throughout the meditation. This helps you enter and stay in the meditative state. This state is different from your waking consciousness that you feel when your eyes are open and your sleeping consciousness that you feel when your eyes are closed.

Count To Twenty
Just after starting meditation, count to twenty or another suitable number, with awareness. As you do so feel your meditation deepening. This will help reduce thinking and allow you to embrace meditation.

Breathe Slowly
While in your meditation, practice breathing as slowly as possible through your nose without straining. Slow, rhythmical breathing is a powerful aid to deep meditation. Be sure to fill your lower lungs first. It helps to pause between breathing in and breathing out. In your meditation it helps to purify your heart by feeling that you are breathing in

pure energy and breathing out all restlessness. This needs to be done consciously to be effective.

Imagine A Flower Opening

When you have centred your awareness on your heart, imagine a flower opening. Allow it to open once, one petal at a time, in rhythm with your breathing. When it is fully open imagine you are that beautiful rose or sunflower. Imagine you have blossomed and you can even smell the scent. This will help open your heart. Then proceed with the next part of your meditation.

Imagine An Enlightened Person

While in your meditation hold the image of an enlightened spiritual person of great significance to you, like your favourite saint, Jesus, or Moses in your heart. This will help your aspiration and draw their meditative qualities to you.

Repeat A Sacred Or Inspirational Word

Inwardly and silently repeat a word that is personally significant and represents a quality you want in your life. Such a word might be Love or Peace. Repeat it in rhythm with your breathing. To deepen your meditation, remain focused on this word as you repeat it more softy until the word is barely present. Allow a place of infinite love and peace to fill your heart.

Alternate Imagining An Enlightened Person And Repeating An Inspirational Word

If you are a beginner and if you are having problems keeping your attention focused within while meditating, try imagining an enlightened person and then when your attention begins to wander switch to repeating an inspirational word. If your attention wanders again while repeating an inspirational word, switch back to imagining an enlightened person. This is a technique beginners can use to help keep their attention focused within during their meditation.

Imagine A Flame In Your Heart

While in your meditation imagine a flame, like a golden candle flame, in your heart. Imagining a flame is very effective in helping open your heart.

Imagine Journeying To The Depths Of The Ocean

While meditating imagine you are going deeper and deeper into your heart. Try and sense a place of great depth and stillness, like the bottom of the ocean. Alternatively try and sense an inner vibration where you are totally at One. This will take you into the depth of Being, the source of your inner call.

Imagine Yourself Connecting To Friends And Enemies

While meditating imagine that you are radiating white light that connects you with family members, friends and even enemies. Then imagine this light spreading out even further until it reaches the farthest horizon. Seek a place of inner vastness and perhaps even sense infinity.

Drop The Method!

Once if you reach a place of total inner peace (this will take practice), drop the method and simply remain in that place of total rest until your meditation is complete. This place of total inner silence is completely fulfilling. Let yourself discover infinity!

Come Out Slowly

End your meditation very slowly. To do this, open your eyes slowly and then practise gradually turning your head to look around the room while keeping your awareness centred in your heart. Take five to ten minutes to come out of the meditation. Slowly emerging from meditation is a pleasant feeling. Practicing this helps take the calmness of the meditative state into your everyday consciousness.

Engage In Quiet Simple Activity After Meditation

If you rush back into your day after completing your session you may not absorb the benefits of your meditation. Leave 10 minutes after your meditation where you engage in simple quiet activity, like sitting still, reading an inspirational book, listening to uplifting music or quietly tidying the house.

Have Regular Daily Practice Times
Practicing at the same times every day will deepen your meditation. To be effective meditation needs to be practised daily.

Create A Meditation Space
If you create a private place to practice meditation this will help deepen your meditation, since that space will absorb the peace of your previous meditations and come to feel sacred. To decorate your private meditation space you can have a small table. If you belong to a particular religion you can place symbols from that religion that are meaningful to you on your table. Alternatively you can place symbols and images of people and places that inspire you.

Take Regular Exercise
Cycling, swimming, walking or jogging regularly will all help deepen your meditation.

Get Your Hands Dirty!
Doing things with the earth like gardening or woodland work will help deepen your meditation.

Things To Avoid While Meditating

Thinking
While you are meditating, your awareness should rest on your heart where inner peace is found, not on your mind, which is full of agitated thoughts. If you are having problems thinking too much while meditating, imagine taking the thoughts down to your heart. This will reduce their power to disturb you or will help them to disappear. It takes a lot of practice to cease having thoughts altogether while meditating. Your first aim should be to observe your thoughts as they pass through. By practicing detached observation, you are able to stay focused in meditation.

Distractions

Maybe you have an itchy nose or there may be a noisy car outside. Scratch your nose if you need to, but it is best to be aware of the distraction without reacting to it. Practicing this will assist your detachment.

Eating Before Or Immediately After Meditating

If you eat shortly before meditating you will find it more difficult to meditate. This is because your body is busy digesting your meal and it is not as easy for you to relax. If you are hungry before meditating, drink a glass of fruit juice. This will not affect your meditation. Try and leave 15 minutes free from eating after meditating. Eating straight after meditation makes it more difficult for you to absorb the beneficial effects of your meditation session.

Meditating For Too Long A Period

This is especially true if you are new to meditation. Do not be tempted to think that plunging in and practicing for long periods will be to your benefit. You will only make yourself unbalanced. It is good to extend the time you spend meditating but you need to do so gradually.

Placing Your Awareness In The Wrong Place

If you are doing heart meditations the correct position for your awareness is the heart. If you meditate with your awareness in other places without proper training you might feel unwell and unbalanced.

Leading A Frantic Lifestyle

Very high levels of daily stimulation will detract from your meditation. The daily practise of meditation will help you get on top of a stressful job or family commitments. A frantic lifestyle is to be avoided.

Drinking Too Much Tea, Coffee Or Alcohol Or Smoking Cigarettes

Any drinks with caffeine, or alcohol, or produces like cigarettes that contain nicotine, detract from your meditation. It is best not to drink or smoke these in the period before or after your meditation. You may wish to avoid these products altogether. Meditation takes us into our still, silent essence, where abiding inner peace is found. Products that dilute mental purity will make it harder for you to enter a state of deep meditation.

You can gradually enrich your meditation experience using the above methods. I have suggested a more advanced meditation below, made up from some of the above techniques. Feel free to develop and make up your own meditation experience from the above techniques. Follow what feels right for you.

TAKING FLIGHT
Using The Above Techniques
To Form A More Advanced Meditation

Light a scented candle. Call in feelings of gratitude and joy. Half close your eyes, letting them rest on the candle flame ahead. Let your awareness descend to your heart. Breathe ever more slowly, counting from one to twenty with each breath. With each in breath imagine pure energy flowing into your heart. With each out breath imagine all restlessness leaving your heart. Stay with this experience for a while. Imagine a beautiful rose opening in your heart one petal at a time in rhythm with your breathing. Feel the fullness of the opened flower. Smell the scent. Stay with this experience for a while. Repeat silently and inwardly the word P...E...A...C...E. Allow this word to resonate within your heart ever more softly. Sense a deep inner peace as you do this. Stay with this experience. Slowly emerge from the meditation after 20 minutes and gradually look around the room. Take 5 minutes to sit in silence and 10 minutes to listen to some uplifting music.

Meditation Is Like Learning To Ride A Bicycle

Do you remember when you learned to ride a bicycle? At the start you had to consciously work at finding your balance and operating the controls. Then one day to your surprise everything clicked and riding your bicycle became easy and natural. Learning meditation is a bit like this. At the start you will have to consciously work at developing the meditation skill by learning to focus on your chosen method again and again. Then one day you may find that it suddenly becomes effortless. If this does not happen do not be concerned. You will still benefit, even though you are working at meditation.

How You Can Tell If You Have Had A Good Meditation

If you have meditated correctly you will feel calm afterwards. You will feel energised and renewed. You will feel balanced and loving. If you are experienced and you have had a very good meditation, you may feel that your body has become light. You will almost feel that you can fly. Afterwards you will feel delight and joy as if someone has given you a beautiful gift. You may also feel positive and dynamic, as if you have some important work to do.

If you are feeling unbalanced it probably means you are moving ahead too quickly with your meditation. To cure this, take a break from meditation for a week or so and then return to your daily practice, but meditate for a shorter period of time than before.

Meditation May Bring up Your Pain

You may notice after meditating that you have unexplained fear or anger that surfaces from deep inside you. This happens because meditation brings up your buried emotional pain to be healed. Simply express the pain and it will leave you. Although this is a difficult aspect of meditation, you can be assured that it is by expressing your buried emotional pain that you will reach new and deeper levels of peace and become more sensitive to inner guidance, (See Your Calling Is Elevated Through The Release of Pain, page 66).

Enjoy experimenting with the above techniques for improving your meditation. Different techniques may suit you at different stages of growth through meditation. Feel free to adapt these techniques to suit your personal needs. It is easily possible to teach yourself meditation. Simply sense what does and does not work for you. Bear in mind that some of the above techniques need practice to become familiar. To learn you will need to persist until you get the knack of meditation and gain the peace it offers.

It is important to have a daily discipline of meditation so that you receive benefits. The best policy is to do it every day at the same time, whether you are in the mood or not, just like cleaning your teeth, unless your intuition guides you otherwise. With time the discipline of meditation becomes easy and enjoyable.

Meditation works slowly but surely. In the short term it may give you a period once or twice a day when you feel really relaxed. As months go by you may notice a calmness descending and you may also find it easier to discern feelings and impressions you are receiving from inner guidance throughout the day. If you wish to explore tuning into inner guidance, sit quietly after your meditation and become aware of feelings, images and thoughts. If you want to focus your feelings, images and thoughts on a particular subject, ask a question inwardly.

By watching our mind, not only during our sitting meditation, but also during the day, we become more aware of our anxieties and fears and discover how these cause us to react in habitual, unconscious ways to the world around us. As we continue to watch our mind working, the one who watches grows in strength, and the power fear and anxiety have over us weakens. We become adept at distinguishing between inner guidance, which comes from a place of peace, and fearful, anxious, negative and unbalanced thoughts. Eventually a day may come when the separation between the watcher and the thing watched disappears. When this happens we discover enlightenment, a state of unity and absolute peace beyond the confines of the mind.

Envoi

As I meditate I drop down into a deep inner world,
Where all is still and all is peaceful.
Akin to floating motionless at the bottom of the ocean
Where thoughts are like fish,
They pass silently by, leaving no trace.

I am Being, the source of my inner calling.

Trees, bushes and shrubs enclose the small grass-covered square. This place is a haven from the surrounding traffic and bustle. Others sense this. People gather to sit. Doves flock to graze. The spacious grass lawn has green and brown shades and is peppered with white daisies. Starlings energetically turn, climb and swoop in the sky above. All around are the growling mechanical sounds of a city at work.

Your Calling Can Increase Creativity Many Thousand Fold

In today's bustling, fast changing world, it is more important than ever to draw on our innate creativity to help us find new job opportunities, create new businesses, master new techniques and methods, and nurture new relationships. Whether you are an artist, businessperson, scientist, government employee, charity worker or politician, inner guidance can really help you with your work. That is because the call comes from an amazing source—the same source as created the stars, the clouds, the trees and the animals—the source that created you!

So whatever your problem you can listen within for an answer. You may feel your problems are huge. Maybe you have a very responsible job and you feel beset by difficulties. Your creative sense can easily solve these problems.

I remember in 1993, when I was working as a volunteer at Oxfam, (a leading charity in the UK for assisting developing countries), I felt strongly drawn to create a project for a developing country. I did not have a country in mind but I knew that if I could raise a large sum of money the project would soon appear. So I had to find a way of raising a significant amount of money without drawing on Oxfam's staff time or resources. Here was a task I really cared about, but what could I do?

I turned to the call.

That evening I went home early. As I cycled through the wet city streets, I reflected on the task ahead. How could I go about raising a large amount of money for Oxfam? I simply did not know. It was raining. The streets were busy with commuters returning from work. As I cycled up Botanic Avenue I could see people scurrying in and out of the many coffee bars, restaurants and hotels. I cycled on up the hill and into Botanic Gardens. It was autumn. The park was resplendent in gold, brown and the kind of rustic red only found at this time of year. I felt a curious potential, as if something significant just might be possible, although I had no idea what.

After tea that evening, I retired to my office upstairs. The room was filled with the clutter associated with my everyday paperwork. I sat in my favourite chair. The clock on the wall was ticking in a regular soothing rhythm as the seconds passed by. I fell silent. I held my intension to raise money for Oxfam lovingly in my heart. I began to listen to my calling.

Initially nothing happened. Then as I continued to listen, I received the feeling that we needed help. I received the feeling that we needed a lot of help. I stayed with this feeling, not trying to change it, or alter it in any way. I simply allowed the feeling to grow and develop.

Then ideas began to form around the feeling. In my mind's eye a galaxy of ideas were swirling half formed, like a giant kaleidoscope. I simply watched as they formed, grew and died. I seemed to be drawing on my whole life experience for inspiration.

Then out of the mists of memory something began to consolidate and take shape—the milkmen of Northern Ireland! In Northern Ireland, as in the rest of the UK, milkmen deliver milk fresh every morning to family doorsteps. They visited hundreds of thousands of homes in Northern Ireland every morning. I remembered that they had run a Christmas appeal by collecting tins of food and shipping them to Eastern Europe. Could this be the help we needed? I resolved to act on my idea.

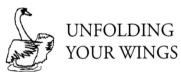

UNFOLDING YOUR WINGS

When presented with a difficult problem that is hard to solve, try retreating to a quiet place where you can relax free from interruption. Hold the problem as a question deep in your heart. Then listen within and notice any feelings, images or thoughts that form in your being. Imagine you are like a giant radio telescope dish, ready to receive even the faintest impression or piece of information. Do not judge or assess the incoming information, simply let the feelings, images and thoughts speak to you in their own way.

A few days later I was sitting in a neat house in East Belfast with the Chairman of the Milkmen's Association. He had a very pleasant manner and received me graciously. He was sympathetic to our need and wanted to help, but he was adamant that the milkmen would not handle money. It was simply too big a security risk. I was left to go away and think of how the appeal might work without handling any money. This had to be an appeal without money! I was stumped.

In the meantime I talked to Oxfam's director in Northern Ireland about finding a suitable project for the appeal. She contacted Oxfam's head office in Oxford where they told us about a refugee crisis on the border of Zaire. A number of families had crossed the border in fear of their lives and were marooned at a railway station. They were starving and in distress.

The media were not picking up the event or the number of people involved; it seemed that many thousands of victims were not enough for a news story. These people were bereft of help. Oxfam wanted to help them but did not have the money. The head office in Oxford was delighted to learn that we were developing a fundraising venture. I really cared and felt strongly drawn to help these refugees. I felt called to take on the responsibility for raising the money.

I was told we needed to raise £50,000 for the refugee crisis. There were no staff available to help and no funds to pay for advertising the appeal. So at Oxfam's Northern Ireland Office we had to raise, in a hurry, more money than from our biggest annual appeal, with no staff time available and no available funds for the project. Such financial and time pressures are typical of many of the charities serving the developing world.

I went home to listen to my inner guidance but without success. What could I do now? I knew from previous experience of solving problems that sometimes two or more people can successfully solve difficult problems by each helping the other tune into their inner guidance.

That evening I rang an old friend who is brilliant at listening to his creative inner guidance and loves an opportunity to explore solutions to seemingly intractable problems. We agreed to meet and discuss the problem.

A few nights later we met and had a few fruit juices together. My friend and I both really cared about raising the money for the refugees. This level of care helped us listen to our inner guidance together. We talked for most of the evening, helping and supporting each other develop our thoughts and feelings. At the end of the evening we had an idea. Why not print a glossy card with the appeal on one side and a space where new unused postage stamps could be stuck down on the other side! The glossy card would be resistant to rain and could be left with the milk bottles at the doorstep. The stamps would be unattractive to thieves, because although unused, they would have been stuck to card.

To respond to the appeal customers would simply stick unused stamps on the other side of the card and leave it out with the milk bottles the next day. We thought we could then reclaim the value of the unused stamps from the Royal Mail. We also felt the timing of this idea was perfect. Christmas was approaching, a time when people are naturally more charitable and have lots of stamps in the house for Christmas cards.

UNFOLDING YOUR WINGS

If you wish you can invite other people to help solve your problems. Working closely with others can be helpful when trying to solve difficult or complex problems. Choose friends or work colleagues to help and support you, but choose carefully. I suggest you invite intuitive people.

The only remaining piece of the jigsaw that remained was that we did not know if the Royal Mail would give us money back if we presented them with thousands of unused stamps! When I rang the Royal Mail they generously agreed to refund the value of the stamps minus a small handling charge. Hey presto, the appeal was a runner!

We had no money, but it didn't matter because the Milk Marketing Board paid for the printing of the leaflets. The appeal was run at the end of November. We were staggered by the response. Box loads of leaflets covered with stamps were arriving in Oxfam's office. The last remaining problem was to recruit enough volunteers to count the value of the stamps as they came in. This proved to be no problem. Success attracts volunteers.

Within three weeks we had raised £108,000! This was £58,000 more than was needed! This meant that we could not only help the refugees, but that we had plenty left over for other urgent tasks. Quietly I gave thanks.

Today the milkmen still run this appeal at Christmas. They devote the appeal to a different emergency each year. It has raised around a million pounds for essential humanitarian aid. All this happened because we listened to the call, the radiant swan within.

Envoi

I have a problem.
It seems huge.
It seems bigger than I am.
It seems intractable.

When my problem seems intractable, it is easy to fear.
When my problem seems intractable, it is easy to doubt.
When my problem seems intractable, it is easy to tense up.

I know of something bigger than my problem.
I know of the call.
Trusting, I relax into its limitless intelligence.
Trusting, I seek inner and outer quiet.
Trusting, I learn to see with eyes of peace.

I gaze inward in wonder at a multitude of solutions
Spinning in the inner caverns of my mind.
I simply watch and wait.
More quiet.
More quiet.

The answer comes.
It has formed out of the mists of my mind,
Ideas inspired by the love in my heart.
I feel empowered and ready for action.

*The large elegant conservatory is reflecting early evening's waning sun-
light. A half visible world of green and terracotta is revealed inside. An
indoor tree fills the central dome. On either side are brightly coloured flowers and dark green shrubs. People enter through a finely decorated arched
doorway between two marble urns. Each urn, topped by small cream leafed
shrubs, is set on a cubic marble podium. The glass is reflecting the setting sun
like a giant multifaceted crystal.*

Your Calling Is Elevated Through
The Release Of Pain

If we are to become pure, strong and true, and able to live out our
inner calling then our character needs to be cut and polished until it
resembles a sparkling attractive crystal. To attain that inner diamond we
need to release buried emotional pain. The vast majority of people and
certainly those who have not explored personal development for years are
full of unresolved pain. Inner pain takes the form of buried emotions
such as fear, anger, bitterness, sadness, grief and sorrow. This pain festers
away inside us like a sickness, sucking the joy, fun and sensitivity from
our lives.

Buried pain blocks us from sensitivity to our calling and explains why
so many people find it difficult to get started on a spiritual path of growth
and healing. If the call is to be our guide in life and we are blocked from
feeling and following its gentle inner prompting, no wonder we feel lost.

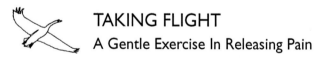

TAKING FLIGHT
A Gentle Exercise In Releasing Pain

Find somewhere quiet where you can be alone. Have a pad of
paper and some coloured crayons or pens handy. Do a relaxation exercise (See Your Calling Responds To Relaxation, page
20). Recall a relationship that is causing you some emotional
pain. Close your eyes and sense the buried emotional pain. Feel
where it is held in your body. Try and picture it as an image in
your mind. What shape does it have? What colour is it? Can

this pain be symbolised by an animal, plant or other object? Stay with these feelings and images. Slowly open your eyes and draw what you visualise. When you have finished drawing become aware of any feelings that are surfacing. Sit and feel these buried feelings surface. You may be feeling a bit raw and vulnerable. The origin of these feelings will lie much deeper than the present difficulty you have with your current troublesome relationship. If you can, recall an incident from further back in your past that may be giving rise to these feelings. You may find it difficult to sense your inner pain. If so, wait until you have an experience that brings your pain closer to the surface (like a row or vigorous disagreement with someone). Then do this exercise when your pain is closer to the surface.

Our pain is held in every cell of our body. This pain is stored from past traumas and hurts dating from adulthood, childhood and even back to our birth experience. To find freedom to be our true, authentic selves, we must release all this buried emotional pain by learning to open our heart. Our calling will help us to do this. We are taken into our pain, through our pain and out the other side into a new joy-filled life by following our calling.

Deep within, we know we have business to attend to that we are avoiding. Maybe we know we should be changing our career, forgiving a friend or confessing to a lie we told our partner. Whatever it is we are called to do, we know it is right and we know it is difficult. It is made difficult by our buried pain. We fear changing our career, we are angry and do not want to forgive our friend and we are terrified of telling our partner the truth. All of this is buried pain at work. No wonder we find it difficult to be truly authentic by having our intuitions, words and actions correspond.

By following our calling's inner prompting and attending to our unfinished business and unheeded challenges, we are taken into our pain. The art of being healed is to attend to unfinished business and to fully experience buried pain and the associated memories as they surface. So how can we release our pain, and become more authentic?

You could try the more vigorous exercise described below for the release of pain.

TAKING FLIGHT

A More Advanced Exercise In Releasing Pain

Find a private quiet space. Become aware of your feelings. Let your awareness of what you are feeling replace what you are thinking. To be successful you must replace thinking with feeling. Sense what your body wants to do and start to do it, gently at first. Maybe you are aware that you are feeling angry. Perhaps you sense that you want to beat a cushion. Get a cushion and start to slap it.

Do you sense that you would like to make a noise? Then make it—again gently at first. As you slap the cushion and growl gently you may sense there is more anger surfacing. So now start to thump the cushion and growl a bit louder. Release yourself from thinking about what you are doing and start to follow your emotions and inner inclinations. Let your movements and sounds take on a life of their own. You are becoming spontaneous. You may find yourself flying into a rage and beating the cushion to bits, followed by a fit of tears, sorrow and grief! This is all very healthy.

By expressing your buried emotions like this they are surfacing to be healed. During or after such an emotional catharsis memories and feelings from your past, including childhood memories, may surface. I always take time afterwards to lie comfortably with a blanket over me and be aware of these memories and feelings that have been locked away. By recalling old memories, and feelings associated with them, I become reconciled with my painful past and the associated pain. After merging with my past memories I then take time to feel loved and cared for.

There are a number of other techniques you can use to develop your ability to release pain.

Catch The Moment

In trying catch the moment you respond to those points in your life when you sense your buried emotions surfacing. Maybe your partner has said something that has really hurt you and brought up anger, or maybe you have just taken on a new job and you are terrified of facing your first day at work. These moments are a precious time when it is easier for you to release pain, so make it a priority to do this, if your schedule allows. This technique is particularly good for people who are new to releasing pain and find it difficult. Catching the moment helps you, because you are releasing pain when it is near the surface and wanting to come out anyway.

Move And Breathe

This technique allows you to release pain even if you do not feel it is near the surface. Find a quiet private space. Start to breathe ever more deeply and strongly. As you breathe start to move by springing up and down on your toes and swinging your arms around. Build up into a strident rhythm of moving and breathing. After about five to ten minutes return your breathing to normal and just stand with eyes closed listening inside for any emotions that may be surfacing. This technique works because it shakes up your buried emotions and helps them to surface. Once you begin to sense your buried emotions surfacing, follow and express them as before. This technique is good for making emotional release part of your daily routine, or to help shift hard to get at emotions.

Write Spontaneously

Pick up a pen and paper, or keyboard if you prefer, and sit down and write about your painful past. Simply let the words and sentences flow. Put energy, feeling and passion into your writing. If you wish you can make your writing a purely private affair. You do not need to write to be published, or even write for others to read, so you can be as open and personal as you wish. Such writing may bring up your buried pain, which you can then release, as above.

Watch Emotionally Charged Videos

If there are films that make you feel sad, or angry, you can watch these and use them to get in touch with your buried emotions. When you feel them you can release them as before.

Listen To Emotive Music
If you have music in your collection that makes you feel sad or angry you can use this music to bring buried emotions to the surface where you can release them.

Let Go of Items Associated With Your Painful Past
Seek out items associated with your painful past and burn or dump them. You may find this brings up buried emotions, which you can then release.

Make Works Of Art That Represent Your Deep Buried Emotions
These do not have to be masterpieces; they are simply tools you can use to help buried pain to surface. Use a method you feel comfortable with. Coloured crayons, paint and clay are good. Be spontaneous. I remember when I was on an art therapy weekend once I made a clay image with sexual connotations. I was embarrassed at the time but it brought up a lot of buried emotion around my sexuality, which I could then release.

Create A Vision
Paint, sketch, write or imagine yourself as a fully functioning, power-ful, peaceful, sensitive person, then allow yourself to feel a longing to be that person. This will help your buried pain surface where it can be released.

We know if we are releasing our pain effectively because we will become lost in the emotional experience and will have stopped thinking about what we are experiencing. Do not under-estimate the amount of buried pain that you have. It takes years of work to clear it. You may find, as your exploration of buried pain progresses, that more pain exists below the pain you have already cleared, like peeling off the layers of an onion. Also as time progresses, the nature of your pain may change from harsh surface pain to more profound deeper pain.

In my own life I have spent years experimenting with releasing emo-tional pain. A great deal of pain surfaced when I had my second mental breakdown and thought I would never be strong enough to ever work again. So much pain surfaced that I was completely disabled by it for two years, (see Your Healing From Adversity, page 179 and Your Healing From Loneliness, page 199). This turned out to be a blessing in disguise, because when I eventually began to listen to my calling and, with its help, commit to shedding my pain, so much of it was near the surface that I was able to make good progress.

UNFOLDING YOUR WINGS

If some event in your life has brought about powerful painful emotions, this is a good opportunity to shed your pain using the above methods. It will take some time, and you may feel overwhelmed by the pain, but you will eventually emerge, renewed and full of life!

Do not underestimate the value and healing power of the above techniques. You may wish to find friends, a local support group (like an art therapy workshop), or a skilled professional facilitator who can support you with your journey into buried pain or, like me, you may feel called to journey into your pain alone.

As our pain is released, we become increasingly sensitive to inner guidance. Our life opens up, we become much more spontaneous and rely increasingly on our feelings to guide our actions. We change to feeling life as well as thinking about it.

The methods in this book and others on www.alifediscovered.org, the web site that supports this book, are all effective in helping you lead a guided life. In particular talking, meditation and the release of pain work well together as a daily discipline for increasing sensitivity within. You can mix and match these methods, as you feel inclined. You may wish to try some of the simpler methods first, like relaxation and questions.

Envoi

I am an emotional being.
I commit to feeling my buried emotions.

As I feel my emotions surface
I find ways of releasing them—harmlessly.

By releasing my pain I become more spontaneous.
By releasing my pain I become more sensitive.
By releasing my pain I am tuning in to the call.
By tuning in to my calling
I am finding the way to a new joy filled life.

The seagull flies low over the busy river bridge. A tall burly man ambles lazily along the pavement. His coat, trousers, shoes, gloves and cap are all black. He has radio ear pieces fitted to his head. A short smart man passes him unnoticed, walking in the opposite direction. His tie is red with a small blue pinprick design and his moustache is neatly clipped. He carries bags with the logo of a nearby designer store. Both men are oblivious of each other and to the seagull's call overhead.

Your Calling Helps You Succeed At Work

The frantic helter-skelter pace of the typical modern office can alienate us from one another, from our environment and from ourselves. Consequently offices are not always the most promising places for solving problems and creating supportive, productive human relationships. To be guided from within we need to be in harmony. Our ability to work together harmoniously as a team increases, and our communication improves, if we care about one another and are being supportive. Our productivity rises when we create the time and space to be guided from within. We are creating harmony by being supportive and solving problems in new and innovative ways as a result. Companies like Microsoft realise this. In Dublin they have time-out spaces in their office where their employees can go to be alone or to discuss problems informally.

You may say, "We don't have time to access inner guidance at work." When I worked as a management consultant I would bring the people who directed companies to my office once a month for three hours. At those meetings I would teach them how to solve their problems by communicating sensitively and by thinking creatively. I was teaching them how to be guided from within. Meeting once a month for three hours was sufficient to have a major impact on the strategy and success of these companies.

I had a client company which sold their product at the low-cost, low-profit end of the market. After learning the skills of inner guidance, they invented an entirely new way to market and present their product. Their improved marketing gave them confidence. They decided to price the same product they were selling at a low cost in Northern Ireland and as the second most expensive in the Republic Of Ireland.

If you have problems finding time to tune in to the call at work, I suggest you start with yourself first. You could choose to do something as simple as come into work an hour earlier on Monday mornings. An hour spent in guided contemplation before work starts is not taking up any of your existing working week. Early on Monday morning will also be a quiet time of day. I suggest you learn to listen within in any way you choose. Perhaps you could use one of five approaches outlined earlier; relaxation, questions, contemplation, talking or meditation. After a period of inner listening you may find it helpful to express what you have heard by either writing down thoughts, drawing images or talking to a colleague.

If you find your early Monday morning quiet time productive and helpful, then you could create other times during the week to listen within by consciously creating space for inner and outer quiet. If you have a private office you could inform the secretary that you do not wish to be disturbed for an hour and hang a "Please Do Not Disturb" notice on the outside of your door. It would also be helpful to find a way to prevent incoming phone calls. You will be more likely to gain the co-operation of other people if you explain why you are taking these measures. This is especially true if you have a boss or line manager.

Once you have seen the effectiveness of harnessing inner guidance to help you with your work, you may wish to extend the benefits to others in your organization. If you are the manager of a department or business you might consider making inner guidance part of your organization's business culture. Four things are needed to make inner guidance part of your business culture. Firstly, your staff needs to be trained in how to listen within. You could do this yourself using this book and the personal development opportunities on the "A Life Discovered" website as a guide. Secondly, your staff needs an environment suitable for listening within. To provide this I recommend the creation of a quiet room to be used only for inner guidance and quiet discussions to assist inner guidance. Thirdly, this room and its environment need to be properly managed. Finally, your staff needs to be encouraged to use the quiet room for the correct purpose. Please see the creation of your quiet room as a labour of love, to be enjoyed.

Once your staff has been trained and the room created, it is then essential that the use of the room be properly managed. I suggest a secretary be asked to manage the occupancy of the quiet room. It should be a rule that the quiet room is only used by members of staff who wish to nurture inner guidance. I recommend that people who are not staff, and are not members of your business or department, no matter how important, do not have access to this room. This is because people who do not understand inner guidance can ruin the carefully constructed atmosphere of quiet and love.

Finally, you may have some work to do educating your newly trained staff to use the quiet room for contemplating problems and other matters. We have such an out of balance work culture that many people have it deeply engrained that to sit and not be rushing around is wasting time. They may even fear being criticized for doing nothing. You will understand what I mean if you see these tendencies in yourself, once you start taking your own quiet times.

UNFOLDING YOUR WINGS

In a rapidly changing business environment we need ways of stimulating creativity and solving problems at speed. Paradoxically we need to learn to slow down so that we can become more efficient. The techniques in this book on using the inner call to solve problems and increase creativity are very powerful. I invite you to experiment by using them to solve problems. You will soon discover their effectiveness.

When I worked as a management consultant, I used to tell my clients that 50% of my effectiveness was due to my input, but that the other 50% was because I provided a peaceful quiet room in which to meet, free from interruptions and the telephone. I'm not sure they believed me but I knew it to be true!

Envoi

I am the first.
All is quiet.
I enter the inner sanctum.

Gentle sunshine falls on the newly opened pink curtains.
The green of nature fills each corner.
The atmosphere vibrates with the old and loved.
I rest in comfort, remembering the day's tasks.
Closing my eyes I ask for help.

How can I perform these tasks?
How can I plan the day?
In the inner sanctum of the room
Resides the inner sanctum of my mind.
Images, feelings and thoughts form and dissolve.
I remain still...listening.
Slowly...slowly...the day is planned.

I emerge ready for action.

Yellow, red, pink, white, peach; the rose garden is full of colour. Air is fragrance-filled. A couple meet to enjoy the garden. They smoothly saunter between beds, engaging in quiet conversation. Occasionally the woman stops to admire a particular colour and scent. Beds resonate with buzzing, as bees and flies flit between abundant petals. A solitary white butterfly flits play-fully as petals, disturbed by a passing bee, fall gently to earth.

Your Calling Helps You Understand Relationships

If marriages are to remain light and playful, then it is necessary that both partners are totally committed to loving one another. I believe that if men and women could learn to really love one another all the world's problems would be solved. I realise this is a sweeping statement, but it underlines the importance of relationships, not only for our own pur-poses, but also for the world at large.

The family and the home are the foundation of life and human civi-lization. If we are able to learn about love in the home and family, then we will have love in abundance to give to our businesses, charities and friends and to the whole of life. Unfortunately relationships are often a source of discord and friction, rather than love and understanding.

Inner guidance prompts us to love unconditionally and with dogged determination. Unconditional love loves before waiting to be loved. When we love unconditionally we pour out our love in all directions, to the hurt, the needy, the difficult and the lonely. Our partner helps us to love unconditionally. This is because our partner is at times hurt, needy, difficult and lonely. Do we stop loving them when they are like this? Not a bit. That is when we dig deep and are determined to love. We need to be able to express our love with understanding and sensitivity; otherwise our love may not have the healing effect we desire. Fortunately inner guidance is there to help.

A healthy relationship has two states—harmony and conflict. Healthy relationships are always growing. They grow when the couple share their love and they grow through conflict, because with sensitive communica-tion and a willingness to learn, matters are eventually resolved. Unfortu-nately most relationships do not have this pattern. Most relationships alternate between conflict and truce. When there is conflict, matters are not resolved and a truce develops. The outstanding issues have not gone away, because they were never resolved, and they continue to influence the relationship. If the outstanding issues continue unresolved and lack of resolution gives rise to resentment and bitterness, then it is increasingly difficult to maintain the truce. Stresses and strains appear and in extreme cases the truce breaks down and divorce results.

This need not happen.

For a relationship to succeed two things are necessary. Firstly, both partners need to be able to grow and learn from the good times together and from the inevitable conflicts. Learning from conflict restores harmony and strengthens the relationship. Secondly, both partners need to honour their inner guidance.

"How can my inner guide help me in my relationship?" I hear you ask.

In a relationship there will inevitably be conflict. Conflict results when two partners are struggling to understand a problem that faces them. Conflict situations need love, patience, sensitivity and determination; otherwise frustration can develop and communication degenerates. Before communication becomes harsh or insensitive we can gain help by saying, "I need time to think this over."

This is the time for us to withdraw from the conflict situation to a quiet place on our own, where we can sense our inner guidance, learn from our insight and conscience and be inspired to find creative solutions.

Of course, in a busy household the children may need to be fed and the laundry done. In this case we could say, "I need time to think this over. I would like to think about what we have said this evening when I have some peace and quiet. Can I talk to you about these matters again tomorrow?"

Then in the evening we could find a quiet place to be on our own, perhaps run a hot bath, and take time to listen to our inner guidance. We can use one of the six approaches outlined earlier, (relaxation, questions, contemplation, talking, meditation and the release of pain). If there are unresolved negative emotions like anger, and resentment, these need to be expressed harmlessly outside the relationship.

We can also talk to friends, consult a book on relationships or seek help from a counsellor, but our final guide should always be our own inner counsellor. Our external counsellor could be wrong. The book could be badly written. Our friend could be giving poor advice. Only our inner guide knows the perfect answer to our situation. Our job is to create the time, space and loving attitude so that we are able to listen to its gentle inner promptings.

Once our guidance has become clear, we are then free to return to our partner and communicate what we have learned with love, sensitivity and persistence. We may need to do this many times before we recreate harmony in a newly strengthened relationship. Our relationship has begun to grow, and so have we. (See Your Healing From A Broken Relationship, page 214).

UNFOLDING YOUR WINGS

Try regarding your relationship as a school and your partner as your teacher. This teacher can help you grow in love and understanding and give you opportunities to practice tuning in to and following inner guidance. Experiment by creating a space in your relationship to talk about difficult and contentious issues. Being part of an ever-deepening relationship is a very powerful opportunity to tune in and follow inner guidance. As both of you tune in you will find an exquisite sensitivity growing between you. The sensitivity you gain by being in a loving and mutually supportive relationship can then be offered to family, friends, work colleagues and the world at large.

When I was 29 I met an attractive young woman at a night-class. I got to know her and eventually plucked up my courage and asked her out. There was an indefinable something that drew me to her.

We started dating. Although I found her an attractive person, there was a side to her nature that was remote and difficult. She seemed to be alienated from life. She had ongoing conflicts at work and with her parents. She was not a happy person. I never felt really close to her. She was angry and defensive and kept me at a distance. I didn't know the real person.

I sensed that my partner had never been really loved. I felt called to give to her unconditionally. Consequently I was the person who gave way most often when there were differences. I was the person who was the most flexible and the most giving, although on some key issues that were important to me I stubbornly held my ground even though I felt controlled and manipulated. When she hurt me with her harsh words, I let her see that I had been wounded by expressing my feelings. After going out for two months, I planned a week's holiday break in a caravan in Donegal in the northwest of Ireland.

On that holiday we spent some intimate times together. Towards the end of the holiday she began to open up to me. I began to see the real person. She told me of her hopes and fears and her despair at the emptiness of her life. We discussed her situation together. I sensed she was taking a real risk telling me these things. I suspected she had never talked to anyone else this way. I saw her vulnerability. Her beauty was revealed. I felt a great love for her; but I sensed that this was only a short relationship. I knew it was not to be a prolonged love affair. I understood from my insight that to have a prolonged love affair I needed a partnership where the giving was much more balanced.

After five days she wanted to return early from the holiday. We left the caravan and drove home to Belfast. Two weeks later she told me she had been given a job abroad. Shortly afterwards she was gone. I never heard from her again.

When I love I give and I receive. Anger and frustration have no place in my love. When I am angry and frustrated it is because I am rigid and dogmatic about getting what I want and need. When I wish to gain something for myself through my relationship I am flexible about what I can achieve and how and when I can achieve it, while at the same time being dogged and determined. This flexibility enables me to be patient and kind. My dogged determination enables me to get my needs met.

We live in a harsh and cruel world. Anger and frustration are everywhere. Maybe our boss is angry or maybe our partner is angry and frustrated. Yet as long as this person chooses to be with us it is important that we love them. This is unconditional love. They may try to control us or manipulate us. Our task is to offer up our kind but determined love again and again even if it is rejected or abused.

Unconditional love is about offering ourselves as kind and determined people in a harsh and cruel world. Such persistent, gentle love is needed because it is so healing of both others and us. Because I have experienced healing I find I can offer up this precious healing love to everyone everywhere.

Giving simply pours out of me in a cornucopia of offerings, presents, gifts, surprises and general helpfulness. This outpouring of love enables me to attract a loving relationship and many caring friendships. I find as I do this others may respond to my love and generosity in unloving, uncaring ways.

I can find myself the target of their anger, bitterness, frustration, resentment, anxiety, and jealousy but I remain kind and determined. It is my possession of this kindness and determination in the face of rampant negative emotion, and my ability to stick to my own calling despite all manipulations, that enables love to work healing miracles. Because I am sticking to my calling it draws the other closer to their calling despite all protests.

This kind of sensitivity will help us understand our relationship. We will feel guided in what to say and when to say it. We will know when to stand up for our viewpoint, when to yield, how to find creative compromises and solutions and when it is appropriate for a relationship to end.

Through my calling to date this woman, I was learning from my insight about the type of relationship that did not work for me and consequently was becoming clearer about what a loving relationship was really like. I went on to have more successful and balanced relationships after this experience. That is the power of the call in helping us understand ourselves and love our partner.

Envoi

At times my partner is awkward.
At times my partner is difficult.
At times my partner is mean.
This is when I need inner quiet.
This is when I need to turn to the call.

You reveal to me the beauty of the flowers,

The beauty of the sky and the beauty of the angry person.

Through you I see the truth.
Through you I feel the truth.
Through you I know the truth.

For it is in

Expressing softness, that I overcome hardness,
Offering flexibility, that I overcome rigidity,
Showing determination, that I have my needs met.

I offer myself as a kind and determined person to the world.

The bed is full of spring's pink profusion, light pink, dark pink, soft pink, strong pink. Some damp flower heads droop and touch the earth where small green leaves populate places between the flowers. Each leaf is bedecked with tiny glistening drops. Bees bounce around dank flowers next to fallen pink petals scattered on brown earth.

Your Calling Can Get You Into Trouble

If we are not skilled communicators we may find our well-intentioned actions lying like fallen and scattered pink petals. When we are able to live a guided life we find, as if by magic, that we are able to meet and make intimate friendships with many people. These intimate friends, we discover, are also living guided lives. They are happy to support us. We will inevitably find that some people will resist our well-intentioned actions.

Why do some people resist the well-intentioned actions of those who are living guided lives? Everyone needs to feel secure. Feeling secure is an important human need. Some people do not know about living a guided life and the security it brings. If people do not know the security of a guided life, they find it difficult to give others the freedom to be themselves. Rather than listening to their needs and responding to those needs in a relationship of equals, they will have a tendency to cajole others into conforming to their wishes.

They feel that by exerting control over others in this way, they will be creating a secure environment for themselves. Subconsciously they are telling themselves, "If only I can manipulate the world to suit my wishes, then there will be no danger and I will feel safe."

It is hard work trying to mould the world to suit your requirements. Relating to the world in a manipulative way is very stressful. Consequently, when a person living a guided life is relating to someone who is not, then awkwardness can result. Fortunately our inner guidance will help through the difficulties ahead.

The answer to being in awkward relationships is to communicate sensitively and lovingly. We may be called to stand up for our point of view and persist in expressing it. Inner guidance comes from our whole being; therefore such persistence will always be tempered with love and under-

standing. Despite our best intentions to communicate lovingly, sometimes it doesn't work. It is at these times that our calling can get us into
trouble and our well-intentioned actions are like scattered petals in the
wind.

When I was 29 years old I was working as an architect in an office
in Belfast. I was put in charge of the design of a family day care centre
to be built in the northern part of the city quite near our office. I had
an assistant, an architect my own age. He was a great help to me and I
involved him in the major decisions and design developments. I appreciated his help.

During the period I was working on this project I took a break to visit
Scotland. One night, while I was away, I was lying awake in my hotel
room with the window open on a perfectly still, balmy, summer night,
when the curtains blew open. This mysterious wind swept over my bed
and I felt my spirit lifted up on a beam of white light into another realm.
There I was surrounded by the loving presence of Beings of Light. While
in their presence I was told to go back to Belfast and awaken people
spiritually. After receiving this guidance I travelled from this realm, back
down the beam of white light into my body lying at rest in the bed. At
the time I did not know what to make of this experience, and it felt too
personal and intimate to share with others. I returned to Belfast from my
break in Scotland to continue my work.

When I returned to the project I no longer seemed satisfied with my
work as an architect. I began to dream of offering work that was more
personal, that could change lives. I began to dream of offering a management training course that combined creativity training with training in
one to one and group communication. I even gave this imaginary course
a name, Creative Action Management.

Eventually our project was successfully designed and the office was
commissioned to carry out a new project, the design of accommodation
for the elderly near the Mourne Mountains. This time my colleague was
to lead the project and I was to be his assistant. There was a reversal of
roles from the roles we had on the previous job. I was looking forward
to us working together again. I felt sure we could do a wonderful design
suited to the special needs of elderly people.

When the project started my colleague went to work on the design by
himself. I was left sitting at my desk twiddling my thumbs. I approached

him and offered to help but he did not want it. I tried a number of times to become involved. Nothing I tried worked. I talked to our boss but he did not want to address the issue. I continued to sit at my desk and twiddle my thumbs. This went on for days. I began to feel that I was drawing a salary for doing nothing. I felt I was not doing my job and was bored.

I knew I needed to do my job. I knew I needed to earn my salary. I cared about the project I had been asked to assist with. I felt intuitively that I did not deserve to be left out. So I began to work on the project on my own to see if I could improve our design work.

Eventually, after a month working on the project, a design meeting was called with our boss. My colleague's design was discussed. Then the proposed improvements I had worked on were discussed. The fact that I had worked on improvements and presented them was an embarrassment to my boss. My colleague was irritated that I had been working on the project and had presented my improvements.

None of my improvements were accepted. I had presented them in a calm manner, although I was feeling rejected. I was seen as a troublemaker, someone who was rocking the boat. A week later I was told there wasn't enough work for me and I was dismissed from my job.

 ## UNFOLDING YOUR WINGS

I f you get into trouble as a result of following your calling and as a result lose your job or your relationship, try and see this as a positive step that is taking you to new improved employment opportunities or a more loving relationship. In this future environment you will have greater freedom to unfold your wings and fly.

I felt a hurt at having lost my job. I had really cared and thought this had never been properly acknowledged. I decided not to apply for another architect's job. Although I felt real fear at the prospect of leaving the architecture profession, I persisted with the move because I felt called to leave.   Once again I was experiencing a transcendental calm when I thought of leaving, a calm that was much deeper and more profound than my superficial fears.

Through my insight I realised there were too few opportunities in the profession to care deeply about the work I was asked to do. I felt boxed in. My sacking led me to rely more on my inner guidance and I accepted the challenge to make my dream of offering my management-training course a reality even though I had a disability. Eventually, by following my calling, I went on to be self-employed as a management consultant. My working life improved dramatically. Although this move brought a lot of fear to the surface, where it could be healed, my sense of freedom increased. I was learning to trust my inner guidance.

Envoi

I am standing up for myself.
I am attracting trouble.
I am at a dead end.
Even at a dead end the call is with me.
With the call as my companion there is no dead end.
There is only a new beginning.

This part of the woodland is less dense. Occupying the space is a giant beech trunk. It expands left then right, each branch adding to the overarching canopy. In the canopy branches divide again and again until they form a dome of small twigs growing skyward. These slender, sky hungry twigs are lined with tiny green leaves. A solitary seagull gracefully glides in the vast empty space above, magically merging movement with stillness.

Your Calling Will Help You Know

There is transcendent reality to which we all belong. This reality is hidden, but it can be known. We are shielded from this reality by a veil of worries, fears, anxieties and preoccupations. This reality is not something that can be understood by the machinations of the mind. It is something we know when we are gliding through life, magically merging movement with stillness.

I find this inner stillness by expressing love. I need to love more and more people and love them more and more intensely. This is what I am guided to do. Loving others intensely, anticipating their needs and offering myself in their service, shrinks my troublesome ego with all its worries and anxieties, opening up the vast, still space within. Once we can carry that still inner space into every situation, no matter how fraught or troubled, then we find that inner space is the doorway to knowing transcendent reality, where everything is meaningful, everything is purposeful and where we realise life is just as it needs to be.

Nature, with its perfect expression of need and response, reflects that reality. Unfortunately we are blind to the beauty around us because our minds are so confused, stressed and filled with fear.

I remember leaving a large Do It Yourself Store in South Belfast late one autumn. As I came out of the main doors and looked across the car park, my heart responded to a magnificent sight. The whole sky was lit up with the most spectacular pinks, reds and purples. A beautiful orange sun was setting on the horizon. I was awestruck. My heart filled with glorious presence.

I looked around at the other people leaving the store, to share this vision of wonder. I stood at that doorway in amazement for five minutes. Of all the people who passed by, it seemed to me that no one noticed that magnificent sight. As they walked urgently with head bowed out of the store, I could see their faces etched with an ever-present anxiety. When I was cycling home that evening I was full of mixed emotions—great love for the beauty I had just seen, and great sadness for the state of humanity.

By loving more we are gradually healed of our fears. Our mind becomes simpler and simpler. We lose the need to rationalize and put words to everything. Then we see the world differently. We enter the present and see the world as it really is. The truth is that we are already living in paradise. It is then that we realize that the exquisite beauty of nature reflects transcendent reality, not as an idea in our head, but directly with tears running down our cheeks.

Envoi

How can I know?

By listening to the call.
By listening to the call I learn to love more and more.
By loving more I lose my fear.
By losing my fear I begin to relax.
By relaxing completely I live in the present.
By living in the present I know.

Below the trees and flowers a turquoise sea surrounds the small brown and green island. People cross by a delicate taut rope-bridge and explore the tiny, white fisherman's cottage that nestles in the only sunny alcove. The fisherman's olive green boat floats undisturbed at the foot of the cottage cleft. Shadows from surrounding cliffs cast dark patches on turquoise water. Beyond the shadows vast ocean reaches to the horizon.

Your Calling Opens Your Potential

To have a life with real potential is to have a life with limitless horizons. Many of us seem resigned to the confined, the mediocre and the mundane. Our life resembles a small garden, with a few attractive seats and some pretty flowers. Outside this garden little is known. There may be the odd visit to another garden, with its attractive seats and flowers, forming a highlight in this drudgery of an existence we call life, but the great wide vistas and the distant horizons where discoveries take place are never explored. We are too frightened of leaving the tried and tested, so we opt to live out our life in this confined little space. But does life have to be like that? Is it possible to share more openly? Is it possible to reach new and unexplored horizons? Is it possible to discover the meaning of life? Is it possible to realise our potential?

To many, such questions are irritating. But such questions persist and if I try and push them away they only persist more strongly. These questions exist not just to irritate me, but also to encourage me to meet the challenge of life, to grow and to become more than I already am. These questions are the very life-blood of the inner call. When I am called forward, it is because I am called to find the answers to these questions, not in dry intellectual argument, but by the recasting and reforming of my character, through offering my life in service, by loving more and more people and loving them more and more intensely.

 UNFOLDING
YOUR WINGS

If your responsibilities are keeping you from exploring your calling, try having the courage to hold on to your dreams. By attending to your duties with love and devotion you are developing a deep and powerful patience. If you wish, while attending to your duties you could ask inner guidance to suggest a few small steps in the direction you eventually wish to travel. You may be able to take one or two of these small steps in the direction of your goal. As your responsibilities diminish you can add more steps. Then when you have more freedom to act, the patience you have gained will be very helpful in fulfilling your dreams.

A life with potential is a passionate life full of purpose and meaning, a life where we really care. If ever there was a time when the world needed people to live such a life it is now. So why not seize the moment. Listen. The inner call is calling us forward to love and to care. What is your calling? Why not follow it? It is by following our guidance, the radiant swan within, that we are empowered to realise our potential.

Envoi

I want to share more openly.
I want to know the unexplored horizon.
I want to realise the meaning of life.
There are answers.

I listen within.
I discover the first step I need to take on my journey.
I take that step and begin to explore my potential.

Would you like help in developing your inner guidance?
If so, visit *www.alifediscovered.org*

- Receive one to one coaching by email from the author on how to develop inner guidance.
- Discover how to solve your problems by tuning into inner guidance on an online tutorial.
- Find out about opportunities for personal development.
- Discuss your calling with other readers.

Your Pass Code is **star**

Visit the home page at *www.alifediscovered.org*. Then, enter through the archway in the home page.

Full details about the website on page 292.

Part Two

Your Potential

"Your Potential" reveals how a life guided from within opens into an exciting destined journey. While reading this chapter you begin to sense that your personal difficulties can actually be the opening to a new joy filled life.

"We must believe we are gifted for something. And that this thing, at whatever cost, must be achieved."
—Marie Curie

Noon

The yellow sun sends its warm rays across the lake. The water sparkles and jumps with reflected sunshine.

The swan glides to the shore to greet an elderly man passing by. He picks at bread and throws the crumbs with pinpoint accuracy in front of the swan. He is intent on throwing each crumb to exactly the right spot. Eventually he becomes bored, tucks his stick under his arm and turns to walk into the woods.

A young couple pass, half walking half trotting, engaged intently in conversation. Clouds of misty water vapour surround their faces.

The water continues to sparkle, like a tray of moving diamonds.

A seagull glides past.

There is a loud slapping of water. Silence stops. The swan is charging flat out along the lake. With wings flapping, feet running along the water and head and neck pointed towards a gap in the trees. She is intent on flight. Eventually she manages to lift her great bulk airborne. The flapping sound ceases. She lifts silently into the air and follows the watercourse through the trees.

The lake returns to its quiet murmurings, silence interspersed with birdsong. In the distance ducks playfully splash each other with water. The trees on the lakeshore are mirrored in the still surface. Specks of grass float silently by.

Great quiet has returned.

Summer Reflections

The large cormorant sits on an ocean rock, wings outstretched, drying in the strong sunshine. She gently contracts both wings to preen with her long yellow beak. Preening completed, one wing is hung out to dry, closely followed by the other. Three seagulls sit motionless, watching from where seaweed grows. The cormorant folds her wings again and turns to face the gentle breeze. Her head darts full circle, to left and right, watching. She beats her wings, tilts her head back and opens her beak to the sky.

Your Potential Embraces The Whole Of Life

When we listen to the call and act on the promptings we are given, then we are opening up an exciting new life for ourselves—a life that becomes deeply meaningful. Like the blossoming of summer we have begun to show our potential. Realising our potential is the only path that leads to liberation.

Our potential embraces the whole of life. It is not a specific teaching that we can apply in this or that part of our life, it is not a method to be practised once or twice a day—our potential embraces the whole of life. Every area of our life offers opportunities to share ourselves more deeply by a committed and joyous giving of ourselves. We create opportunities to share with others by expressing our many different talents and gifts in our marriages, families, working lives, hobbies, spiritual interests and friendships. We are healed of our fears through this profound sharing of ourselves.

Unfortunately many people do not know about their calling and their potential. Many people are stuck in a rut of their own devising. Others are following a path they believe to be their potential, like ambition for career goals or rigid adherence to a religious dogma, which are only causing them lots of stress and strain and not delivering the healing they so badly need. Their potential embraces the whole of life.

As we embrace our potential we change. How we change is very individual; we might change our career, hobbies, daily routine, marriage partner or friends. Throughout, our calling guides us in the changes we need to make and because we sense these changes intuitively, altering our life is easy and natural. For example, my TV had been sitting practically unused in my lounge for some time. My sister needed a TV and I felt prompted to give the TV to my sister and use the money I spent on the license fee on cut flowers for the house instead. I did this and felt much better as a result.

As we seek to change, we apply will power to developing our character and pursuing our ideals. We do this because we think it will do us good. Changes of this kind always require persistent effort. After a while we often revert to the good old ways anyway. When our potential changes, it is because there has been a change of heart. When we have a change of heart, it is because we are in communion with the purity of the radiant inner swan. Our love has grown and we need never go back.

Envoi

I listen to the call.
As I listen I open up to
And follow its gentle inner promptings.
My life changes and I face new interesting challenges.
My life is going in new directions.
I have opened up to my potential.

The ocean is completely calm. Stillness is suddenly disturbed by the distant sound of wings against water. The solitary cormorant is intent on flight. Eventually she climbs and turns shoreward skimming the calm water. The sea rises rhythmically, fills a tiny rock hollow and falls spilling and tinkling to the ocean. Water sighs deeply, fills the gully and slithers seaweed. Little bubbles form. Each tiny bubble offers itself to the vast flat ocean.

Your Potential Is As Unique As You Are

If we are to offer ourselves to the limitless ocean of life then we need to acknowledge that our destiny is an individual one. There is no prescription. What is right for one person at any one time is not necessarily right for another. This is because our guided life mirrors our relationship to the call and the call speaks to each of us with a unique message.

One of the most wonderful characteristics of living a guided life is its surprise element. From the age of 12 all I wanted to be was an architect. I realized my dream and might have spent my whole working life in the profession had I not decided to follow my star. When I was 30 I changed to become a self-employed management consultant. When I was young I had never dreamed I would be a management consultant. I was genuinely surprised to find that I made a much better management consultant than architect! I went on to lecture in personal development at Queen's University. I am 44 now and I am working as an author writing this book. When I was younger I never dreamed I would ever be an author. Each time I have made a change like this, I have been delighted to find I could do the work and that I enjoy the work much more than my previous occupation. This has happened of course because I am leading a life devoted to my inner call.

For those in a relationship, each partner will have their own call and their own destiny. It is in the nature of a relationship that destinies are shared. For a successful relationship it is preferable that those parts that are shared are discussed and agreed together before being implemented. (See Your Calling Helps You Understand Relationships page 77).

UNFOLDING
YOUR WINGS

It is an advantage to have a major project at the heart of your relationship that you both care about and to which both can contribute. For a time raising your children might be your joint project; however, this will only be a temporary phase of your marriage. There will come a time when it is healthy and natural for you both to move on. A suitable project might be the husband's, or wife's work, in which the partner could be involved in a supporting role, or a joint project like a shared business venture. If you are established in separate careers you might have a shared voluntary or charity project that means a lot to both of you. This project will create a shared destiny and will help hold things together when other more peripheral issues are in conflict.

If you want to support others in realising their potential be aware that it is misguided to try and coax others to take up this path or that cause. By cajoling people in this way you are only taking them away from their own calling. To many people coaxing others is a sign of concern and friendship. Such behaviour only reflects our own insecurities about the path we have taken in life and our lack of understanding about the call. It is preferable to draw out their interests, inclinations and skills rather than attempt to foist our ideas on them. This is especially important when we are raising our children.

Envoi

My friend seeks my advice.
She is lost.
"Show me my potential," she pleads.
She seems so helpless.

It is tempting to tell her.
She wants me to tell her,

But I know she must find the way for herself.
Despite her pleading I keep silent.

Acknowledging my silence she turns inward.
She turns inward to her calling.

A steady gentle breeze sweeps over the rocks. Three ducks float past in the slightly choppy water. The jewelled surface glints in midday sunshine. A solitary seagull soars out from the shore. He keeps low over the water, then climbs, turns and drops to land on the blue ocean. On the distant horizon the deep blue ocean meets the powder blue sky, forming a perfect straight line.

Your Potential Is Not A Method (but may employ methods from time to time)

Many people explore life in a straight line, looking to methods, systems and exercises to grow spiritually and enhance their lives. There is no harm in this provided we realize that our potential is not the method. Our potential embraces the whole of life.

Some people pray twice a day, others use rosary beads, some people eat a special diet, do yoga, or fast at certain times of the year, take vitamin pills, or go to church every Sunday. Some of these people think that because they use rosary beads or attend church on Sundays, this will change their life and lead them to salvation. This is a much too narrow view of spiritual development.

Near where I live there is a centre that teaches meditation. Many fine people attend this centre to learn meditation. I have met a number of them. Some of these people really believe that by meditating twice a day for 20 minutes their lives will be significantly transformed. They are unconcerned that their work is meaningless and their marriage is a mess—their life is going to be revolutionised by meditation alone!

I know because I was like that myself once. Years ago I suffered from extreme depression and stress. My life was so unbearable that I had to find something to relieve the pain and give me hope of a cure. In desperation I hit upon meditation as the solution. This was going to save me and bring me back to normality. I enquired in this local meditation centre in Belfast, only to be told the teacher would be away for a number of months. They didn't seem sure when he would return.

I was distraught. The method I had pinned my hopes on was unavailable. In my despair I contacted the headquarters of this meditation organisation in the UK and arranged to travel across the Irish Sea to England. Although I was very short of money at the time, I spent all my savings staying in a bed and breakfast accommodation for a month until I was trained in their meditation method.

After the month was over I returned to Belfast and began practicing the method. After a few months practicing I could see no significant improvement. I quickly realized that to restore my health was going to be a long involved process that needed work on all fronts, not just sitting meditating twice a day. I stopped feeling desperate to find a cure and began listening to my calling, which guided me to make changes that affected many aspects of my life. Shortly after starting this life-embracing process, I gave up their meditation method in favour of a broad sweep of other approaches. (See Your Healing From Adversity, page 179.) I did return to and explore meditation at a later period in my life, when I had shed some of my inner pain and was feeling less distressed. Their meditation training was useful, but was not appropriate for me at the time.

There is a deep-seated desire in each of us for the quick fix, the easy option, and the simple answer. Life is complex. We need help to work it out. In order to make a significant difference we need to apply the lessons learned from our inner guidance to the whole of our lives. We need a life born of devotion to the inner call.

UNFOLDING YOUR WINGS

Methods, systems and exercises are useful provided they are part of a guided life and you are using them for as long as your intuition suggests they are useful and helpful to your personal growth. When you sense that they have had their day, it is better to drop them permanently or temporarily and move on.

Please feel free to explore methods as we follow our destiny, but be aware of their limitations. Our potential embraces the whole of life.

Envoi

As I explore my potential
I discover new exciting methods.
I search the most promising.
I find the method helpful.
I find the method interesting.
I find the method healing.
But I always remember my potential
Embraces the whole of life.

The honey hue rock shelf rests close to calm ocean water. The tide is out. Tiny encrustations cover the rock. Moisture collects in small hollows. Here limpets stubbornly cling in clusters. Small ridges radiate on each stony shell. Bright green seaweed ties itself to the tip. Around this rock shelf the calm ocean breathes gently.

Your Potential Needs To Be Understood

Many people find it difficult to stay calm and breathe gently because they are afraid of making mistakes. We are bound to make mistakes while exploring our potential. Making mistakes is natural and normal. We learn by making mistakes. If we do not learn from our mistakes then we will simply repeat the mistakes until we do learn from them.

We follow our star to learn about love. We learn about love through lessons from mistakes we make along the way. These lessons teach us to understand love, which underpins the whole of life. Understanding lessons presented while exploring our potential will also greatly help us to discern our calling. This is because the call is suffused with love. It is vital that we learn from mistakes we make while following our star. If we fail to learn then we fail to grow and we will be fruitlessly repeating outmoded patterns of behaviour.

Our potential needs to be understood.

Sometimes it has taken time for me to learn lessons I received from following my star. All my life I have felt drawn to undertaking freelance projects. Doing freelance projects has been an important part of realising my potential.

I remember when I undertook to design a glider. I always loved flying and thought I could create a better motor glider than was available on the market. The project failed.

A few years later I met an aeronautical engineer at Queens University. He had a project to design and manufacture a light aircraft. I decided to help him by producing a marketing plan to launch the project. The marketing plan got nowhere.

The following year I decided to design a new type of vehicle for developing countries. I spent 3 months on the design but the project failed to progress beyond the report stage. (See Your Healing From Arrogance page 165).

Why did all these projects fail? The first project failed because I didn't:

- Involve others in the project
- Gather together the necessary resources
- Acquire knowledge needed to carry out the project
- Cultivate contacts to make it a success
- Respond to a proven need
- Have a humble approach to carrying out the project

Interestingly, the second and third projects failed for exactly the same reasons. I didn't learn the lessons that were repeated from the first project. That is why these projects also failed.

I hadn't understood my life-path because I hadn't used my insight.

After the third failure I decided to take a serious look at why I was failing in my freelance projects. I reflected on my past projects and I wrote down what I had learned from the lessons they presented.

A few years later I decided to research running a business exhibition in Northern Ireland as my next freelance project. This time I decided to learn from my insight. I wrote down lessons from my three previous failed projects and made sure I had learned from those lessons.

- Involve others in the project:
I involved the Federation of Small Businesses.
- Gather together the necessary resources:
I organized major sponsorship from an international telecommunications company.
- Acquire the knowledge I needed to carry out the project:
I talked to others who had organized exhibitions.
- Cultivate contacts needed to make it a success:
I worked alongside an exhibition company with a proven track record.
- Respond to a proven need:
I carried out a questionnaire to establish that the small business community would support such an initiative (the questionnaire showed they would).
- Have a humble approach to carrying out the project:

I did not think I had all the answers. I involved others and acted as a facilitator for other people's efforts.

When the time came to decide to go ahead with the project my inner guide was absolutely clear. It said, "Do this project." We received many appreciative letters from exhibitors. It was a great success. I had learned my lessons. I could now apply what I had learned to any future freelance projects.

 UNFOLDING
YOUR WINGS

Experiment in fulfilling your potential by pursuing activities that you feel guided to undertake. This is the best way I know to grow as a person. If you are afraid of failure try and reduce the power of that word by seeing failure as an opportunity to learn something new. If you feel attracted to a particular activity but are afraid of the risk involved, ask your guidance to show you a simple first step where the risk is minimal.

Our potential needs to be understood. When we follow our star we will fail and we will attract lessons. These lessons will apply to every aspect of our lives including hobbies, friends, family, work and relationships. If we reflect on our failures and difficulties and learn our lessons, our understanding will grow. As a consequence we will learn about love and we will become more sensitive to the inner call.

Envoi

I am opening to my potential.
I have made a mistake.
What am I to do?

The mistake has been made. What is past is past.
How can I make the mistake into success?

I can learn from the mistake.
I can learn the lesson given from following my potential.
I can learn about love.

I learn my lesson.
My mistake is transformed into success.
Next time I know how to behave,
And I am grateful.

A great curving crescent of golden sand runs from the town to the pan rocks. The air resounds with children's laughter and lapping waves. Families are gathered in small groups to build sandcastles and sunbathe. A few have taken to the water. Dark patches of seaweed are visible through the azure blue sea. Out on the ocean a single white yacht leaves harbour. Two men shout and laugh as cold water stimulates their warm bodies.

Your Potential Needs Persistence

If we are to enjoy a swim in Ireland we have to persist, undressing on a windy beach and pressing on despite the shock to our bodies, wading deeper and deeper into cold water. Persistence is a vital quality to cultivate when following our potential. The way is difficult, especially in the early days. As we open up to our guided life we are confronted with our deepest fears. Our existing assumptions about life and how it can best be lived are fundamentally challenged.

If we don't persist, what hope have we of travelling such a journey?

 UNFOLDING
YOUR WINGS

Try not to engage in blind persistence. When living a guided life endeavour to understand what is happening and to divine the meaning of the lessons with which you are being presented. When you combine persistence with understanding in this way then your journey will be really fruitful.

In the example under the previous heading I had failed at three projects in a row. At this point I could have given up carrying out freelance projects. However, I knew that I was strongly drawn to freelance projects. Pursuing them was crucial to the development of my potential. It was when I combined persistence with understanding, by undertaking the fourth project differently, that I was rewarded with success.

If we fail, and respond by blaming others, cultivating a cynical attitude to life, then all progress will be halted. We will remain stuck and miserable. We need to remember that no matter how other people

behave towards us, we can control only our own behaviour. Therefore we
need to persist while at the same time always remaining open to learning
and to changing our responses as situations grow and develop.

This approach will benefit us in our relationships and in our projects.
No energy will be wasted. All efforts at change will be directed inwards
to changing ourselves. Even if others remain cynical and negative we
will prosper and win through in the end. Positive energy applied with
understanding and persistence is an unstoppable force. We are adopt-
ing an approach which is in harmony with the principles of evolution.
Consequently we will be supported by life.

 UNFOLDING
YOUR WINGS

Once you begin to explore your potential and learn the lessons
they offer, you will notice that a mysterious force is helping
and supporting you. Things will begin to fall into place. You will
experience coincidences that help your life develop. You may even
start to feel a loving presence travelling with you. As you feel and
experience this help, your faith will strengthen and you will feel able
to take bigger risks.

Persistence is a rare quality. We will gain immeasurably by cultivating
it. When I worked as a management consultant I used to be surprised
at how easily professional business people would give up on a project.
Sometimes they would even do all the hard bits, and yet fail to follow
through to completion. I can think of marriages I know where one of
the partners has been astonished to find that their spouse wants a divorce
after only one year. In some cases the person didn't have it in them to
persist. Consequently they failed to develop their character and to reap
the rewards.

Whether we are engaged in our work, are building a better marriage
or working to improve our health, persistence and understanding applied
together yield amazing results.

Envoi

Exploring my potential can be tough.
Developing my potential can be hard.
Realising my potential can be long.

That is why I need to persist.

When times are rocky I dig deep.
When I dig deep I develop my character.
When I develop my character I mature as a person.

When I mature as a person
I do not complain about my destiny.
I know I am receiving help and support
From a mysterious source and I am in love with the journey.

Rocks lie like flat plates, linking pebbles to still ocean water. Their honey-coloured smooth surface is patterned with glistening green seaweed. Brown sea moss contributes colours. Beyond the rocks, shelve shallows with free-floating weed and sandy floor. The patterns in the sand echo the patterns in the weed, etched by wandering waves.

Your Potential Absorbs Unusual Happenings

As we wander the way, we are hoping to improve the quality of our lives. We quite naturally seek out relationships, work and friends who we think will make our lives happier and more fulfilling. , although we try to avoid it, eventually we are bound to encounter unusual happenings.

Unusual happenings are events that happen to us along the way, that are not of our conscious choosing and involve loss, grief and heartache. Examples include diseases, accidents, divorce, becoming bankrupt, being a victim of crime, experiencing the death of a loved one, etc.

How can we make such difficult experiences part of a fortunate life?

When we meet with unusual happenings we are inclined to experience feelings of bitterness, cynicism, self-pity, anger, resentment, and a host of other negative emotions. These are all part of a natural grief reaction.

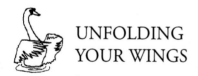

UNFOLDING
YOUR WINGS

Healing takes place when you allow these feelings to surface and be expressed. You can go into the woods and scream, do artistic drawings, write, talk to a friend or simply sit alone and cry. If you express these feelings fully they will eventually leave. (See Your Calling Is Elevated Through The Release Of Pain, page 66.)

This is the vale of tears. It is the way we cope with loss. It is important to remember that the vale of tears is not all pain. We open our hearts through this grieving process and we become aware of a deeper reality.

When a loved one dies, or we have a disabling accident, our favourable outer circumstances are shattered and we are grief-stricken. For a while we may think happiness is no longer possible. We grieve because we believe our happiness is dependent on our lives having these favourable circumstances. By fully experiencing this grief, happiness eventually returns. We then discover that our new-found happiness is more durable, because it is closer to real happiness—a happiness that is independent of our circumstances. This is one of the purposes of following our calling—to come upon happiness that is independent of our circumstances. This happiness endures, no matter what life throws at us.

 ## UNFOLDING YOUR WINGS

You open your heart through this grief process and give birth to deeper compassion and empathy. This means you are more able to empathise with others who suffer. You will find you are more inclined to reach out and help. You are becoming more loving.

Aspects of our lives that were important may not now hold the same prominence in our mind and in our values. We are more in touch with the durable, timeless and dependable. We are more in touch with reality. We are also more sensitive to our calling.

In my own life I have been touched by two unusual happenings, schizophrenia and depression. As a result of these two diseases I lost my career, my income, my friends and my happiness. Because I eventually embraced these illnesses and worked through the grief associated with them, I became a much stronger person. I now have a new set of values, a new understanding, a new compassion and a new more durable happiness given by the beauty of the radiant swan within.

Although I did not consciously choose them, these were the most significant events to happen to me as I explored my potential. Looking back on that difficult period of my life, I can honestly say that it was a blessing in disguise. (See Your Healing From Adversity, page 179.)

If we embrace the feelings of loss and work through the associated grief, unusual happenings that we encounter along the way lead us to a happiness that is independent of our circumstances.

Envoi

I am exploring my potential,
And I have had an unfortunate accident.

I am suffering loss
I am grief stricken.
I am in mourning

The grief can be held in no longer.

I express my pain.
I exorcise my loss.
I embrace my grief.

Through my grief I am healed
And find a new kind of happiness.
In my newfound happiness
I am aware of the timeless, indestructible reality,
An inner diamond,
Unaffected by the rigors of loss and decay.

Brown rock forms a sloping shore. Close to the ocean, where tidal waters touch, a million tiny, conical crustaceans cling. Seaweed clings in clumps to crevasses. Blue ocean water gently laps, flowing into small rock gullies. The water gently tinkles and gurgles. Seaweed surfaces sensuously before dropping down deep.

Your Potential Is Illogical
(when judged by outer criteria)

The journey is directed from deep within. Guidance comes from the call. Inner guidance often leads us to make decisions that are not to our material advantage and are materially unproductive, but will yield spiritual fruits. When following our destiny we are often asked to give up situations that benefit us materially, so that we might gain other inner benefits like the presence of more peace and love in our lives.

Just recently, in my own life, I felt drawn to close down my business and go into retreat by withdrawing from the world and spending more time sitting quietly in my own home. I followed this guidance and as a result found great depths of inner peace and contentment. This book was also written as a result of that period of withdrawal. I have a friend who recently sold his "proper house" in a local town and moved to a mobile home so that he could fulfil his calling to live in the village community where he works. He has felt much greater levels of contentment since he has made this move. I frequent a local vegetarian café. The owner gave up a lucrative job in a major corporation to pursue his love of cooking. The café only yields a minimal income.

 UNFOLDING
YOUR WINGS

If you feel drawn to a project that is important to you but may yield a smaller income, trust that you will find a way to have your needs met while pursuing your project.

A materially unproductive activity I felt drawn to was to take off most days for a walkabout. When on walkabout I would wander for hours aimlessly. There was no material benefit to this walking. I was not trying to get anywhere. I was not doing it to become fit. I wasn't doing it to enjoy the scenery. I wasn't following a pre-planned route. I was just doing it. I did not know why I was doing it. In time I came to realize that going on walkabout was helping to break up my rigid ways of relating and thinking and increasing my sensitivity. We don't always have to know why we are doing something for the activity to yield benefits. What is important is that we feel guided do it.

Sitting in silence "doing nothing" is a materially unproductive activity. People in our western materialistic society find this particularly difficult to cope with. I often hear parents say to their children, "Don't just sit there—do something".

From an early age we are indoctrinated to be active "doing something." "Doing nothing" is regarded as unproductive, irrelevant and for wasters. As we progress through school, college and work, our lives are increasingly filled with things for us to do.

When I worked as a management consultant and was involved with the business community in Northern Ireland, the first thing business people would ask me was "Are you busy?" I felt an obligation to say yes, even if I wasn't. Then one day I was asked the usual question, when I was out at a convention. I wasn't particularly busy and I decided to experiment and said "No, I'm not busy at present." Well you could have heard a pin drop. The group of business people I was with did not know how to cope with my answer. They parted and drifted away. To them not being busy was a sign of failure.

Many of us reach such a state of inner compulsion, that we cannot exist for a minute without some sort of noise or other activity to distract us from our inner silence. When we are busy, engaged in activity, with no counter balancing periods of inner quiet and reflection, we are running away from our own healing. It is during periods of inner quiet that our pain and angst will surface to be healed. By sitting silently, we find that presence that makes our lives truly meaningful.

Be still and know.

Pursuing our potential is illogical, but only if judged by outer criteria. Following our potential cultivates our highest qualities. If we value our inner world, the world where we can nurture peace, harmony, freedom and love, then pursuing our potential makes perfect sense.

Envoi

I give a loan to a friend who cannot repay it.
My other friends do not understand, but I understand.
I change to part-time work and pursue my love of sculpture.
My friends do not understand, but I understand.
I spend the day mowing my elderly neighbour's lawn.
My friends do not understand, but I understand.

The inner call guides me to live from the heart.
I am happy to oblige.

There are no waves. Sunlight picks patterns on the calm ocean. Two seagulls sit motionless on honey coloured rock. There is only gentle gurgling as still ocean laps water-bound boulders. Brown seaweed slides slowly near a single submerged rock. The rock touches the surface, radiating ripples.

Your Potential Can Be Crazy To Family And Friends (but sane to genuine friends)

As we follow our dreams the effects of our journey will ripple out and touch family and friends. It is important to have friends with whom we can share our journey. If we are new to the journey, we can be disappointed to discover that our existing friends will often not support us in the decisions we make about our life. We may even find that family and friends disagree vehemently with decisions we are making.

Most people judge the value of the decisions they make by their benefits in the outer world. Just recently, when I closed down my business to enter a quiet space and retreat from the world, some of my friends did not understand the move and a few advised against it. Such a move appeared irrational to them. That is because they did not understand my calling. My genuine friends, with whom I shared my inner life, and who are living intuitively, did understand and were supportive.

 UNFOLDING
YOUR WINGS

If you find your support withering in this way, endeavour to persist with your decision, provided it is guided from within, and find genuine friends who will understand and support you in the difficult decisions ahead.

As we travel the journey we will make more and more genuine friends. Close friends are people with whom we share intimacies, like our deepest fears, highest dreams, personal philosophies on life, doubts, failures and successes. Genuine friends try to help us understand our lives, so that we are able to make the best decisions. When we do make those decisions they happily support us. Close friends are much more valuable than financial riches.

Before I started on the spiritual journey in earnest, my hobby was hang-gliding. I had a lot of hang-gliding friends. When we met we would discuss hang-gliding and nothing else. We did not share our inner life. Eventually I gave up hang-gliding and took up charity work as my hobby. When engaged in charity work I made new friends. These friends were willing to talk and share their inner world. They were also more supportive and did not try to put me down as my hang-gliding friends did. Eventually I met other friends who were also living their dream. These became my genuine friends. With these close friends I was able to share more and more of my inner world, including my doubts and insecurities. I really value friends with whom I can be intimate.

Do not be surprised if you decide to cultivate new friends as you lead a life devoted to listening to and following inner guidance. Be open to encounters and associations that arise from your new interests. By inviting genuine friends into your life, you will be able to share more of yourself and feel really supported. You will be a truly rich person, no matter what your financial circumstances.

Envoi

Dear friends—Where would we be without you?
In a harsh and cruel world
Your friendship brings softness and love.
With our close friendship we have
Understanding when we are confused,
Compassion when we are hurting,
Sympathy when we are sad
And joy when we are glad.

Dear friend, I turn to you, heart open, vulnerable,
Needing to share and you welcome me in.
I have a secret never told; you hear it.
I am in pain; you feel it.
I bring glad tidings; you are full of my joy.

Although my life may appear strange to another,
You do not reject me.
Although it may be difficult to understand,
You do not judge me.
Although I may have failed and be thought stupid by others,
You do not criticize me.
Although I may be in pain and unattractive to others,
You do not shun me.

We know that we are travelling inward to the great beyond.
We share our pain, that we may be healed.
We share our secrets that we may be forgiven.
We share our glad tidings that we may be full of joy.
We give to each other freely and without reservation.

I know that in giving to you, I am giving to myself,
For we are as one.

A beautiful pond lies ringed with rock and surrounded by ocean. The bottom is visible in strong summer sunshine. Long stringy seaweed floats close to the pond's edge. A small brown fish glides from under the seaweed. She moves with a sudden deft flick of her tail near a stony shelled crab creeping sideways. Blue sky and white cloud are reflected in the pond's gently rippled surface.

Your Potential Can Make You Feel As If You Are Lost

When we start to walk the way, we become less certain and our outer life begins to reflect that uncertainty. Old goals and ambitions may not have the same appeal. We may not feel the same connection with the career path we have chosen in life. Whether or not we live in an up-market part of town may not be so important. Getting a new car may no longer be so attractive. This is happening because we are changing our goals from outer goals concerned with amassing material wealth, to inner goals concerned with increasing our ability to experience peace, love and happiness.

As I made this move from outer to inner goals, I decided to change the plans I had for my life. I have changed my plans twice, from being an architect to a management consultant and from being a management consultant to a writer. Making these changes was rather unsettling. I needed to acknowledge that my present career path no longer satisfied me spiritually. I had to admit this before an alternative path opened. As a result I felt lost as I made the transition from one career path to another. Feeling lost for a period was an inevitable part of my transition experience.

When I took time out for healing, I felt lost for extended periods. Creating an open space for my own healing brought forward my ability to nurture and be creative. I moved from having my day structured by my job or my commitments, to having a day I could structure any way I pleased, or even had an absence of structure, by letting the day unfold without a predetermined plan.

Being in a healing space like this was highly experimental. How was I to spend my day? What activities were best? How did I know if the way I was spending my day was healing for me? I felt as if I was drifting in the ocean without a paddle or rudder to help give me direction. Listening to my inner mentor helped me answer these questions and structure my day. I needed to remember that during these healing times my direction and purpose was inner healing. As long as I felt I was making progress with my inner healing, it did not matter that my outer life lacked direction and purpose.

During the years I spent on experimental healing I went on walk-about, allowed fears and tears to surface, nurtured myself with quiet times and read spiritually enlightening books. For most of this period I felt lost, yet deep inside I knew that what I was doing was meaningful, so I kept going. Throughout this difficult period my close friends were supporting me. I did not concern myself with the opinions of others. At that time I was a single man. If you have a partner it would be wise to gain their support if you feel drawn to enter a healing period. This could be difficult if they do not value inner healing and the spiritual life.

During my period of inner healing I often wondered if I would ever emerge from these lost feelings. The openness of healing periods and periods of transition helped me gain the trust and sensitivity I needed to become ever more dependent on inner guidance. Eventually I emerged with a new expanded sense of purpose and direction and with new, more rewarding outer world goals given by my new, more purified calling.

UNFOLDING YOUR WINGS

If you are entering a healing period or a period of transition try and embrace the unfamiliar open-ended feeling that will be arising. Ask your calling to show you new possibilities that may be found in your transition period. Do not be in a rush for answers. Periods of transition usually herald profound changes in your life. Lots of open space and inner quiet may be needed for these new possibilities to become clear.

Periods of transition and inner healing are not easy. But they are necessary if we are to go through a personal metamorphosis. During these times we are a bit like the caterpillar retreating from the world to build a cocoon and settle inside. To the onlooker nothing seems to be happening. Then one day, to everyone's surprise, a beautiful butterfly emerges.

Envoi

I feel lost, floating in mid-ocean, rudderless.
My friends do not understand.
My family does not understand.
Sometimes I do not understand.
But I know it is right to be here.
I am casting my gaze inward towards peace, love and truth.
It is painful.

My close friends understand that pain and are there for me.
My days go by.
Their only purpose is the one I give them.
I reach inside to the gentle murmurings
From my ever-present heart.
Its voice is so soft, so delicate and so quiet.
Can I really rely on this still small voice
To carry me through to a new life?

I doubt.

But deep inside there is a knowing.
My friends doubt me but I know.
My family doubts me but I know.
I even doubt myself, yet still this inner knowing persists.
Truth lies at the heart of trust.
Emptiness harbours healing.
That is how butterflies are born.

Golden sand is pockmarked from gentle rain. Among the pockmarks, half-buried in the sand, are white, buff, orange, grey and black pebbles. They are as numerous as the stars. Their colours blend perfectly with the sand. A wavy line leads away from the small pebble area. This wandering line marks the meeting of pockmarked rain danced sand, with smooth wave washed sand. It runs for a mile.

Your Potential Can Make You Feel As If You Are Losing Control

When wandering our lifeline, we are challenged to change from outer goals, like amassing material wealth or cultivating status, to inner goals like the reformation of our character. As we make this transition we feel as if we are losing control. The truth is that we are losing control—we are letting go of our old materialistic values and increasingly listening to and following our calling. When we do this our lives become motivated by love.

Previously we may have been motivated by status, money, power, or by cultivating the good opinion of others. The plans we had for our life were a reflection of these values. When I trained and worked as an architect, I harboured a secret desire to be rich and famous. I saw architecture as a way of making my mark, gaining attention and earning lots of money. At the time I was not aware I was motivated in my career choice by these values. When I lost these values, I became more sensitive to my calling and being an architect no longer had the same appeal.

When I began to realize that architecture was no longer satisfying, I was uneasy. I felt pulled forward by a hidden inner force into an uncertain future. Rationally it made perfect sense to continue developing my architectural career. I had studied seven years to become qualified. It was secure and the prospects were good. But my heart was no longer in it. The call was guiding me towards being a freelance management consultant because I could bring forth more love in that role. As I let go of my commitment to architecture I felt a very real fear in letting go of the secure profession that I knew well but which no longer fitted my life. In letting go of my architecture career I felt as if I was losing control. Then enthusiasm grew as opportunities to get started in management consultancy appeared. Following my inner guidance was taking me towards a new working life.

As we let go of old outmoded values and are motivated increasingly by love, we become progressively more dependent on our inner guidance for the decisions we make and the direction for our lives. Life becomes simpler. When faced with difficult decisions there is an inner knowing that we can depend on. It may take us to some strange places, but we can rely on its wisdom. I have come to trust the inner call implicitly.

Envoi

I listen, heart open.
I hear the call.
My calling is soft and persistent.
Slowly it wears down my stubborn attachment
To all that is not love.
Like water flowing around a boulder in mid-stream.
I am that boulder.

For years I have sat immovable.
I feel the soft water.
Slowly it is washing away my grip.
I feel as if I am losing control.
Then the flood comes and I am washed away.

Now I am flowing with the water.
Now I am living out of love.
Now love has control…and I am free.

Wisps of high cirrus cloud are painted against the milk blue sky. Between the shore and Rathlin Island a line of small grey and white clouds hangs motionless, close to calm ocean water. On the horizon across the Irish Sea, fluffy white clouds are towering. The cloud base lies low, just above the land. The towering tops reach into the blue in great boiling columns of cotton white.

Your Potential Can Be Frightening

Like watching thunderclouds form, feeling lost and out of control can be frightening. The old certainties are gone. They will never come back. We can no longer rely on our old goals. We need to learn to have faith and to trust. This is especially true when nothing seems fixed or certain.

Being lost and out of control are means adopted by the call to bring our fears to the surface. When our fears surface they leave us and we receive healing. We may have quite understandable worries. We may be worried that our partner disagrees with what we are doing, or that our family members do not understand, or we may be worried that we will run out of money. Following our potential will challenge us to trust in a fundamental way. Trust stops being a concept in our heads and becomes a central feature of the way we run our lives.

As I followed my potential I had money worries. I went for long periods without working and had to rely on small amounts of money I received from the government. I worried because I did not seem to be achieving anything (I was achieving inwardly, of course, but this was not always obvious). I was worried that I no longer had any status in society (this was good for me and taught me not to be dependent on status for my self-esteem). I also worried if I would ever come out of my healing period (this taught me to have patience).

In the end I did not so much move away from feeling lost and out of control, as enter fully into it as a permanent state. I adapted to it. It felt comfortable. In that settled state I discovered freedom, true love and security. I had found a life centred in love and in the call. I had gone beyond my fears and was at peace.

Envoi

I have fears...inside.
They are buried deep.
How can I be free of my fear?
How can I live a life free of anxiety?

I follow my potential in trust.
As I travel the inner journey my fears surface.
I never knew I had such fear.
No wonder I was stubborn.
No wonder I was arrogant.
No wonder I could not love.

Like a volcano my fears surface and I am terrified.
Anger, jealousy, bitterness, resentment, and great sadness
All pour out.
It comes from fear.
I am emptying all negativity.
What do I have left?

Love. Only love,

...and great peace.

The rain stops. Land and ocean reawaken. Over the ocean sky opens to the blue beyond. Sunlight picks out the white, green and brown cliffs of Rathlin Island. A cloud's dark grey shadow moves imperceptibly across these colourful cliffs. The air sings with cascading sounds of breakers on the beach, as the blue ocean sparkles and shimmers in the distance.

Your Potential Is Full Of Joy

I am just back from my morning walk along the beach. My face is glowing with the warm fresh air. The ocean was overflowing with beauty in the July sunshine.

I was amazed at a bird which simply dropped out of the upper branch of a beach side tree and fell in a controlled swoop, opening its wings fully before landing. She was an interesting colour, blue grey and black. She was with her mate. The mate found a piece of shiny silver wrapping paper, picked it up and hopped over a tuft of grass to examine his new discovery.

How many of us love life enough to find joy in simple things, the flight of a bird, the smile on a friend's face, the silvery whiteness of frost on the grass? Most of us are far too preoccupied.

Many people look forward to find joy. They look for joy in holidays, dates, parties, a new car or Christmas day. Of course we can and do find joy in these, but joy can be much more than an occasional experience, interspersed with drabness. Joy is all around.

Exploring our potential helps us to go beyond our pre-occupations. Following our star helps to heal our worries, anxieties, fears, ambitions, strivings, comparisons, addictions and our continual need to turn everything over in our minds. When we go beyond all this we see things as they truly are, in all their glorious simplicity.

 UNFOLDING YOUR WINGS

Joy is your natural state.
Try to believe this and to aspire to this.

Joy is the natural state for human beings. Joy is an inevitable outcome of healing. We know we are making progress when we find a spontaneous joy arising in our hearts for no apparent reason. This is the joy that has no cause.

This is the joy that is present when we have love in our hearts.

Envoi

Today I feel an expansive overpowering joy
That resides in my heart.

I was not given a present.
I did not go on holiday.
I did not meet my lover.

This joy is a mystery,
For it knows no cause
Other than the love I carry within.
A love that blossoms
As I endeavour to explore my potential.

Along the coast Fair Head stands majestic in the afternoon sunshine. Even at this distance great boulders are visible on the headland's steep sea slope. Above the slope a serrated sea cliff pierces the sky. In places the headland is covered with gleaming green and outcrops of rusted rock. Far off, beyond the sea cliffs, a distant dog barks suddenly.

Your Potential Is Full Of Surprises

When following our potential we notice that our daily life is filled with an increasing number of surprises. Before, much of the day may have seemed rather drab. Now we can't wait to get out of bed to see what the day will bring.

As we listen to and follow the inner call, our lives are filling up with surprises, because we are becoming more open, flexible, discerning and creative. We start to attract new happenings. We discover we have new talents. We receive new gifts. Friends make surprise visits more often. We make new discoveries. We are introduced to new interesting people. We express ourselves creatively in new ways. We reach new levels of understanding. These new happenings add a great richness and diversity to our lives. These surprise happenings also hold great personal meaning.

In addition to attracting new happenings we also notice many more existing happenings, like the flight of a gull, or the bark of a dog. These happenings are very interesting and surprising. We would have completely missed them in earlier times.

When I began to live intuitively I discovered an abundance of new talents. Some formed gradually and some arose almost instantly from nowhere, almost fully formed. I discovered to my surprise, that I had a talent for helping business people. This was all the more surprising because I had no background in business. I discovered I was good at working with groups of people who were gathered together in teams or in committees. I discovered I was a good counsellor to my friends. I was surprised to discover that I could write. It was especially surprising to discover that I could write poetic prose. I had never tried it before. I discovered that I really enjoyed woodland work and working with trees.

I also began to receive increasing numbers of surprise gifts, not just at Christmas, but also throughout the year. (With the exception of one picture, I have been given everything I've hung on the walls of my home.) These wall hangings are all personally significant to me. I am invited out to the cinema and invited for meals. I am continually invited out for coffee.

Often I will receive a new gift and find that it is exactly what I need. While writing this book, I have been loaned two books on how to self-publish, a book on how to source commercial publishers and given a manual on how to promote my book on the Internet. I didn't even have to ask and I have obtained all the information I need to get my book published!

I have received many surprise visits from friends. Some call regularly, some drop in when they are passing and some call occasionally. Some call round for a coffee and a chat, some want to invite me for a walk and some want to use my computer. All are welcome.

While following my potential I have made many new surprise discoveries. I am discovering new teachings, new websites, new books and new music, all of them personally significant.

I have received a surprising number of new introductions. These become new friends, or new associates connected with my hobbies or my work. I have reached new heights of creative expression. This has led to surprising new projects, hobbies, work and new forms of artistic expression.

 UNFOLDING
YOUR WINGS

If you feel denied a life of surprises, try being more open. Experiment. The next time a friend offers you something, say yes, followed by thank you.

As I have followed my destiny, I have been surprised at how my understanding has grown. This has been the result of new discussions, surprising fresh insights, and sharing new intimacies with friends.

Attracting new happenings are not the only surprises that have entered my life. Every day I encounter surprises which are a normal part of daily life, but which previously I would have missed.

In the early morning I go alone for a walk along the beach. This walk is never the same. Each morning it has its surprises. This morning there were three birds, each sitting in a different tree. They were calling out to one another. First one would call, from another tree there would be a reply, then the third bird would respond from the third tree. I looked but could not see the birds, so it seemed as if the three trees were engaged in a triangular conversation. It was most amusing.

This was one of many surprises on this morning's walk. It's the same when I go for a cycle ride up the river or take a walk through the city at midnight. Sometimes I sit and just listen to the sounds of the city around me at night. These sounds are always changing.

I can be really surprised by the expressions on peoples' faces. People have such a range of facial expressions. I love to be surprised by a shop assistant's radiant smile. It makes me light up with a smile in return. Nature and people are full of surprises. It was all happening before I began to lead a life devoted to following my inner call, but I was too busy to notice.

As well as lots of new surprises in the outer world, I receive an abundance of surprises within. These include new insights, understandings, creative ideas and visions of the way forward. When we follow our potential we are delighted at the number of surprises. So much is new. Even the old are new! That is because we are evolving and so we see the old with new levels of understanding and heightened awareness. Being surprised is an integral part of leading a life guided by the beauty of the inner swan.

Envoi

A precious new day has dawned,
I cannot wait to begin.
I wonder what the day will bring,
A visit from a cherished friend,
New discoveries in the bookshop,
A breakthrough at work,

A visit to the quiet riverbank?

I rise and greet the dawn.
Pink and rose red fills the horizon.
I can feel the vibrancy of the morning sun fill my veins.
Sitting quietly before breakfast,
I listen to the emerging sounds of the ocean.
My day is pregnant with purpose.

The mouth of the small dry riverbed lies open to the sea. Waves run up the beach and enter the river's empty channel as a barely perceptible movement. On entering, each wave banks higher against the reverse flow of water, creating sensuous smooth surges that caress the riverbank. In time the wave slowly changes from a single mass into a series of short steep waves with breaking edges sparkling in the sunshine. Eventually the wave withers and dies, the water stretching like a rubber band, as it returns sliding into the ocean.

Your Potential Reveals Genuine Friends

Our friends are people we return to again and again to find and offer support, love and understanding. Close friends are precious. Real friends are interested in you. They understand, sympathize, offer practical support, listen, don't judge, give of their time, give of their money, share intimacies and bring joy.

Genuine friends are hard to find. They are not easily found in the places where people normally socialize, like pubs, bars, clubs, churches, work etc. It is possible to find real friends in these places, but such finds are rare. Close friends are found by following our potential. When we lead a life with increasing potential we are living our lives by listening to and following inner guidance. By living this way, we mysteriously find that we will recognize and automatically be attracted to other people who are living the same way. Following my potential is the only way I know to find and make genuine friends.

There are many ways close friends can come into our lives. Sometimes existing friends turn into close personal friends. This can happen with old friends who begin to follow their star at the same time we do, or who begin sometime before or after we have started. Sometimes family members turn into genuine friends. This is particularly satisfying, because we then have both the bond of sharing a family and being close friends together in the one person. Sometimes we are led or are introduced to new people while following our potential and we quickly know that they could become real friends.

My friends have changed and evolved as I have travelled the inner journey. Before I led a life devoted to the inner call I had friends through work, hang-gliding, squash and tennis. These were not genuine friends.

At the time I thought they were close friends, because I was not clear what real friends were like. Still, deep inside, I had nagging doubts about the quality of their friendship. Although I saw them often, I did not feel that I really knew them. This is because we talked about what we did, not about who we were. We did not reveal our dreams, doubts, anxieties, joys and insecurities to one another.

When I took up charity work as a hobby, I began to lead a devoted life. Through charity work I met people who were closer to being genuine friends. I felt I knew them better than my other friends because they discussed personal matters. They did not reveal enough to be close friends. They were half way between everyday friends and genuine friends.

In time a few of my charity friends introduced me to some of their friends. A few of these people became my first real friends. I made other close friends by attending personal growth activities, workshops and classes. I discovered that these places were quite good for meeting genuine people. During this time family members were becoming close friends. One old friend also changed into a genuine friend. This was happening because I had started to explore my potential.

UNFOLDING YOUR WINGS

If you would like to make more genuine friends try some of the personal development opportunities available on www.alifediscovered.org or visit the website's Discussion Forum. Alternatively you could join some local personal development workshops or night classes.

Eventually I became so delighted with the benefits of having genuine friends that with a close personal friend as my partner, I started a club called New Horizons, a friendship club for people interested in personal development. As a consequence of starting this club the number of real friends I have has really grown. I feel intimately involved in my close friends' lives. Sharing my life with so many caring people is deeply enriching.

It is important that we can share intimacies with our friends. We need friends to help us find, share and understand our potential. Genuine friends are precious. They are precious because they bring love. We love them in return and we know we would lose our way without them.

Our intimate friends act as our everyday counsellors. A friend once put a note in my office. It said, "It takes two to know one fully." We cannot know ourselves on our own. We need to share ourselves with others. When we share our lives with another openly and honestly and that person is a genuine friend who loves and tries to understand us, that very act of sharing will help us fulfil our potential. In my conversations with my close friends the way opens up before me and becomes clearer. We can do this for one another because we are both listening to the call. Love and understanding blossom within each, because we are living intuitively.

Through sharing we discover that "A problem shared is a problem halved" and that "A joy shared is a joy doubled." No wonder genuine friends are so precious! Lets look more closely at the characteristics of close friends so that we will know whether or not we are able to share creatively.

Genuine friends are interested in you.

When we are with a close personal friend we will talk about many shared interests. We may both be interested in horse riding, so of course we will talk about that. We may both like to go to the cinema, so of course we will both go and see films or watch a video together. Both may have children, so we will discuss our children's lives. The one thing that cements our friendship, more than all these shared interests, is that our real friend is primarily interested in us and we are primarily interested in him or her.

Genuine friends understand.

No one will understand us fully. No one will understand us perfectly. But close personal friends will do their very best to understand. They will be interested in hearing about the intimate parts of our life and not be embarrassed, or think it silly to talk about such things. They will think about our problems, even when we are not there. They may ring us up if they think they have something to say which will help. They are there to assist and they are actively working for our own highest interests.

Our closest friend will be the one who understands us best. Therefore he is well placed to help. A genuinely close friend is particularly good at assisting in exploring our potential.

Genuine friends sympathize.

Close friends really care. When we are in trouble or having a difficult time, they don't dismiss our problems as unimportant; they sympathize. They are right there with us. As we tell them of our difficulties we may be surprised to look up and see tears running down their face. This is because they are feeling what we are feeling. They not only sympathize verbally but emotionally as well.

Genuine friends listen.

Close friends meet our needs. This means that when we both meet and we feel a burning desire to share something, our friend will sense this, become quiet and simply listen. He/she will listen attentively, picking up on every word. Nothing will be missed. If we feel the need to share but are hesitating, perhaps out of fear, or because we don't know what to say, our real friend will lovingly and gently offer support and encourage us to speak. When we do so they will immediately switch to listening attentively. If neither of us needs to speak then real friends are not embarrassed to be in our company silently.

Genuine friends don't judge.

Close friends will refrain from telling us whether they think what we are doing or thinking is right or wrong or good or bad. Instead of judging, they focus on helping us understand our situation, so that we will know what course of action to take. When we come to a decision they are happy to support us, even if they do not think the decision we have made is correct.

Genuine friends offer practical support.

Close friends are happy to share their resources. I couldn't afford a car when I had very little income. I had a friend who lived nearby. He knew I was a bit stranded and offered to share his car with me. He charged a small fee per mile. He calculated this fee to cover the cost of the car only. There was no financial benefit in the deal for him. He simply wanted to help.

Another friend has a bicycle workshop in his house. Whenever I need my bicycle fixed he often offers to do it for me free of charge.

Genuine friends give of their time.

The other day I went for a coffee with a close personal friend. We spent three hours over two coffees talking, helping and supporting each other with our lives. We do this regularly, at least once a week. Real friends are happy to give of their time to be with us and offer support. That is because we are a number one priority.

Genuine friends give their money.

When I was in a tight financial corner, a close friend asked me to draw out some sketch plans to help him get permission to build a new house. He had money and I had not, so although I was doing the work privately from my own home, he offered to pay the full professional fee. The final bill was quite steep, but he was happy to pay. I did a wonderful job for him and he was granted permission to build.

Genuine friends share intimacies.

With close friends the central pillar of our friendship is sharing our hopes, dreams, fears, doubts, successes, failures and loves. The extent to which we can share these intimate parts of our lives, determines how close we are.

Genuine friends bring joy.

When we are happy, our real friend is happy with us. When we are successful our close friend is there to celebrate. By being present our close friend is there to share the joy that only love can give, the joy that knows no cause.

Genuine friends help you find your calling.

If we are in doubt about what is and is not inner guidance, we can share our uncertainty with genuine friends. They will give us different perspectives on our situation or problem. By being open to these different perspectives, while continuing to listen within, we will find it easier to know what we are being called to do.

At times following our potential can be tough. It is natural to have doubts, fears and insecurities. It is in times like these that the love of close intimate friendships keeps us going. Genuine friends are much more important than financial wealth. Genuine friends give us unconditional love. It is the quality and number of our close friends that is a true indication of our wealth.

Of course the best way to discover genuine friends is to be a genuine friend to others!

Envoi

I am lost.
I am confused.
I am distraught.

I tell my story of lost love, harboured bitterness,
And deep loneliness.
I look up.
His soft eyes engage my own.
Tears of sympathy stream down his face.
I know I am loved.
The call has come to me, in the gentle words of a close friend
Speaking from the heart.
He speaks.
Words of great wisdom flow from his lips.
His gaze is full of love and compassion.

Slowly...slowly...my confusion dissipates.
Slowly...slowly...my mind clears.
Slowly...slowly...my heart begins to sing again.

I am freed of bitterness.
The chasm of loneliness closes over.
Love has returned.

Great gratitude.

Sunlight sparks off kelp-clad rocks.   Colours dance, mauve, pink and brown.   These rocks are washed with foam-filled water by the ocean's eternal rhythm.   Each wave approaches as a quiet ocean swelling that rises over rocks before cascading ocean bound with a deep sucking.   Brown kelp weaves back and forth and up and down with each beat of the ocean's heart.

Your Potential Is Deeply Meaningful

We may not realize it, but everything encountered while following our potential follows the eternal rhythm of life and is significant—every feeling, every thought, every person, every happening. These events are the heartbeat of our lives. As our understanding develops we become increasingly able to read the meaning of these signs. Signs that we encounter along the way can be either positive, drawing us to a particular course of action, or negative, taking us away from a particular course of action.

I had been hang-gliding for six years. I was spending less time with my hang-gliding buddies. I also felt, through inner guidance, increasing dissatisfaction in having hang-gliding as my hobby. Then I had an accident when taking off and, although unhurt, could easily have been killed. I decided from these signs that hang-gliding was no longer a suitable hobby for me. So I left and took up charity work instead. These were examples of negative signs taking me away from a particular course of action.

My existing business had entered a quiet period. Clients were not contacting me. Being at home alone and sitting quietly in my chair felt right. On the basis of these signs I put my business on the shelf and withdrew from the world. While I was in that quiet space I received the inspiration to write this book! The negative signs of clients' lack of interest in my existing business and the positive signs coming from inner guidance about spending long periods on my own at home, combined to encourage me to take this course of action. As we follow our potential we will be given many signs. These signs will help us find the way ahead.

UNFOLDING YOUR WINGS

Endeavour to become a dispassionate observer of the events unfolding in your present life. What are these events pointing towards? What are the positive and negative signs suggesting? Let the meaning of these events speak to you. You may learn something valuable about the road ahead.

Events, happenings and incidents in the outer world can help us understand the promptings we are receiving inwardly from our calling. All we need to do is learn to read their significance. As we follow our potential we encounter many meaningful coincidences. These coincidences help us to have our needs met, even if we are in tight financial circumstances.

During my healing period I was not working and had very little money. Although I lived in the centre of the city at the heart of the public transport system, some journeys were proving difficult to make. I made two new close personal friends. One of them helped me buy a bicycle adapted for carrying heavy loads and offered to service it for me. The other friend shared his car with me. Between the public transport system, my bicycle and the shared car, all my transport problems were solved, even though I had very little money.

As we see these meaningful coincidences at work in our lives, it helps us to develop faith and trust, not as an abstract theological concept but as a living reality at the heart of how we live our lives. Developing this faith and trust is important, because sometimes following our potential can feel like walking a tightrope. This applies whether our guided life path is currently a business project, a time of withdrawal and healing, or the ending of a relationship. At times we may have very little room to manoeuvre, especially financially. We need not worry because while we are following our potential an invisible force is supporting us, which will not let us fall. That force is love.

As we begin to transcend our worries fears and anxieties, we find ourselves in a flow of ever increasing love and significance. What is the significance? What do the signs point to? Where is our star taking us? Our destiny is taking us back. We are returning to wholeness. Travelling the inner journey has much more meaning than any other life path we could take.

Envoi

As I follow my potential
I am supported,
And I am loved.
Therefore I follow with faith.
Therefore I travel with trust.
Whenever I am really in need,
What I need comes to me.

My destiny opens before me
Like a long winding country lane.
I cannot see the extent of the journey
But I know I am right to travel it.
If I feel lost, the signs are my guides.
My potential is full of significance.

The great ocean is flat to the horizon. Near the shore, ridges of water rise from the surrounding flatness. Each watery ridge rears steeply as it nears the beach, held up by a gentle but persistent wind. Eventually the top hesitates, then drops with a crash. The wave is transformed in an instant into a broth of bubbles. This place between golden sand and blue ocean is filled with these rhythmic crashing sounds and foam-filled waters. Another ridge of water rises, guided by an unseen force.

Your Potential Is Being On A Roll, The Opposite Of A Rut

We need discipline to successfully run our lives. Unfortunately, many people associate discipline with harshness and severity. They have never experienced a discipline guided by an unseen force that sets them free.

Whether our discipline is harsh or freeing depends on whether we are in a rut or on a roll. If we are in a rut we will experience the discipline in our lives as severe, stressful and harsh. We will feel imprisoned, unfulfilled and sad. Our lives will be permeated with gnawing discontent. We may seek escape in vigorous hobbies. We need these hobbies to dissipate the anger and frustration we have inside.

This anger and frustration arises because we have not fully accepted the discipline we have in our lives. We do not accept it because we do not love the discipline. We do not love it because the discipline does not come from inner guidance.

If we have a job to perform, or duties to undertake for others, and these duties do not sit comfortably in our hearts, then we will rebel against the discipline these duties require. If these duties are unavoidable, like caring for a disabled child or elderly relative, then we need to find that place in our hearts where we can love and accept these duties. If our duties can be changed then we need to look at how we can change them.

UNFOLDING
YOUR WINGS

You can choose to redesign the discipline in your life and develop a more loving and positive approach. If you accept your inevitable duties, change other inappropriate duties and build some simple spiritual activities into your life, like quiet times for contemplation or meditation, then you can change from being in a rut to being on a roll. Listening to your calling will help you decide what to accept lovingly and gracefully and what to change courageously.

When we are on a roll our attitude to the discipline we have in our life is totally different. Our discipline is a natural outcome of listening to and following inner guidance. We know our discipline delivers freedom, fulfilment and happiness. We are increasingly embraced by inner peace. Order comes into our life easily and naturally. In the beginning, when we are new to this different kind of discipline, we have to strive to attain it. Later we find an increasing effortlessness as we slip into the natural unfolding of our life.

When I was working for a particular architect's office in my twenties I was in a difficult rut. Uncaring people staffed the office. The bosses made no attempt to vary my work, so I was required to sit at a drawing board all day doing meticulous pen work under severe performance pressure. My opinion was never sought. I did not feel that I counted as a human being. Producing drawings as quickly as possible was my only value. I started hang-gliding at the weekends. I was desperate for a release valve. After a year of suffering this abuse, I plucked up my courage and obtained another job in a more caring architect's office.

Today I am on a roll. My day has a simple discipline. I rise and have some quiet meditation before breakfast. After breakfast I plan the piece I intend to write. Then I head out for my walk along the beach and write when I arrive home. After lunch I do some household duties, and read a favourite spiritual book or listen to some classical music. After my evening meal I usually meet a friend, returning home in the evening for some meditation and a prolonged quiet time that may include some emotional release. I then talk to the most elevated part of myself before going to bed. I do not follow this pattern precisely every day, but it is the backbone of my ordered life. At this point it is the perfect discipline for me.

A discipline suits us if it is guided from within. Discipline that emanates from our calling releases us to enjoy the simple virtues of everyday living. Intuitive discipline nurtures love. This is the discipline we use to expand our potential.

Envoi

The sun rises and sets with complete regularity.
The tides rise and fall with unerring predictability.
The leaves fall in autumn and the buds form in spring.

Nature, you are full of rhythm.
I belong to you.
I too need to find my natural tempo.

Listening to the call I slip slowly into silent submission.
I learn to love what must be done.
I learn to create what needs to be changed.
With no other guide than the call, I expand my potential.

My potential is born out of relaxation.
My potential is born out of service
My potential is born out of love.

As I remould my life to the inner promptings of the call,
I am reunited with the rhythm of nature and I am free.

Paths of sand meander down the grassy bank. Each path opens to embrace the beach. The golden sand is pockmarked with patterns of playing feet. The beach slopes gently to the ocean shore, where the gentlest of waves run ripples over sandy surfaces. Beyond the ripples, calm ocean stretches to the horizon.

Your Potential Leads To A Calm Mind Undisturbed By Change And Uncertainty

Many of us struggle to maintain calmness and equanimity in the fast changing modern world. Change creates uncertainty and uncertainty creates stress. It is possible to live in a changing world and be free of the inner turmoil and strain that so many face.

I remember when in transition from being an architect to freelance management consultant; I was suffering from a great deal of stress. I worried that I would not be able to be an effective management consultant and I was anxious because I thought I would not earn enough money. Despite an inner knowing and calm, I was filled with surface fear and anxiety for the first year of my new occupation.

Fourteen years later I changed from being a management consultant to a writer. This transition could not have been more different. I decided to leave the business world without having any other direction for my life. I went on a retreat by staying in my own home for five weeks, only going out for walks alone, or to do some shopping. Instead of being filled with fear at the uncertain future ahead, I was completely calm. In truth I had never experienced such peace. In the fourth week of my retreat I received the inspiration to write "Unfold Your Wings and Watch Life Take Off" and begin my new career as a writer of personal development books.

Why was the first transition so stressful and the second so peaceful? In my first transition I had the call to leave architecture and be a management consultant, but I did not fully trust my calling. I struggled with it. I doubted. I tortured myself with worry. This anxiety was all unnecessary. I turned out to be a competent and capable management consultant. If only I could have trusted my intuition and happily followed my star, I would have had a much sweeter changeover.

The peace I felt in my second transition can be summarised in one word—trust. Although I was being called out of the business world and into an uncertain and unknown future, I trusted that call. While on my retreat I was unconcerned that my life had reached a dead end. In the silence of my retreat I opened up to any and every possibility and let my inner call speak to me. I needed the fourteen years experience of following my potential to enable me to make the second transition with such grace.

UNFOLDING YOUR WINGS

If you are entering a period of transition and are unsure of the direction ahead, try the following. When the time is right, let go of your old life. Trust the calling that is taking you into this transition period. Open to all possibilities and let inner guidance speak. Follow gentle inner promptings with action.

By trusting our calling and following our potential we receive healing. Through our inner healing we are given the gift of a calm mind undisturbed by uncertainty and changing circumstances. This calmness of mind allows us to live more fully in the present.

When in the present we find the peace that passes all understanding. I remember once seeing a bird protecting its eggs in a tree. All around a storm was raging. Twigs were flying past. The wind was howling. The rain was lashing. Yet in the middle of the gale the bird sat calm and still, unconcerned at the turbulence. Inner peace is like that. It is present even in the midst of a storm.

Envoi

My life is changing.
Outside a storm is raging.
I do not know what the future holds.

In silence I retreat from the world.
In silence I listen within.
I am suffused with silence.
Then in that inner place of peace
I become inspired.
In my inspiration I know what the future holds
And I am ready for renewed action.

The sea is slightly choppy. On the surface, between rock outcrops, is a carpet of bubbles. Beneath the choppy surface a forest of seaweed disappears into the depths. The air is filled with lapping and gurgling. Close to the shore small waves slide on and off winkle-encrusted rock. Carpets of bubbles foam and dissolve with each wave. Here seaweed slithers and slides sensuously.

Your Potential Leads To The Discovery Of True Love

What is love? We talk incessantly about love. We watch films about love. We read about love. We dream about love. We pine after love. But how many of us really know love? How many of us can hold our hand up and say "I have discovered true love?" I suspect very few.

True love is not dependent on being with a particular person. It exists beyond the need to have a particular person as the object of our affections. True love is a spiritual state in which everything is appreciated as being sacred and worthy of our veneration.

Living a guided life helps us reach this state. It is a state with which you are already familiar. Do you remember how the world appeared when you were a child? Every day was filled with wonder. Do you remember the time you played for hours fascinated by a simple colourful stone? Do you remember the time you lay in the long grass and gazed aimlessly at passing clouds above? Do you remember rolling down a hill with your friends to see who would reach the bottom first? When you were a child the world seemed a place full of marvel and wonder, a special place where every day held new promise and new discoveries. When you were a child you were in love with life.

How a child feels the world is very close to the state of true love I am talking about. You may also have touched on this state as an adult. Maybe when on a camping holiday you decided to rise at 5 am and saw the sun rise over a silvery, still lake. For a moment, just for a moment, you stepped out of your normal everyday world of goals, targets, disputes and struggles and became lost in the beauty of a precious gift—today. Maybe that experience touched your heart and you realised that life has a meaning beyond the mundane. Nature is an expression of love. When we are deeply touched by nature's beauty then we are beginning to discover true love.

By following our calling we are constantly challenged to expand the circle of our love.   Starting with our immediate family, our love and commitment to serve others expands to embrace our neighbours, our local community and humanity at large, eventually embracing everything that lives and grows.   As we explore our potential, we move from less love to more love, from narrow love to expanded love.   This growth of love, expressed as a hunger to serve, attracts challenges and trials that strengthen our character and helps us mature.   We realise that by travelling this journey, we learn to have higher and more all-embracing visions and ideals.   Meeting the challenge to ground these visions and ideals in the world around us is the only path to happiness, because these challenges and trials bring our buried fears, doubts, prejudices and anger to the surface where they can be released.

As we are healed we find it easier to appreciate, find wonder in, and fall in love with every day.   In this state of love and appreciation we no longer have to chase after happiness, because it permeates our daily experience.

Envoi

I am blessed.
A new day is dawning.
The sun is rising beyond the trees,
Mirrored in the lake's still water.
All is quiet.
All is still.
The orange ball is reflected in the gently rippling water.

I forget my worries.
I forget my troubles.
I am faced with the dawn.
In the city I could not see it.
In the midst of my woes I did not value it.
In my hectic schedule I did not look for it.
In the end I forgot about it.
But now I have fallen in love with today

And gratitude penetrates my preoccupations.

Now, just for this moment, I am fully alive.
Now, just for this moment, I am in love with life.

Little clumps of bubbles hug the rocks. Rippling patterns run across still waters. Slithering seaweed separates the surface. Down in the depths brown seaweed wobbles. Clear turquoise waters reveal their world. The wobbling weed has long brown fingers, like underwater palm leaves. Beyond the weed, water delves deeper into turquoise mystery.

Your Potential Leads You Back To Where You Belong

There is a great mystery in the depths of life. This mystery exists because life cannot be known by the mind. We cannot delve deep into life's mystery through analysis. To plumb these depths and discover their secrets we need to be like the drop of water that returns to the ocean. We fall to earth and blend with a mountain stream. The stream journeys down the mountainside seeking to return. As the stream joins with other streams it tumbles in youthful waterfalls and ponds, journeying homeward.

Eventually the stream becomes a river, meandering more gracefully but with great power along the valley floor. Then the meandering river joins with the ocean and disappears. While on this journey, the drop of water has not become lost. Through merging, the drop has grown in power and presence, and has been led back to the Source from where it originated.

By loving more and more people and loving them more and more intensely, we merge with the river of love and are led back to the Source. This merging of our destiny with the Source creates transcendence. What is it that we transcend? We transcend the worry, confusion, irritation, hatred, bitterness, jealousy, resentment and anger of a troubled life. We achieve enlightenment and perceive the truth. We see that everything is precisely as it needs to be and that love permeates experience.

By becoming more proficient at listening to and trusting inner guidance and acting on its promptings our lives develop this momentum that carries us onward and inward. We are able to relax, secure in the knowledge that this river is leading us home to a place of peace, power, love and security.

Envoi

I am being called.
I am being called to make the return journey.
I long to merge with the ocean of love and know its secrets.
I long to be led back to where I belong.

The ridge of water rises, folds and crashes. The rushing wave surges shoreward, running up the beach as a foaming carpet of bubbles, sparkling in summer sunshine. The flattening water burbles and gurgles as it bubbles. Then stretching like an elastic sheet, it slides smoothly under the next foaming torrent. The beach is empty. On the sheltered slope nearby the chill wind ripples leaves that are starting to turn from green to gold and brown.

Your Potential Creates Wonderful Healing

As we step out on our journey eventually fear, anger and insecurity turn to peace, power, love and security. We are healing. To make this transition we need to stick to our path, learning to share and express our fears as they arise from within by being more honest and open with others and with ourselves. Such expression will nurture healing.

If on our journey we are emerging from a particularly dark place, progress may seem slow. Patience and persistence are required. Throughout our journey we will be accompanied by the feeling that our potential, however difficult, is deeply meaningful. All other paths will seem empty by comparison.

By surrounding ourselves with close friends, the journey is made easier because it can be shared. With close friends as our allies we will find ourselves part of a healing community. This will create opportunities for further advancement and discovery. As we continue to heal, our healing community will grow larger and larger. Our extended family may also become part of our healing community. This community forms our healing resource, to which we can contribute and receive from as needed.

To contribute with power and vision to our local community we must lead an inspired life. We need to look within for guidance, trust our intuition and follow it, wherever it leads. As we heal we draw closer to Creation and sense a living presence that permeates the whole of our existence, where we are united with the radiant inner swan.

Envoi

Home.
That is where I long to be.

Not a home of bricks and mortar,
But a home inside my own immortal heart.
Hear lies my source of security.
Hear lies my source of love.
Hear lies my experience of the transcendent.

As I follow my potential I ask,
Please take me home to security,
Please take me home to love,
Please take me home to the Source.
Please give me wonderful healing.

Would you like help in developing your inner guidance?
If so, visit *www.alifediscovered.org*

- Receive one to one coaching by email from the author on how to develop inner guidance.
- Discover how to solve your problems by tuning into inner guidance on an online tutorial.
- Find out about opportunities for personal development.
- Discuss your calling with other readers.

Your Pass Code is **star**

Visit the home page at *www.alifediscovered.org*. Then, enter through the archway in the home page.

Full details about the website on page 292.

Part Three

Your Healing

Using moving personal stories from the author's life, Your Healing demonstrates that by opening to your potential, your wounded heart will eventually be healed.

"Instead of seeing faults in others, search for those in yourself."
—Sri Sathya Sai Baba

Afternoon

A single seagull glides effortlessly across the lake.

The swan sits motionless, watching. She then turns gracefully to travel across the lake. As she paddles she looks from one bank to the other, occasionally flicking her pointed tail.

A small, black, water bird scoots from the long grass on one bank across the lake and disappears into the reeds on the far shore.

The swan reaches down. She bends her long neck to preen feathers with her orange beak.

A solitary man runs past in a bouncing uneconomical manner, his long thin white legs exposed to the chill air.

Another runner appears. He has red bottoms and a green top.
He has a short jerky stride.

There is a distant flapping on water. She takes off across the lake, making a rhythmical whistling sound as she flies by. Her body is stretched like an arrow in the direction of flight.

The sun is hidden behind newly formed cloud. The skeletal trees are reflected in the brown water, their reflections distorted by the ever-present ripples.

The powder blue sky has filled with a blanket of thick grey cloud. A single area of blue and light is visible over the tree-lined horizon.

The air is still, sombre and cold.

Peace hangs like a benediction on the lake.

Autumn Reflections

Great banks of spent leaves lie in brown shaded quilts, beneath a copse of ancient gnarled oak trees. The wind rises. The driest leaves are caught by the icy blast and carried across the jet-black path where they spin, revealing each invisible swirl. The leaves drop and with a delicate scurrying sound tumble along the path and are gone. The wind dies, all scurrying stops. The path is empty of both sound and movement.

Your Healing From A Wounded Heart

If we empty our heart and examine the contents, most of us will find it filled with impatience, addiction, greed, insecurity, shame, meanness, stress and fear. It is easy to feel enslaved by falling victim to these negative characteristics. Is it any wonder that we are far removed from having a life filled with joy? We need to have the courage to refine our character, so our heart can be healed from these enslaving feelings.

A joy-filled life is only possible when we are free of these undesirable characteristics. To experience joy every day our heart must be simple, pure and loving. Listening to our inner call and following our potential will purify and simplify our heart.

When our heart is unwell we feel compelled to fill our lives with all kinds of complexity in order to try and feel fulfilled. Immersed in complexity, we are driven to participate in hobbies that do not really fulfil us, relationships that are unsatisfactory and jobs that are draining. To fill the resulting emptiness we surround ourselves with entertainment, possessions and expensive holidays.

When our heart is simple and pure all compulsion leaves us. We feel fulfilled by simple work, fulfilling relationships and a devoted life. We no longer need to be entertained. Having a plethora of possessions becomes a burden. We do not hanker after expensive holidays to make our lives fulfilled. Instead we find joy, inspiration and fulfilment in an enlightening conversation with a friend, a walk in the woods or a simple expression of gratitude at the end of a joy-filled day.

The healing we obtain as we follow our potential is very comprehensive. It heals our bitterness and resentment, our lust for fame, money and power, our lack of confidence, our fear, anger and grief, our relationships and our stress, to name but a few. This is because as long as we listen to our calling and explore our potential, love, the most powerful healing medicine, will be growing within us.

Our life-path can be like a mountain river, steep and full of rocks and boulders that we have to navigate. If we stick to the task we will eventually reach that still, calm lake where we can be filled with joy, creativity, relaxation, peace, humility, and love. These are the inevitable rewards of a life well lived.

Envoi

My wounded heart,
You have suffered so much.
How can I heal your open wounds?
I know my calling will guide me.
I know I will be healed by realising my potential.

I resolve to follow my calling
And expand my potential every day.
I know that by travelling this journey,
I can heal my wounded heart.

A mother is walking with her son. She is tall and her son is only half her height. They are both wearing the same kind of blue woolly bauble hat. A flock of smoke blue pigeons are grazing nearby. The couple's collie sees the flock, scampers, slows and stops. He is ready. Mother and son are lost in conversation and do not notice the unfolding drama. He creeps forward, like a trainee tiger, then charges. The flock explode into a flurry of flapping, lifting the pigeons almost instantly above the surrounding trees. The collie hurries over to where the pigeons were pecking and looks up in amazement. The mother calls the collie with a loud angry voice, her face contorted with rage, but he does not respond.

Your Healing From Bitterness And Resentment

When we feel wronged, when we feel our life is unfolding beyond our control, when hopes are quashed, it is easy to feel bitter and resentful. When I became disabled by schizophrenia I blamed it on my tutor. (See Your Calling Needs To Be Trusted, page 26). I was very bitter and resentful. I remember sitting up in bed in the Mental Hospital, where I had been taken to recover, and shouting abuse towards my tutor, (who was 200 miles away in a different country). I think the staff thought this behaviour was caused by a schizophrenic delusion, but I was simply angry.

When I returned to college a year later, unsure if I could survive the rigor of university life because of my newfound vulnerability, I could not even look my old tutor in the eye. Whenever we had the opportunity to meet or make eye contact I avoided him. I never did manage to make peace with my old tutor, at least not in person.

What upset me most was that I had trusted him. In my eyes he had broken that bond of trust and had let me down. Now I had to take powerful tranquillisers to prevent me from having destructive hallucinations and to subdue paranoia. Taking the medication was making me feel drowsy, sapping my spontaneity. I had little tolerance of pressure and stress. Levels of stress that others found quite normal would cause my mind to seize and I would slip into dark depression. I also had to live with the possibility that if I experienced a very stressful event I could once again be thrown into madness. Medical authorities advised that I would have to live with the after-effects of schizophrenia for the rest of my life. I felt enslaved by the limitations imposed by my disability. I was angry, bitter and resentful. How dare he do this to me!

By spending time alone in nature, and by going for walks in the mountains, I began to contemplate the events that led to my illness. Through discovering my solitude I learned to live with my disability and gradually came to see things differently. I realised that I was the one who had decided to trust my tutor and to place his opinions above my own. I had opened myself up to his influence and had willingly placed myself in his power. In the end I had to admit that I had played a prominent part in my own downfall.

Eventually I realised that if I had been more discriminating and more aware, then I would not have chosen this tutor to help me with my design thesis and would not have suffered as a consequence. As a result of these contemplations I became wary of taking risks and more interested in developing my awareness, so that I would not find myself in a similar situation again. I became more reflective and began to study books on personal development.

The episode with my tutor became my wake-up call. I grew fairly quickly into an aware, mature adult, who knew how to handle tricky situations and difficult people. I also became softer and more compassionate.

Before the incident with my tutor, I had always felt as if there was some strange glass screen between other people and myself. Despite my bubbly hyperactive personality, I felt fundamentally alone and separate. Once I began to see the lessons for me in the incident with my tutor, the glass screen that had kept me apart from others began to dissolve and I felt a new connectedness. Although I was now a disabled person, I definitely experienced more love and peace. This made it easier for me to forgive my tutor for treating me badly.

Forgiving my tutor has not been easy. I have also had to learn to forgive myself for hating him. It has taken many years and many tears, especially as I am left with a disabling legacy that I am told will last a lifetime. My newfound vulnerability and awareness has propelled me along the path of mature adulthood and given me wisdom to share with others. Paradoxically instead of being the great disaster it appeared to be at the time, this seminal life event has proven to be my greatest blessing.

UNFOLDING YOUR WINGS

There is a great blessing to be found in traumatic life events. If you have suffered an injustice try going with the experience. By allowing the injustice to work within you are challenged, through quiet contemplation, to find deeper meaning and a more profound understanding of life. You open your heart through this process and become more connected to life in all its abundant glory. As you reflect on, learn about and receive the blessings from this apparent injustice, you will find it easier to forgive the person who has committed the wrongdoing. Someday you may even want to thank them!

Life is not always as it appears on the surface. If we have been wronged, we can allow ourselves to become enmeshed in bitterness and resentment, or we can choose to learn from the radiant inner swan and grow. By learning and growing we are eventually able to forgive our abuser, discover a much greater connectedness and experience a deep, heartfelt joy.

Envoi

I have been wronged.

By turning inward,
By grieving,
By offering compassion to my abuser,
I am freed of a need to blame.

By freeing myself from a need to blame,
I grow in awareness.

By growing in awareness
I grow in joy.
By growing in joy
I grow in forgiveness.

By growing in forgiveness,
I am healed of my bitterness and resentment.

Water tinkles from below rocks as it flows into the open. Around the spring, water seeps sideways into moss, before disappearing underground again. Reappearing, it flows past two grass-covered rocks. Tall grass grows where a tiny rock strewn stream forms. Water meanders between these small rocks, hesitates to form a little pond, and then tumbles over brown stone to spill downhill, gurgling on its way to the foot of the mountain and beyond.

Your Healing From Arrogance

When we are arrogant our vehemently expressed views spill into our relationships with family, friends and beyond. Do you know where vanity and arrogance come from? They come from the Me. The Me that says, "I am more clever than she is, more intelligent than they are, more beautiful than that person, more alluring than she is, more wealthy than he is."

The Me that says, "I Am Someone Special."

This need to elevate ourselves above others is driven by a need to compensate for an unconscious belief that, "I Am Not Someone Special At All—I Am Pathetic."

So I have to prove myself, drive myself. This arrogance can burn like a huge log fire at the centre of our being, causing us to choke on acrid smoke that fills our living space, blinding us from the source of our calling. With arrogance it is our sense of inferiority that is the real illness.

In its extreme form it can drive us to spend money we don't have on clothes we don't need, become addicted to work in the pursuit of wealth, and amass qualifications, rank and status, all with the aim of feeling important and impressing others.

Is there a way off this torturous treadmill of our own devising? If we turn within for guidance on how to conduct our life we are admitting the truth that we are not so smart after all. By admitting we need help then a measure of humility can enter our character.

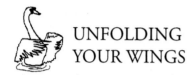

UNFOLDING
YOUR WINGS

If you would like to be more humble, then seek to empathise with others by really attending to what they say. Help them develop their point of view by asking questions. If someone is saying something important, ask a question that helps develop their point of view. If they say, "I don't think you understand me," you could reply, "Why do you think I don't understand?"

Asking questions and then listening attentively to the answers will help you understand their viewpoint and empathise with their needs. Taking quiet times where you can tune in to your guidance and releasing your pain will also help.

I speak from experience. I was returning from Donegal after a weekend-break with a friend. On the long run home the conversation turned to the transport problems of developing countries. We both engaged in a lively debate on the topic. It went on for several hours.

On returning home I thought I would try putting some ideas down on paper. I began to sketch out proposals. As I worked I began to think that I really had the answer. I was thinking this way even though I had no experience of transport problems in these countries and did not know anyone who had.

On I pressed, becoming more and more convinced I was right. I was someone special, after all. Wasn't I a great designer, with a list of talents too long to mention? If I couldn't solve this problem, who could?

I worked on in my office every evening until the small hours, for three months. I did not consult any research findings. I did not visit any of these countries. I did not canvass the opinions of experts in the field. The people affected by poor transport infrastructure were not contacted by me. I did none of the things that make for a well-balanced piece of research work. I did not need to do them because I was so convinced I was right. I was going to make a major contribution to solving the world's transport problems right there on my own in my office in Belfast.

Eventually the work was completed. It was very clever. My idea involved buying old second-hand trucks in the developed world, taking the back off them, and converting them into vehicles that could carry both passengers and small containers for mixed freight at the same time. This design would reduce freight and passenger transport costs because it would always be so full there would be little wasted space. The eventual report ran to over a hundred and fifty pages. I had even designed a system of bicycle transport to ship the small containers to remote villages along small tracks.

When it was completed, I contacted the Centre for Appropriate Technology in London. They said they were always interested in new ideas to do with transport for developing countries and offered to see me. I also contacted the overseas transport division of the governments Transport Research Department.

I flew over to London the following week, my report carefully stored in my briefcase. It was valuable after all and I was being very careful not to lose it. I arrived on a hot August afternoon and found the Centre for Appropriate Technology without much difficulty. The organisation was in a small modest first floor office near the city centre. I was received graciously and was led into a private room. There I met two of the organization's experts on rural transport systems for developing countries.

I got out my report and began to propound at length about the merits of my ideas. The two experts listened in silence. They didn't stop me or ask any questions. After I had been talking almost continuously for half an hour one of them stopped me and said, "But Mr Huey, they don't need any new trucks to solve their transport problems. They have all the trucks they need. What they do need is a reduction in corruption. It's corruption and poor management that is the root cause of the transport problems in many developing countries."

They then pointed out the many ways in which my existing idea would not have worked anyway.

I was flabbergasted. I couldn't say another word. The entire edifice of my argument had disintegrated. I didn't know what to say so I thanked them, gathered up my papers and left. The next day I went on to the government Transport Research Department. It was the same story there. I left for home feeling rather stupid and more than a little embarrassed.

If I had been more intuitive I would have known it was not something for me to take on. I would have sensed that I was not experienced enough, that there were too many imponderables, that I lacked
the resources and that I did not have the knowledge. I would also have
listened to my friends who considered this an inappropriate project for
me to undertake. I was so full of my own sense of importance, so arrogant and vain, that I was totally out of touch with my inner guidance and
missed all its quiet inner promptings, which I now realize were always
there.

All was not wasted, because I learned from this mistake and vowed
never to repeat it. As we follow our potential we can learn from the
feedback of others about our vanity and arrogance. By learning to turn
increasingly to our radiant inner swan, listening to the call for guidance
and direction, we acquire humility and become both a better friend to
others and more successful at choosing and managing projects.

Envoi

Maybe I am not so clever.
Maybe I am not so intelligent.
Maybe I am not so wise.

Maybe I need help
Maybe I need help from the call.

In that place of inner quiet and absolute stillness
I learn to listen.
The call guides me.
In what projects I am able to do.
In what clothes are appropriate.
In how much money I need.

By my calling's gentle inner prompting
Nurtured by a humble listening attitude,
I am gently guided to a simple, honest and straightforward life.
Slowly, gradually, my arrogance is healed.

A canopy of lush green leaves covers the grass. Streaming sunlight travels through the covering and lights the earth. Flowing sunbeams mark each grassy undulation. Crows and magpies peck here. They make myriad movements married to the grass. A crow breaks into hopping and stopping. Suddenly wings explode in slapping and flapping. The crows energetically rise, skim the flat grass and leave.

Your Healing From Lust For Fame, Money And Power

Some time ago I was in town and as I was leaving a shop I met my old boss from the days when I worked in his architect's office. He was an energetic guy then, full of fun and vigour. He used to drive in late to the office in his expensive sports car, bounce in through the doors and annoy most of the staff by telling them how much he had spent taking his friends on expensive dinners the previous night.

I was wondering why he looked so forlorn. He told me his business was almost bankrupt. When I worked for his office he employed about fifteen people. Now he told me all the lucrative government contracts had been cancelled and that he and his partner were the only ones left. He confided that he had to sell his expensive sports car and I presumed there were no more expensive dinners. (I wondered if the expensive friends were still around, or if they had left too!) Greed is a charade. It does not lead to happiness. My one time boss had lost his materialistic trappings and he was struggling to cope. I could see that these troubles were encouraging my former boss to change. He had let his defences down by sharing his vulnerability. I was being invited inside his ring fort.

Unfortunately our society is built on greed. Financial institutions and private investors, whose only concern is to make money from their investment, support many great corporations. Most of these investors do not care if the corporation they are investing in is kicking indigenous people off the land in their search for mineral wealth, or if the corporation employs child labour in a developing country. In truth they may never know that these abuses go on. They don't know because they are focused on making money.

This heartless attitude toward investment creates an all-pervading business culture where greed is not just ok, it is positively celebrated. The best company bosses are the ones who make the most money, the best companies are the most profitable, the greatest entrepreneur is always the wealthiest and the best salespeople are the ones who sell the most. Where in all of this does our worth as a human being come into play? What part does our character play in business?

A friend who works in a telephone call centre for a major international corporation told me a story recently. At this call centre the staff are paid to ring the company's customers and try to persuade them to buy more telephone services.

One telephone sales lady was on the phone to a blind, vulnerable and elderly woman who was on a small pension. The telephonist realized on talking to the lady that she was blind, vulnerable, elderly and poor and did not need the services on offer, so she did not really try to persuade the old lady to buy. At these call centres managers listen in to calls like spies. After making this call the telephonist was taken aside and lambasted for not really trying to sell the company products to the blind, elderly lady. It's disgusting, isn't it? This sort of thing is going on all the time.

It is said that we should be proud of our capitalist system and the people who run it. Many people think we have to base our society on greed for it to function. Competition for money and profit, they tell us, is essential to make people work hard and get ahead. This is a complete fabrication. Do not be tempted to believe these lies. Some fight the system, rebel and protest and even resort to violence. I agree with not giving corrupt institutions my allegiance but I prefer to support those who are doing things differently. I would like to tell you of a place that does not correspond to these precepts.

I do my voluntary work on Wednesday afternoons in a village community just outside Belfast called Glencraig. This village has a farm, a woodland area, a small commercial pottery, a room for weaving, a school, a church and offices. It is a go-ahead place. The farm uses up to date techniques of organic agriculture. Some techniques are ahead of their time. The potters and weavers produce the most exquisite work. The woodland is preserved as a conservation area but produces timber for carving and for wood-burning stoves. In the village many of the houses are home to adults with learning difficulties. Everyone works in the village, commensurate with their skills, interests and abilities.

The other week I was leaving Glencraig in the early evening. It was dark. The work of the community was carrying on, even in the cold and dark. There were jobs to be done and people were mucking in. They were not doing this to get a pay rise. They were not working hard to get promotion. They were not doing it for the overtime pay. They were working these long hours in the cold and darkness because they cared.

You can care, too. If you are investing some money to provide a small nest egg for your family you might like to consider one of the many excellent ethical investments available today. Wherever you are working you can stand up for caring—even if it doesn't lead to bigger profits for the company and higher wages for yourself. Caring is what business should be all about. We are drawn intuitively to care about our work and how we earn a living. The business you work in can start to care and this caring can start with you.

UNFOLDING YOUR WINGS

Would you like to be the start of a caring revolution in your work place? Your inner mentor will show you how to achieve this. In your workplace pick an issue you would like to champion, even if it does not make higher profits for the company. Share your enthusiasm for this issue. Nurture support—then try to lead this body of opinion to bring about the changes you seek.

Caring is infectious. When one person starts and persists, others follow. Our working life is a very important part of our potential. Developing our potential will heal us of our lust for fame, money and power.

Envoi

My calling guides me to care.
My potential requires I risk so that I can care.
I care so that I can grow.

I grow so that I can know the beauty
Of being surrounded by love.

I know now
That work is not primarily about making money.
That work is the means I use to express my caring.
Through caring I am healed of my lust
For fame, money and power.

The black tar-macadam path and handmade palisade fence run to either side of a small grassy dip. This hollow is home to a rounded pond ringed with small mature trees. Strong sunlight casts bands of shaded tree trunk across its mirrored plane. Only tiny ripples, stirred by an invisible wind, mark the shiny surface. In this little pond, blue sky and white cloud live among trees and grass.

Your Healing From Prejudice

In the little pond that is our life, why do we live with prejudice? We judge others because they are different and we fear that difference.

Prejudice is based on fear.

The truth is that others are no different from ourselves in their essential nature, because we all share the same humanity. The difference that we imagine exists is created in the mind. We create these differences because our mind is full of fear.

We fear our common humanity. To embrace our common humanity is to admit that we share that person's poverty, we share this person's disability, we are open to marrying that black person or white person, we share this person's pain and that we share this person's terminal illness. Prejudice is a means we use to keep people we fear at a distance. Prejudice runs counter to love. We need to learn to love those we hold at a distance, especially if we imagine that they are controlling and imprisoning us.

I used to be prejudiced against poor people and people with disabilities. I was frightened of being poor and disabled. In 1979, when I was just 24, I was at architecture school. I had my life mapped out. I was going to be a rich and famous architect.

My studies were going well and everything was on target. Then I was given the devastating news that I had schizophrenia. I struggled on with the condition for several more years, eventually completing my studies, but in the end it got the upper hand and I became disabled by it. (See Your Calling Needs to Be Trusted, page 26 and Your Healing From Adversity, page 179). Then, because I was disabled and unable to work, I became poor as well. My worst nightmare had come true. I had become poor and disabled myself.

What did I feel when I admitted the truth, that I was poor and disabled and there might be no escape? Fear. I was feeling pure unadulterated fear. I was terrified. All my dreams, all the plans I had for my life had evaporated.

As time passed I came to accept my condition. Then after more time passed I came to learn from it and to improve. Eventually I came to see having schizophrenia as an advantage! It had taught me so much. By accepting my condition not partially but fully, something powerful began to happen. I not only learned to live with it and improve but I lost my fear of disability and poverty in both others and myself. I lost my prejudices.

I also learnt that there is beauty in disability. When we are disabled we do not have it in our power to do what we please. Therefore we are more open to help. We discover a beautiful, quiet place within, like a still, pure tree-bound lake, where we become more receptive to our calling. We identify with other people who are disabled and disadvantaged and we reach out to help. We become more loving.

I learnt that there is wealth in poverty. Poor people often share more. They know what it is like to be without and are more inclined to happily share what they have. This not only creates wealth but also helps build friendships. There is dignity in poverty. I learnt that the most crippling kind of poverty has nothing to do with material wealth, but comes from a poverty of love. I found love in abundance when I was poor.

I lost most of my prejudices. I felt a freedom and openness I had never known. There were few barriers. Now everybody was my friend. I shared a common humanity with the world.

At Glencaig, where I do my volunteer work, there are many village residents who have been born with brain damage or are mentally handicapped in some way. They are the most loving of people and they communicate in whatever way comes naturally to them, be it sign language or by repeating a few often used words or sentences.

I feel very at home with the villagers of Glencaig. I communicate with them in simple ways we can both share. Being with them expands my repertoire of free expression. I feel liberated. If I had visited Glencaig before I had schizophrenia and before I was freed from my prejudices, then on meeting the villagers I would have cringed with embarrassment and looked for somewhere to hide.

We can lose our prejudices. Inner guidance will help us do this. Our calling increasingly guides us to draw close to those who are disabled and disadvantaged.

UNFOLDING YOUR WINGS

If you are seeking healing from prejudice, try befriending the people you are prejudiced against. If you are prejudiced against criminals, volunteer to work in a prison. You will lose your prejudices if you actively establish relationships with the people you are holding at a distance. This can be a richly rewarding pursuit.

As we follow our potential our radiant inner swan draws us to befriend the downtrodden, diseased and disabled. These friendships bring great riches. By encouraging us to reach out to those who are different, the call heals us of our prejudices.

Envoi

You are different and I fear that difference.
You are black and I am white.
You are Muslim and I am Christian.
You are poor and I am rich.
You are disabled and I am able bodied.

With the call as my guide,
I reach out across the illusion.
I reach out across the illusion that we are different.
We share and as we share our common humanity is revealed,
And I am healed of my prejudices.

Lush lawn, damp from recent rain, has been lovingly cut. The grass varies from bright emerald green to duller beige and brown. Little tufts of longer greener grass grow here and there. The lawn is decorated with light brown leaves that are being blown and scattered by the wind. The grass flows, undulating with the land. Each hollow and curve is emphasised by these ever changing shades of green and brown. In the distance a solitary gardener is raking the leaves into neat piles.

Your Healing From Distaste For Work

Unfortunately many people dislike their work. This is sad. Work should be a source of great joy and personal fulfilment. It is important that we learn to express the love we feel in and through our work. If we dislike our work, we can change our perspective. Instead of seeing work as a means of earning a living, we can see it as a vehicle to express love by being of service to others.

When at work we can be like the patient shepherd, ever watchful and devoted, ready to meet the needs of his sheep. Becoming sensitive and responding to unmet needs while at work is one of the primary means we can use to increase the flow of love in our lives.

UNFOLDING YOUR WINGS

Try to see your workplace as a school, where you can learn to communicate more effectively, anticipate and meet colleagues' and customers' needs and happily conform to a discipline. By changing your outlook, jobs that were previously unfulfilling may become satisfying.

Changing our outlook is the vital first step to a satisfying working life. We may wish to change our job as well as our outlook. There are several guidelines we can use in assessing the suitability of our work. Our work should harness our strengths and not stress our weaknesses, be of personal interest to us, create enough income and provide a personal challenge in our ability to express love and caring.

Fortunately there is more scope and opportunity than ever before to find a job that really suits. Such jobs rarely drop into our lap; we have to do the necessary groundwork. In my last occupation I was working part-time as a self-employed management consultant. This work suited me very well except that living with schizophrenia meant I found it difficult to concentrate for long periods during lengthy business meetings. If I overdid it, I found it impossible to work for the next two days due to mental exhaustion.

My work as a management consultant was putting undue stress on one of my key weaknesses, an inability to concentrate in meetings for more than 90 minutes in any one day. This meant that although I could do the work easily, I often felt unsure of my ability to cope with the demands that were being placed on me.

By acknowledging that I had these weaknesses and accepting them, I became open to the possibility of a change in career direction. After a period of voluntary effort I constructed my present occupation as a writer, webmaster and personal development trainer. My new career is even more creative than my old one. It still uses my strengths to advantage but does not pressurise my weakness, because I can now control precisely the amount of concentration my work needs each day. I love my new occupation even more than my old one.

To create or find a job we can fall in love with, we may need to work voluntarily to get things going. It took me four years of unpaid effort to set up my current occupation. I have a friend who works with me in the woodland in Glencraig. He was offered his current job, which he loves, after working in the woods for two years as a full time volunteer. He made himself so indispensable to Glencraig Community that they offered him employment.

 UNFOLDING
YOUR WINGS

If you wish to change career direction, I recommend you get a big yellow file (yellow is such an optimistic colour), and fill it full of notes that will help you find a suitable job. These notes should include your strengths, weaknesses, and your interests. Your strengths, weaknesses and interests will suggest a project or job type. Ideas for projects and job opportunities can then be added to the file. You can use these notes to explore options for voluntary work in suitable fields or for further education and training.

In life some types of work are of our own choosing, and some are not. We all have duties to perform. Our duty is work that we need to do but which we have not consciously chosen. Looking after elderly parents or a severely disabled child are examples. Work that is our duty needs to be gracefully embraced and carried out with love and devotion.

Our inner call will tell us when we can give our employer loyalty and support, how we can select and find a better job and what constitutes our duty. By changing our perspective on work and with the call as our guide we are well equipped to find fulfilment and joy in our working life.

Envoi

I do not like my work.

My supervisors annoy me.
My customers annoy me.
My deadlines annoy me.

I decide to experiment and change my perspective.

My supervisors teach me.
My customers teach me.
My deadlines teach me.

As I learn I discover more about myself.
As I learn about myself I am better equipped
To improve my working life,
And I am healed of my distaste for work.

The broad path is open with views of river and lawns. As the path rises and turns gently left, it passes through overarching trees that line the route. Here the path is protected from excesses of wind and sun. There is a womb like security. All around branches sing in the fresh autumn breeze.

Your Healing From Adversity

If we want our lives to sing with vitality and optimism then we have to work for it. All of us face adversity in our lives. The question we need to ask is, how can I learn and grow from adversity? Maybe our marriage has broken up in disarray, our business has gone bankrupt, or we are living with a debilitating illness or disability. Whatever our adverse circumstances we can use them to develop our character. By developing our character we become stronger, wiser, more joyful and more loving. Growing through adversity is challenging. We may need a special friend or relative who, like a wise old Druid, can help guide us to see beyond our current difficulties, so that we pass through a gateway into a new more abundant life.

 UNFOLDING
YOUR WINGS

You can choose to learn and grow from adversity. Try regarding it as a challenge. If you meet the challenge, you will uncover a priceless blessing.

I experienced three mental breakdowns, two straight after one another. I was disabled for a period, but eventually these breakdowns became the most valuable learning experiences I have ever encountered, leading to a new life of profound peace, love and happiness.

I had my first breakdown with schizophrenia when I was 24. (See Your Calling Needs To Be Trusted, page 26.) I recovered and struggled on with the condition working as an architect and then for a short period, as a management consultant until my second serious mental breakdown when I was 30.

My second breakdown happened because I decided to stop taking my medication. Ever since I had been placed on medication, I had questioned my need for it. This lack of acceptance and the constant questioning blinded me to evidence available from doctors and health care professionals, that people who have schizophrenia need to take medication to remain balanced and healthy. I never really accepted that I was a disabled person with special needs.

By not accepting the advice given by the doctors I had distorted my inner guidance, so that when I met a practitioner in complementary medicine who said he could successfully take me off my medication I readily believed him. Slowly, gradually he weaned me off my medication by giving me acupuncture and other treatments. Initially I felt much better, without the damping effects of tranquillisers in my system. I lost all of my drowsiness and felt really alive and alert.

Then slowly, gradually, to the consternation of my family, I began to become deluded once again. When my mother and other family members suggested I keep taking my medication I treated their ideas with disdain. I refused to listen. I was becoming arrogant and distant, a symptom of the condition when not treated. I went without medication for two years. During those two years my family had to watch in horror as I slipped further and further away from the real world and into a fantasy world created by my deluded mind with its unbalanced brain chemistry.

In those two years I spent all my savings unwisely and walked the streets pointlessly. As my mind became increasingly filled with fantasy places and people I began to behave in bizarre ways. I felt sure people were trying to harm me. One weekend my parents were so distressed they called to take me for a break to my uncle's home 50 miles outside Belfast. I remember stopping for something to eat half way through the journey. While my parents sat waiting for their meal I was busy in one of the public toilets praying to God for all I was worth. I had gone insane. My parents had no idea how to get a mad man to see sense and take his medication.

That night at 3 am I awoke at my uncle's house in a state of blind terror. All I could see were flames surrounding me. I felt I was drowning. My uncle heard the commotion and entered the room to find me rolling around the bed screaming with fright. At this point grace intervened.

My uncle was a country doctor with a dispensing practice. He seized the moment, collected some tranquillisers from his store and suggested I take them. My deluded mind thought that he was trying to poison me with these drugs, but some tiny sane space inside my head knew that my uncle would never poison me. I decided to take the medication.

By the morning the hallucinations had died down and I was feeling much more normal and open to reason. When my parents suggested I go into hospital I agreed. With the help and care of the hospital staff and the medication, I was able to start the long road to recovery. I had to nurture my ability to socialise once again and learn simple skills like developing the concentration to read. My mind was shattered and it had to be reintegrated and healed. This was an on-going process that took many years.

After recovering from the second breakdown I had lost my confidence and my dream of being good at something and becoming rich and famous. As a result I had a third breakdown caused by the development of deep depression. (See Your Healing From Fear Anger And Grief, page 223 and Your Healing From Loneliness, page 199). I was suffering depression as well as schizophrenia and was in a right mess.

When I was depressed I would get up at midday and lie on a couch all day in my lounge and do nothing, except the bare minimum needed to survive. This went on for two years. After a year living with my house-mate struggling to keep my head above water, my mother offered to take me under her care. When living at my parent's home I did not want to face up to how unwell I was. I just wanted to escape. (See Your Healing From A Meaningless And Pointless Existence, page 220). After two years suffering this mental torment my mother helped me realise there was no escape and I would somehow have to find a way out of my pit of despair. I fell quiet and turned within for an answer.

I began to listen to my calling.

I sensed that, no matter how difficult, I would have to stop spending so much time thinking about myself and instead think outwardly about other people. I knew I would have to get some fun and laughter into my life. After listening to these feelings I thought of approaching a charity shop to work as a volunteer two mornings a week.

After two enquiries, I was accepted as a volunteer. It can be very difficult to get off a couch and work for two mornings a week. People who have been depressed understand this. It was difficult, but it wasn't impossible.

Oxfam ran the shop. Its purpose was to raise funds to assist Oxfam with their overseas programme for developing countries. The shop had a gifts section; with imported crafts from all over the world, and a furniture section selling donated furniture, tables, chairs, wardrobes and beds.

On my first day there I was rather down in the mouth and morose. I went home just as fed-up as when I arrived. Then I remembered the guidance given to me intuitively. I remembered to create some fun in my life, no matter how difficult this was going to be. I resolved that evening, that for as long as I worked in the Oxfam shop, I would be the life and soul of the party. The next day, as I walked through the shop door, I put a big smile on my face. When I was behind the counter I joked and laughed the whole afternoon. Underneath I was still severely depressed. My jovial exterior was a complete act.

That evening when I went home I felt as depressed as ever. I persisted with this act for years. I gradually increased the amount of time I spent in the shop. Each time I went I acted out my jovial performance. I still felt depressed. Slowly, very slowly, I began to change. I was beginning to take a genuine interest in other people. Just for a moment, now and then, I was beginning to forget how miserable I was.

 UNFOLDING
YOUR WINGS

If you are suffering from depression, consider cultivating activities that will improve your mood, even if the effect is only temporary. Willing yourself back to a positive attitude, while engaged in enjoyable activities, will help you rise above depression.

Eventually I was working a good part of the week at the Oxfam shop and helping upstairs in the office occasionally as well. After a number of years in the shop I received another suggestion from within, that I work upstairs as a full time volunteer. I acted on this inner prompting and spent the following year working in the office. During that year I organized the most successful Oxfam Week appeal they had ever had, put together a rock concert for Africa and invented the stamp appeal, which turned out to be the most successful Oxfam appeal ever in Northern Ireland. (See Your Calling Can Increase Creativity Many Thousand Fold, page 60). It raised so much money it was even featured on television.

One Friday evening in January I went to the television studio to see the programme featuring my appeal. It was being broadcast live on Ulster television's prime Friday evening slot. I sat in the studio gallery watching the presenter and his guests from Oxfam on the stage. I had a big smile on my face. But this time the smile wasn't a fake. It was genuine. I had been cured.

Now that my depression was cured I wondered what I might do with my life to earn a living. A standard nine to five job was too much for me because of my sensitivity to stress, a side effect of living with schizophrenia. I turned within for help. I sensed that I needed to be gentle with myself. I felt guided to find work that was personally meaningful. Before my breakdown I had developed a modest interest in management consultancy. I thought I might start up as a self-employed management consultant once again.

Returning to being a management consultant would allow me to use creative talents I had developed as an architect and apply them to business. Being self-employed would allow me to control the workload and pressures I was feeling. But how could I start? I was not sure I had the ability. I had no contacts and had very little money.

By listening within, I sensed that I needed to go to business events and be involved with business people. I felt I would pick it up as I went along. I decided to act on the feelings I was receiving intuitively.

The first business event I attended is still fresh in my memory. It was at the Culloden, a five star hotel and the most prestigious in Belfast. I arrived at the hotel on my bicycle, parked it in the car park among all the Mercedes and BMW cars, dismounted, gathered up my papers and walked with gut wrenching trepidation toward the main hotel entrance. I walked down through the main hotel foyer, into the conference centre.

There were hundreds of senior business executives milling around. They were all dressed in blue pin striped suits and crisp white shirts. I looked down at my clothes. I was wearing a large white, baggy Arran sweater and brown corduroy trousers. I felt rather conspicuous. I was about to fold with embarrassment, when I remembered a famous British businessman who nearly always wears casual clothes and tried to forget about my eccentric appearance.

During the conference I seemed to be more concerned about my appearance than the others present. I met some interesting business people and began to feel involved in the business community. It was a good start.

In time I made a number of contacts and eventually received my first two contracts for consultancy with an Arts Centre and a freight forwarding company. I was very nervous undertaking these two contracts but deep within I knew I would be able to do the work. After starting each of these contracts I was delighted to find that I could do the work easily. Both the chairman of the Arts Centre and the managing director of the freight forwarding company wrote excellent references. Indeed the managing director said that as a result of working with me he had changed to having a positive opinion about business consultants.

My career opened out from there. I began to specialise in teaching personal development skills to people in business and went on to lecture in personal development at Queen's University. As a result of these developments in my career, my confidence, self-esteem and energy all grew. My new found working life, combined with my continuing personal development, resulted in further improvements in my ability to live with schizophrenia. The psychiatrists were able to progressively reduce the quantity of the drug I was taking to control my condition. I then felt better and improved still further. Indeed my psychiatrist commented that, even as a professional in mental health, he would never have known I had a mental illness unless he had been told first.

This process continues today. I can honestly say I have never felt better in my life. I am still taking medication in moderate amounts. A psychiatrist closely monitors this medication. Despite taking powerful tranquillizers and having a mental illness, I am no longer disabled by the condition.

I have come to the conclusion that schizophrenia is a shattering of the Self. This shattering is commonplace in humanity but perhaps takes its most extreme form in the schizophrenic condition. When I was lying on the couch, a broken and shattered person, I was stripped of everything and left alone trapped inside my deluded mind. The only resource I could draw on was the radiant inner swan, and because she became my only hope, I saw her in all her glory and splendour, calling me out of the pit of despair. Since then I have never let go of her. Through listening to and following my inner calling, my Self is gradually being reintegrated, healed and made incredibly strong. Indeed I have learned so much from my radiant inner swan that I have been vastly empowered.

When I was discharged from hospital 12 years ago, I started life again by attending a daily drop-in centre for people with schizophrenia. I still meet people in the street whom I then knew and who still attend that centre today. Many of them are still imprisoned by its debilitating effects. I am in no doubt that it was through the support of my father and wisdom of my mother that I began to listen to my calling, found the courage to follow my potential and experienced the healing that has set me on an upward path to personal freedom and fulfilment. Why not experiment with inner guidance yourself?

Envoi

I am unwell.
I have lost hope.
I have nowhere to turn,
Except to a close friend,
And the call.

Even in my darkest moments
You are there to support and guide me.
You set me challenges,
It is up to me to respond.
You teach me about life's highs and lows,
It is up to me to learn.

Slowly, slowly I accept, learn from and embrace my condition,
And I am healed from adversity.

Patches of sunlight play on a carpet of gold and brown. Green and gold are reflected in nearby puddles. Wind rustles the branch's dying leaves. A dog, with tinkling bell, slaps through the puddles, disturbing each still reflection. At the path's end sunlight shines on a small tree's golden leaves as they rustle in another billowing blow.

Your Healing From Fascination With Sex

In modern western society we are fascinated by images of gold, glitz and glamour. Sexual images are portrayed everywhere. The marketers, advertisers and ratings managers know we are fascinated with sex and use this fascination to attract our attention. We are fascinated by sexual images on billboards, newspapers, magazines, cinema and television. These media managers lead us around like poodles. They know we are suckers for a good sexual image. These images deface our civilization.

At a personal level our fascination with sex can lead us into having the wrong motives for relationships and lead to relationships that are not nurturing. Such relationships can be a source of conflict and misunderstanding between the sexes.

 UNFOLDING
YOUR WINGS

If you are troubled by a persistent and inappropriate fascination with sex, redirect that energy into a higher purpose, like voluntary work for a worthwhile charity or offering more assistance to your family and friends. By persistently and joyfully expressing love within your personal relationships and by offering services to others without expecting anything in return, you will be awakening unconditional love in your heart. This awakening of love will gradually sublimate your sexual urges.

I too have exhibited inappropriate sexual behaviour. I had a robust sexual drive that sometimes led me to approach women in inappropriate circumstances. I remember once I showed a keen interest in three different women who were members of a club I belonged to. One evening I was sitting quietly at home when I received a call from the chairman of the club. He wanted to meet me but would not say why. The next day the chairman knocked at my door. I opened it to find two other leading members of the club in attendance. I was surprised and invited them in for tea. After some minor chit chat the chairman broke the news. Three women in the club had complained about my inappropriate level of interest in them. I was shocked. I was not aware I had been behaving insensitively. I didn't like to think my behaviour towards these women was inappropriate. I was deeply embarrassed.

I offered to write a letter to each of the three women. In the letter I apologised for my inappropriate behaviour, reassured them that it would not happen again and thanked them for drawing my insensitive behaviour to my attention so that I could address it. All three women accepted my apology and assurances. I then had to learn to forgive myself for behaving insensitively, which I did by vowing to behave much more sensitively in the future.

I was no more immune from behaving insensitively due to my sex drive than anyone else. Inappropriate behaviour, in this regard, has been found at every level of society from Presidents to parking attendants.

Today I have no problems behaving appropriately with women and have many female friends. In the course of time, expressing love by listening to my calling and following my potential led to a transformation experience that made peace with my sexuality. I am no longer fascinated by attempts to win my attention through revealing images in advertising or films. Although I appreciate womans' physical beauty, I choose to befriend women only because I am interested in their spirit and soul. I experience an inner innocence and enjoy the freedom that comes from that.

With this transformation has come a great increase in my level of inner peace. My mind is quieter because it is no longer affected by sexual longing. Because my mind is quieter I am much more aware of the beauty of nature. I notice fairy trees and play with laughing children.

Envoi

My calling and my potential,
You have transformed my heart and brought great peace.

Now I see dewdrops on grass at dawn.
Now I feel chill autumn wind in my face.
Now I taste the salt in sea spray.
Now I hear the gurgling of ocean waters.
Now I smell the dank earth after rain.

Now I am at peace.
Now I know that I am loved,
And I am healed of my fascination with sex.

*White and grey cloud shines through the gap. All around, the branches
and leaves are dark and still. A gentle breeze begins to flow. Around the edges
slender drooping branches waver in the wind. The longest branches bob. The
leaves vibrate and shimmer. Quiet whispering accompanies the wavering.
For a moment the gap sings with life and movement. Wet leaves waver in
the wind. The gentle breeze disappears. Now only a few leaves vibrate in the
barely noticeable cool autumn breeze.*

Your Healing From An Inability To Give And Receive

In the English-speaking world, a cool breeze is freezing the people's
wallets. We live in an incredibly affluent society, yet meanness and miser-
liness are rife. How many of us turn charity collectors away when they
knock at our door or approach us in the streets? They only want a few
pence, yet some people think, "No I can't afford it."

Paradoxically it is often those with the most money who have the
greatest problem in being generous. Poorer people have, in my experience, a greater understanding of the need to share. Why are we so mean
and miserly when we have so much? The answer is because we are afraid
that if we are generous we will not have enough for ourselves.

Meanness is born of fear.

It is not only charity collectors who suffer from our meanness; it's
our partners, our friends, relatives, and employees, indeed everyone with
whom we come into contact. So many of us are simply plain miserable
when it comes to giving of our time, money and interest in the service of
others.

How many times when we are engaged in a conversation do we give
of ourselves to be interested in the other person's hobbies, passions and
life story? How many times when we leave a shop after being served do
we say thank-you? How many times do we say thank-you for a lovely
meal and complement the staff, after we have eaten at a restaurant or
café?

Meanness doesn't just apply to money; it applies to our whole life.

Being generous is important. When we are generous we are free. It is
completely natural for us to be generous, open, loving and giving. When
we are miserable we are crippling ourselves as well as others.

When I worked as a management consultant, I was told by the managing director of a company that his staff were always pressing him for a pay raise. He also said his staff were discontented. He asked me to find out why.

I had private meetings with each member of staff. I asked each person to list in order of priority what he or she wanted from his or her boss. I expected them to put more pay top of their list. I was wrong. Top of the list they put more appreciation!

On further enquiry I discovered that their boss hardly ever appreciated anything that was done in the business. I was also told he never missed commenting critically when something went wrong. When they were asking for more pay, what they were really saying was, "Why don't you appreciate us more?"

Over lunch the boss asked me what I had found out. I could tell he was a little nervous of the answer. When I told him the result of my enquiry he was genuinely shocked. He was simply unaware he was behaving in such a mean and miserable way, and vowed to change his approach.

Our inner mentor encourages generosity. I am inspired to give freely. Giving as I am guided, freely and abundantly, takes me beyond my selfish little desires and awakens love in my heart. Sometimes I am able to develop giving into a creative relationship of mutual giving and receiving. What is given and received is not always the same, but is a creative relationship that is mutually enhancing.

I used to do woodland work for a local charity. This involved hopping on a minibus, driving out into a woodland area and doing conservation work. It didn't last long. I was not being supported in this work. I could not make friends with the people I was working with. The whole experience felt dead.

Today I still do voluntary conservation work in woodland. I even pay for my own transport to and from the conservation area. The difference is that the person I work with has become a good friend. I bring my own lunch and eat with him in his home. We have great chats about life. When he works in the woods I carry his equipment, lift and lay logs and plant trees, all for free. Sometimes I'm invited to stay for tea and look at the stars through his telescope. This creative relationship is at the heart of my current voluntary work and I love it.

Many of us also find difficulty in receiving the help and support we need and deserve. We may find ourselves in relationships where giving has become a duty or obligation. We give out of guilt because we feel we should.

 UNFOLDING
YOUR WINGS

You will know if your giving is genuine, because you will be empowered by offering gifts and giving support. True selfless giving, prompted by inner guidance, is a spontaneous act of love that enhances the giver as well as the receiver.

If you are in a relationship where you give out of a sense of guilt and where giving has lost its spontaneity, perhaps your relationship has become unbalanced. You may be doing most of the giving and providing most of the support but are not receiving what you need in return. It is vital to know that you deserve support and appreciation. When I find myself in such a relationship I discuss the balance of giving and receiving with my partner, friend or employer, to make sure that my needs will be understood and met. If the relationship continues to be unbalanced after a number of such discussions, I would begin to review the relationship and reassess the role it plays and the value it has in my life.

When we are able to give and receive in this way we feel our creative power. This is because we are supporting life and being supported by it. We are called to give more to our creative relationships. Our gifts become buried treasure that we offer to create abundance for everyone. We know that by giving more to our creative relationships, we are really giving more to ourselves. I invite you to give and receive, create relationships and find yourself in the ever-growing embrace of the radiant inner swan.

Envoi

I am fearful of giving,
But the call helps me see I have so much to give.
Before I thought I was poor, now I realise I am rich.

Committed I give of my money.
Inspired I give of my time.
Beloved I give of my love.

By persistent, abundant and fruitful giving
I open up a channel for love to flow,
Both out and in!
And I am healed of my inability to give and receive.

Patches of sunlight play on grass. Thick tree trunks define distance. The short squat trunks disappear into a low-lying canopy of decaying leaves. The leaves are as still as the trunks. A solitary magpie pecks the grass and joins the stillness. The lawn is touched by a single soft white feather floating earthwards.

Your Healing From Stress

It is possible to live with the sensitivity of a feather touching the earth. But an excess of stress in our lives blunts our sensitivity. Recent research has shown that stress is now affecting every level of society. The rapid pace of change is shaking old securities and we are living with uncertainty. As a result we are changing friends, jobs and marriage partners more often. We are being asked to adapt to an insecure world.

I find the stress of modern living even more of a challenge than most people, because living with schizophrenia has made me vulnerable to stress. If I am in a stressful or stimulating situation, I lose the ability to concentrate and can easily become exhausted. I then slip into a dark depression and have to do nothing for two or three days to recover. I have managed to adapt to my disability by creating work that suits me, and by managing my life and my medication wisely. I actually believe that my sensitivity to stress is an advantage, because it has stimulated my creativity. In the middle of a hectic and uncertain world, by listening to my inner guidance I have created a life where I often visit the still lake of inner peace and tranquillity.

Having to adapt to uncertainty can be good for us. To adapt successfully we need to learn to detach more from our preoccupation with jobs, families and friends and live in the present moment.

 UNFOLDING
YOUR WINGS

If you wish to reduce stress, endeavour to detach by realising that you are not dependent on your job, family and friends, while still remaining committed and involved. Instead try to become more

dependent on inner guidance. By learning to have faith in your
calling and depending on it, you are provided with a peaceful foundation in a turbulent world.

Living intuitively like this teaches us to live more fully in the stress
free present moment. Stress results when we are emotionally attached to
jobs, families and friends. This attachment causes us to use our imagination destructively to conjure up all sorts of fearful and negative outcomes
that are wild distortions of reality.

When I let go of my commitment to the architecture profession
to become a freelance management consultant, I was riddled with fear
and consequently was very stressed. My mind was filled with negative
thoughts. I worried about how I could earn enough money and whether
I was capable of doing the work. I imagined something terrible might
happen. The stress resulting from these worries impaired my performance and I am sure excess stress impaired my judgement on some occasions and I lost important business deals. I was once offered a training
contract but at a very low price. I refused the deal, but on reflection
realised that had I accepted this contract would have been an opening
into a steady supply of high paid work.

In contrast, when I let go of my commitment to the business world
fifteen years later to enter an unknown future, the transition was much
easier because I was in touch with that beautiful, quiet place within
where I had learned to completely trust my inner calling. To discover
freedom we are sometimes called to risk letting go of the past and invited
to step out into an unknown future.

We can escape the worry trap by gradually learning to have confidence in and trusting our inner guidance. When we start responding
to our calling and taking our first few risks, it can seem very frightening
and stressful. If we persist, we learn through experience that our calling
can be trusted. We begin to relax, become more comfortable and display
greater wisdom when going in new directions.

If you are experiencing stress, it is helpful to share your thoughts and
feelings with a few close friends or family members. Unfortunately, managers and employers often do not encourage employees to talk about the
stress they are under. Instead they expect employees to improve their
personal coping. I had a friend who complained about being under too

much stress. She was invited by her manager to attend a time management course. She thought the course might be useful, but she knew that insufficient resources and management support were the main cause of her problem! Because she was unable to have her needs acknowledged and then met by her managers, she felt sidelined. She did not have a significant say in the decisions that created her working environment and eventually had to leave the job for over a year on stress leave.

If we do not participate in the major decisions that shape our world, we will experience stress. This applies equally well to the home and work environments. Let your intuition guide you in becoming a participant in important decisions that affect your life. You have a right to be involved. In extreme cases where you have tried everything, you are not being listened to and you are suffering chronic stress, consider changing your environment. Let your calling guide you to the appropriate solution.

If you are still overstretched and stressed, I would like to ask you a simple question. Why is it necessary for you to do so much? Life is best kept simple, but we have an uncanny knack of making life complicated. Listening to inner guidance will help simplify your life. When your life is simple, it is easier to relax.

My uncle once asked me, "What do most people want?"

"I don't know," I replied.

"A little bit more," he giggled.

There is so much truth in that punch line. Most of us are never satisfied.

One holiday in the year isn't enough; we want two. One car isn't adequate; we want two. One television isn't enough; we need two, or even three. One house no longer satisfies us, we are getting a second. One bathroom isn't sufficient; we need two. Then soon of course we say, one job isn't enough. And then, one pay raise isn't enough; we need another. It's all a vicious circle of stress.

Doing so much and having so much is an illness. We need to be cured. Following our potential is the cure. It may be a different life-path from the one we are used to, but it is a certain cure for all the complication we build into our lives.

Of course we need to have our needs met. I am not advocating a life of want and hardship—far from it. We may need a second home or a second car, but we will have less stress if we pay for these needs by carrying out work that is personally meaningful. There may be times when we are called to take our career in a new direction by developing new skills, or take time out for personal healing. At these times we may be drawn to satisfy only our most essential needs. In circumstances like these we need to remember that meeting our basic needs in life can be simple. It is we who make it complicated.

One of the biggest stresses in modern society is paying the mortgage. Even though many houses are a ridiculous price, they still seem to find buyers. Why is that? Why do millions of people every year cripple themselves with exorbitant mortgages?

People have high ideals of the home they want to buy. They want a certain style. They want a certain area. They want all the modern conveniences and they don't want to use their imagination or do much work. I would like to offer this story, in all humility, as an illustration of how I used my imagination creatively to furnish myself with a beautiful home.

When I bought my house I was thinking differently. I wanted to meet my needs simply. I wanted a house that I could pay off easily. I wanted a house with enough space and plenty of sunshine. Although I had a car, I wanted a house that was in easy reach of everything I needed and was close to good public transport facilities—this was because I wanted the option of not having a car.

I found the perfect house. It was near Belfast city centre, beside the river Lagan. (I'd always wanted a house beside a river.) It was not in a sought-after area; in fact, it was in a housing action area (a designation given to areas where houses are run down and in poor repair.) This meant it was eligible for a grant. When I visited the house I was struck by its atmosphere of love. I believe the last resident was an elderly lady who had since left to live in a nursing home. The house had no modern conveniences. It even had an outside toilet. It was over a hundred years old and as far as I could see had never been upgraded. Despite all this the elderly lady had obviously cared for her home. I knew this house needed imagination and it needed work, but I felt powerfully prompted by my intuition to buy it.

The house cost me £7,250. I collected some second hand furniture and let the house to some students while I applied for the grant to do it up. The profit I got from the rent, I put into a separate account. After some delays the grant came through. By coincidence it was £7,250, exactly the same as I had paid to buy the house! This meant I got the basic house for nothing!

I used my imagination to improve the house. I borrowed some money from the bank to pay a builder to build on a new kitchen and bathroom. I also paid the builder to revamp the interior and put lots of new windows in the gable that faced the river. This gave me wonderful river views and also lots of sunshine. When the house was complete, I spent the money I had put aside from the students' rent to pay for decorations and furnishings. I added a final touch myself by building a tiny conservatory overlooking the river. When the job was finished my total mortgage was £15,000 to be paid off over a twenty-year period.

I knew that for the next twenty years I was free of the burden of an exorbitant mortgage. I knew that for the next twenty years I had greatly increased my prospects of leading a low stress life. I also had a beautiful home. A year later I lost my job and had to give up my car, but it did not matter because everything I needed was within easy reach and I was at the centre of the public transport system.

Meeting our basic needs in life can be simple. We make it complicated.

There is nothing wrong in taking on heavy financial commitments, provided meeting them is not a burden. You may be in a well-paid career, in which you feel completely at home, and find your work easy and natural. If you are in a career path you dislike or find excessively stressful, then I suggest you think very carefully before committing to a large expensive mortgage. You could be entering into a commitment that may drive you to remain wedded to a working life that is no longer satisfying.

This matters, because some day you may get fed up with your stressful career and want to try a new path. As a result you may need to live on a smaller budget for a period, while you experiment with new means of earning an income. If you are already committed to an exorbitant mortgage and are struggling to meet the payments, you have my sympathy. Even if you are in this situation there are many other ways you can simplify your life and reduce your stress levels. Relax and let your intuition guide you.

Finally, not being open and honest causes a great deal of stress. We are at peace when we have a high degree of personal authenticity. To be authentic we need to live out of our calling. If we feel guided to forgive our husband or wife, then we need to act on that prompting and not hold back out of a false sense of pride or vanity. If we have a dream, then we will suffer if we hide our passion under the carpet and try and forget it exists. To lead a stress free, authentic life we need to act out our intuitions, follow our dreams, explore our creative ideas, understand our insights and adhere to our conscience. When we commune with the radiant inner swan our intuitions, words and actions are one and the same.

Envoi

My life is complicated.

I want an exotic holiday.
I want a second home.
I want a new car.
I want.

As I follow my potential I experience healing.
I want to have less.
I want to give more.
Wanting is wasting.
Giving is fulfilling.

I am joy filled.
I am creative.
With joy and creativity I simplify my life.
With joy and creativity I gain control of my life.
With joy and creativity I lead an authentic life.
As I simplify, gain control of and authenticate my life,
My stress is healed.

Under a solitary, soaked tree the air oscillates with the gentle pit-pat of dripping water. The green canopy is changing to brown. The trunk crevasses and cracks are havens for snails. Their brown and black striped skin blends with the colours of the trunk. Around this isolated tree, fallen leaves scatter the ground.

Your Healing From Loneliness

Isolation and loneliness are endemic in our society. Why, in our modern technological age when we are connected to each other as never before, by telephone fax, email, car, bus, train, airplane etc., do millions of us suffer from loneliness? Why do we have more societies, clubs, associations, dances, parties and social outings than any other civilization in history—and yet loneliness is rife? It's strange, isn't it?

Loneliness has nothing to do with how many friends we can reach in our car, or how many clubs we belong to; loneliness is in the heart.

Loneliness is born of fear.

Loneliness is born of the fear that separates, divides and isolates. When we are obsessed with our worries and anxieties, when we are obsessed with ourselves, then we are lonely.

I lived through a period of crushing loneliness. It was during the years when I was depressed. When I was depressed I was obsessed with myself. Indeed I found it almost impossible to think outside myself. I remember during my three months stay in hospital for the condition, I used to go for runs in the grounds. Before I became depressed I was very fit and ran regularly, so when I was in hospital I tried to keep this up.

I remember asking my mother to bring in my running gear. I would put on my running kit, trot down the hospital stairs and burst out through the front door. It was a huge shock to go in my shorts from the overheated and closeted hospital ward, out to a freezing January winter night. The mental hospital was called Windsor House and was in the grounds of the larger City Hospital.

Windsor House itself was a rather attractive, if slightly forbidding, old stone Victorian building surrounded by other nondescript modern buildings, black tar macadam roads and car parks. This somewhat desolate environment was lit by yellow sodium streetlights, which gave everything an eerie colourless hue. Mist hovered above the yellow streetlights. Damp hung in the air. The place was deserted. I ran out into this gloom …alone. I trotted around the dimly lit grounds for half an hour, occasionally putting in sprints to warm up. I must have looked a surreal sight to any onlooker.

When I returned to the hospital I was fine…for a while. I would be able to chat to the nurses and the other patients and take an interest in them. Then after about twenty minutes the crushing isolation would close in; I would go and lie on my bed exhausted, disconnect from the world and think about nothing but myself all over again. Although I sensed the running was doing me good. It was simply too much effort to keep it up. The loneliness would not go away. It went on for years.

I know about loneliness. It's a terrible affliction.

The call healed my loneliness, and it can heal yours. When we are lonely we feel disconnected from the world. I was guided to counter that loneliness by countering the disconnection. This meant doing things that would involve me with people, by participating in activities and events that took me out of my self-isolating world. It meant devoting at least some of my time and interest to serving others. Doing this was difficult. I was frightened. I lacked energy. Because I was self-obsessed, I felt I had nothing interesting to talk about. I thought that if I talked to someone else they would find me boring. I lacked confidence. These fears were a natural by-product of being self-obsessed.

UNFOLDING YOUR WINGS

If you are lonely I suggest you examine all aspects of your life for hints of a possible new direction, or the development of an existing opening that will help reconnect you to the world and to other people. Allow yourself to be guided to your most promising activity.

Loneliness casts a dark shadow. We must commit to walk out of the darkness into the light. By nurturing activities that reconnect us to other

people and by consciously taking an interest in this world outside ourselves, we will find the way out of loneliness and despair.

Envoi

Loneliness, you are a mirage
You arrive when I think about myself.
You leave when I think of others.
I do not accept your dark despairing days.
I do not accept your selfish, self-possessing ways.
I know I can be healed.
I know my heart can sing again.
And I can be healed of my loneliness.

Shadows from puffy white clouds move slowly and silently across the sun-lit fertile plain. Small reflections mark farm buildings. A turbulent breeze whistles through the grass. The valley is filled with the plaintive bleating of grazing sheep and the gurgling of small streams. Sun sparkles off fast flow-ing waters. Tall, spent thistles vibrate in the whistling wind. A single piece of thistle down fails to cling and floats by, carried out into the valley's vast emptiness.

Your Healing From Insecurity

People cling to all manner of goals and aspirations to feel secure. They cling to career goals (when I get promotion I will feel secure), money goals (when I earn $1,000,000 a year I will feel secure), relation-ship goals, (when I get married I will feel secure) or family goals (when I have children I will feel secure). We might ask ourselves—what do we cling to in order to feel secure?

If we cling to having anything in the outer world to feel secure, we are going to fail in our bid to find security. We need to learn to find security here and now even if our life is a bit of a mess. Have you ever picked up a ball that is too low in air pressure and tried to press out a hollow on the ball's surface? You succeed only to find the ball has developed a hollow somewhere else! Our outer lives are like this. We gain our money goal only to find we are facing divorce, or we achieve our career goal only to find we can't have the third child we wanted.

Today on the cover of a magazine I saw a picture of a famous English football player. The caption read, "The Man Who Has Everything." A few lucky people will achieve all their goals, money, fame, a family or whatever, but that will still not bring them security. We will never find security by trying to fix our life so that everything is perfect on the out-side. A few famous people may have everything outwardly but they will still have to look elsewhere to find security. If we are to trust the passion of our calling, risk escaping the self-made confines of our existence and climb through life with the freedom and power of a swan in flight, then we need to admit that security is an inside job.

We begin to feel secure when we turn away from our outer world attachment to goals, possessions and people, and turn within to live in the abiding peace of the present moment. How can we achieve this?

I do this by retiring early to my bedroom around 10:00pm. Before I retire I put the heat on in my bedroom to make it nice and cosy. I then clean my teeth, wash etc. so that once I enter my room I do not need to leave it again. I also take a glass of water with me so I can have a drink.

I put my favourite rocking chair beside the window and turn on the table lamp that I keep on the windowsill. I relax and feel the warm glow of the radiator beside my chair. I gaze lazily out the window onto the river below or watch the play of light and shade on the old beams that support the sloped ceiling. These beams are painted sage green, a beautiful, restful colour.

In time I take out a favourite spiritual book from a few that I keep handy upstairs and read for a while. After reading I contemplate the passage and then write an entry in my private personal development diary. This is a diary that I keep of insights I have had that day, or aspirations I currently have for my own personal development. After writing the day's passage, I read a few past entries as a reminder of past commitments and understandings. Then I light a candle, turn off the light and sit and watch the reflections of light and shadow on the ceiling. Once I feel an inner peace descend I move to face the candle and do half an hour's meditation. Then I get changed, give thanks and ask the most elevated part of myself to help make the inner changes I am trying to bring about in my life. Finally I get into bed and go to sleep in a state of total inner peace.

I invariably have a good night's sleep. The peace and sense of security I feel from my nightly routine increasingly permeates my daytime experiences. During those evening retreats I often feel the great peace and security of the present moment and an awareness of Being Alive.

During my bedtime retreats I like to think that I am engaged in building a shell of peace around myself. This is totally different from carrying around a defensive shell. A shell of peace keeps unwholesome influences out but lets people in. With my shell of peace comfortably in place, my outer life can go up or down and I am unaffected.

UNFOLDING YOUR WINGS

I suggest you consider giving some time to building your own shell of peace. Here are a few ideas that you can choose from, to practise with each day. Practising any one of these may help you find the security you seek.

• Sit quietly each evening and read a book that will enhance your personal development.
• Talk to the most elevated part of yourself at a regular time each day.
• Meditate at a regular time each day.
• Sit quietly and listen to the sounds outside your home.
• Contemplate the beauty of nature from a window.
• Go for a walk in the local park or in the countryside.
• Listen to beautiful relaxing music.
• Keep a personal development diary and contemplate its contents.
• Review the day's events before going to bed and contemplate their significance.
• Nurture peace in your mind and heart before going to sleep.

The time you need for building your shell of inner peace needs to be protected from the rigours of the day's demands. You will manage to protect your daily practise if you value it highly enough. This is your time to feel truly secure.

As we develop and expand our protective shell of peace we become increasingly sensitive to our calling. Guidance comes from communion with the beautiful swan who lives in that place of inner peace and security.

Envoi

I feel the rigors of the day weighing heavily on my mind.
I feel insecure.

Retiring to my cosy bedroom early,
I sit and contemplate the day,
Then as inner quiet grows
I naturally listen to the sounds of the city.
The soft yellow candle flame casts shadows on the ceiling.

Slowly, slowly, the concerns of the day fade.
Slowly, slowly, peace descends.
Slowly, slowly, I return to the present moment.

Now there is only now.
I feel suffused in peace.
And I am healed of my insecurity.

Beyond the trees a group of golfers walk like a small herd of deer, down the fairway, towing their golf bags silently behind them. Each golfer stops in turn where his ball landed. There is the swing of the club and the sharp crack of the ball being struck followed by a deeper clunk, as the spent club is arrowed into the stationery golf bag. Then each golfer hitches his golf bag and disappears beyond a dense grove of young birch trees. A bird sings with vibrant delight somewhere overhead.

Your Healing From Inability To Solve Problems

If we are to experience vibrant delight then we need to feel confident we can meet the problems life throws at us. All of us have problems to solve. Life would be boring and meaningless without problems to inspire and challenge us. Problems are to be embraced, not avoided. We gain a great deal of pleasure from solving our most pressing problems.

For many of us, problems are burdens to be borne rather than challenges to inspire. When faced with our problems it is easy to fall into the worry trap and become immobilized by fear. Worry and fear undermine our confidence in our ability to solve problems. We need to be able to approach our problems with the joy, abandon and playfulness of a group of children.

If we feel enslaved by our problems, then we need to create an escape plan. Fortunately help is at hand. Our problems will be solved when we are in touch with inner guidance. The inner mentor can help us solve any problem, no matter how large or intractable it may appear. Guidance comes from the source of creativity. Our task is to tune in to its child-like ever-present intuitions.

I remember about six years ago meeting up for coffee with my friend Mark. We were talking about our friendship and how much it meant to us. I was telling Mark about a social club I had joined in Belfast for single people. With a heavy heart I explained that I had decided to leave the club because I was unable to make any friends there. Mark commented that Belfast needed a social club where people could make genuine friends in safety.

As I was walking home that winter night through the dimly lit, wet streets of Belfast, his comment reverberated within my mind. Once I arrived home I made a cup of tea and relaxed in my favourite armchair. As I relaxed I began to strongly sense there was a real need for a social club where people could have close intimate friendships. I knew I would find freedom and fulfilment in being a member of such a club. This feeling grew quite quickly and I became inspired.

I did not hesitate. I followed the feeling. Skipping upstairs to my office, I brought down a pen and a large pad of paper. Ideas were starting to flow. I scribbled joyfully. That night in the heat of my inspiration I created the idea for a social club with a difference. The club was to be for people interested in personal development. It was to have one event a week, each event chosen and organised by a member. By ringing an answer phone where the details of each month's events were to be announced, members would learn what was on offer. I even thought of a name—New Horizons.

That night, I cycled over to Mark's house, put my proposal through his door and left. I heard nothing for six days. Then the phone rang. It was Mark. We discussed the proposal on the phone and he invited me round to talk about it in more detail. We worked together to improve the proposal one evening and then decided to hold a first meeting with our friends. A second meeting followed. Finally we held our first event, a launch party where everyone we knew who was interested in personal development was invited.

Today New Horizons has about 35 members and has been going for over six years. A committee elected by the membership runs the club. We have enjoyed fun weekends away, gone horse riding in the rain, visited the theatre, lost our balance while ice-skating, walked in the mountains and enjoyed boat trips. In addition to our weekly social events we hold one event a month specifically on personal development. We have organised and run over 300 social events in our six-year history. One of these events was held in the Wellington Park Hotel and attended by 180 people. As a club member I have never had such an active social life and have made many close friends.

All this happened because I had a dream to create such a club in Belfast and trusted and followed that dream. The call is a feeling, a thought or a dream. I have learnt to trust the feelings, thoughts and dreams I receive from inner guidance.

I succeeded in that project because I visited the still lake where I could commune with the radiant inner swan. Fear, worry and the resulting stress separate us from our inner guidance and we become deaf to her youthful promptings. If we remain out of touch our problems can mount because they remain unsolved. We can find ourselves in a vicious circle of not coping.

 UNFOLDING
YOUR WINGS

If you are finding it difficult to cope, try reversing this vicious circle of mounting stress and unsolved problems. See if you can turn your life into a virtuous circle of increased relaxation and solved problems. You can do this by learning to relax and by tuning to inner guidance. (See Your Calling Can Increase Creativity Many Thousand Fold, page 60 and Your Calling Helps You Succeed At Work, page 73).

When we do this, inner guidance can easily provide answers to our problems. We then change from seeing problems as a threat to be feared, to seeing them as a challenge to be enjoyed.

Envoi

My problems are mounting.
I cannot cope.
Fear and worry begin to infect my mind.
Tension builds.

I am entering the circle of despair.
I need to act.
I need to have faith in my calling.

As I have faith, I relax.
As I relax,
I am filled with the creative promptings of the inner call,
And I am healed of my inability to solve problems.

Wings, barely visible among leaves, beat in a short fervent burst. Between tree trunks, tiny insects play among shafts of sunlight and shade. A single thread from a spider's web floats upward, glistening in sunshine. Tufts of quivering grass mark the passage of wind along the ground. The wind nears. The canopy comes alive with responsive rustling, as fingers of leaves sway sensuously. A hidden dove takes to the air and leaves.

Your Healing From Compulsion

To live free of compulsion we need to replace addictive behaviour with peace. A compulsion is any activity that is driven and unrestrained. There are the well-known compulsions of heroin, nicotine and alcohol abuse, where the addictive behaviour is further strengthened by chemical dependence. There are other serious compulsions which are also life threatening, like the addiction to slimming (anorexia nervosa). Then there is a host of other troublesome compulsions that, although not life threatening, impact the quality of our lives in a major way.

Thankfully, the serious life-threatening compulsion is still fairly rare in our society. More common are the multitude of other troublesome compulsions. These include golf, gambling, overeating, work, television, sailing, sex, shopping, music etc. Our compulsive tendencies are always on the hunt to turn something into an addiction.

We may consider golf to be a relatively harmless compulsion. Our view would not be shared by the mother trying to raise a young family on a tight budget and with few opportunities for relaxation, who finds her husband spending $600 on a golf club and who takes off every Saturday and Sunday to the golf course with his mates. This type of compulsion can split up families and ruin marriages. So compulsion is a serious problem.

Why do we feel compelled? Why do we choose to continue engaging in activities when they are not in our own interests or the interests of those dearest to us? We are compelled because we do not sense the timeless, the eternal and the ancient.

We are compelled because we are not at peace.

When we are at peace we are able to see things in their true perspective. When we are at peace we are able to listen to and understand our wife's need for a break and some relaxation. When we are at peace we are able to respond to our children's need for our attention and we are able to buy a golf club for $60 and devote the rest to the family, where it is so badly needed.

When we are at peace our insight helps to lead us away from our compulsions.

When I was in my twenties, I was very keen on hang-gliding. I remember getting up early every Saturday and Sunday and going outside to study the clouds and the winds. Even if it looked as if the winds were not favourable I'd get in the car and drive 70 miles to sit on a hilltop, just in case the weather would improve. When I was with my mates we would talk about hang-gliding and nothing else. If I was out with some non hang-gliding friends for a social day in the park, I'd be studying the sky to see if I was missing a good day's hang-gliding. In the office, I'd be dreaming about the weekend ahead and the prospect of doing some hang-gliding. Hang-gliding was a compulsion.

In my twenties, love grew in my heart as I began to discover my potential. Gradually I was becoming more and more peaceful and contented. I was beginning to pay more attention to inner guidance. I noticed that I was gradually becoming less interested in hang-gliding. The hang-gliding banter with my mates began to bore me. I didn't fancy driving 70 miles to sit on a hilltop to see if the weather might improve and I began to be more interested in my work when at work. I didn't feel the need for an adrenalin rush every weekend. Through my insight, I realised that sitting on top of a hill for hours waiting for the wind to change, talking endlessly about hang-gliding, was a waste of my precious life.

Then one day I noticed my hang-glider had been lying unused in the garage for some months. I mentioned to a few hang-gliding mates that I wasn't using it so much any more. A few weeks later a car pulled up in the driveway. It was one of my mates.

"Would you be interested in selling your hang-glider?" he asked.

I thought for a moment. Why not, I concluded.

"OK," I said, "I'll get it out of the garage."

In fifteen minutes we had agreed on a price, and as a free bonus I threw in my instrument panel, crash helmet, and flying suit.

We loaded the hang-glider onto the roof of his car and put the other things in the boot. In a moment he sped off down the driveway and was gone. I walked in a bit of a daze back to the house. I made myself a cup of tea and sat in the lounge. I sat sipping the tea in pensive mood. Some time later my mother walked in.

"Where's your hang-glider gone?" she asked.

"It's been sold," I replied.

"So you won't be doing that again?"

"No," I said.

I had been cured.

As I have embraced my destiny, similar healings have happened to my other compulsions. Gradually I watched television less and less to kill time and eventually gave it to my sister. A vase of flowers now sits where my television once was.

As well as the easily visible compulsions like gambling and golf, there are the multitude of invisible personality compulsions that ruin lives and relationships. These include feeling compelled to be nice, or be strong (addictively avoiding our vulnerability), be successful, be right, be perfect, be a carer, helper, giver, or be responsible, etc. There are so many personality compulsions.

I used to have a personality compulsion that drove me to be successful. I found it difficult to contemplate failure. To move away from this particular compulsion I first needed to become aware of my unbalanced attitude through contemplation. Then I needed to learn to embrace failure as an opportunity to learn and grow, instead of the disaster I imagined it to be. I did this by learning failure's lessons from my inner mentor.

UNFOLDING YOUR WINGS

To discover if you have a personality compulsion, reflect on your behaviour. Is there a type of behaviour that you are drawn to again and again? Is there a type of behaviour you shy away from? In family life do you feel compelled to be responsible all the time? What would it be like to occasionally hand responsibility over to your partner? If you find that difficult, then your difficulty would suggest a compulsion towards feeling responsible.

By reflecting on our compulsions we can become aware of their existence. We can then address them by actively seeking to restore more balance into our life. As we listen to our inner guide and follow our potential, our life becomes more balanced. This leads to greater peace and contentment. As we come to rest in the peace that passes all understanding the kind of peace I sense when I visit an ancient stone age monument, our compulsions gradually fade, leave us and we are cured.

Envoi

The call blossoms when I am at peace.
Exploring my potential leads to inner peace.
When surrounded and suffused with peace
I am free of all compulsion.

When I was not at peace I felt compelled.
How can I know love when I am compelled?

Slowly, slowly my destiny
Leads away from my addictive behaviour,
And I am healed of my compulsion.

Ahead a copse of textured tree trunks stand motionless. Above are myriad clusters of dark green needles. All is still. A slate grey dove lazily drops, opens her wings and climbs, disappearing into a swathe of green leaves. Stillness returns, then parts as a solitary black and white magpie moves across sheltered space. In the distance leaves dance to a gentle breeze. Another dove swoops down from a neighbouring tree and lands beside the first. Both doves coo gently together.

Your Healing From A Broken Relationship

If we are to heal our broken relationships, we need to learn to keep our heart open to our partner and our creativity flowing, even though we may be discussing and attempting to resolve difficult and potentially contentious issues. By keeping our heart open and communicating honestly we avoid the trauma of feeling separate and remote from our partner.

This is difficult because open and honest relationships challenge both people to grow. When each person in the relationship is growing, then the relationship also evolves to ever-greater levels of harmony, love and understanding, strengthening unity. The most effective way to promote harmony, love and unity in a relationship is for each person to make a vow that they will keep their heart open, commune with the radiant swan within, and return to communicate with their partner about difficult issues creatively and sensitively.

I remember when I fell out with my girlfriend and ended our relationship. We had been dating for 18 months and had just begun to pull our lives closer together pending engagement. In doing this we discovered we had diametrically and heart felt opposing views on a matter of central importance. I did not want to try for a child and Carolyn did. It was difficult to see any way through. We struggled with this issue for some time. Eventually we reached a point where we did not talk for weeks. Our communication had degenerated and we were both feeling hurt and aggrieved. There seemed to be no resolution and the pain was becoming unbearable. After five weeks leading separate lives my girlfriend phoned and I broke off the relationship.

Seven months later Carolyn called me. We met socially a few times and then, fifteen months after we broke up, we forgave one another and decided to renew our relationship. The issue that separated us was still there, but we had both taken time to refresh our inner guidance. A few months after we had re-established our relationship, we went for a weekend in Carlingford, a quaint seaside village in the heart of the Coolie Mountains. We spent a lovely weekend together, walking, dining out and talking. The same issues that had plagued our relationship before came up again. This time we made a vow to talk more gently and sensitively as we explored this painful issue together. That night we went to bed as friends.

The next day we walked through farmland along the shore. We stopped and looked out at the sea together. I put my arms around Carolyn and discovered she was crying. Nothing was said. We stood and watched the waves flowing in and out, united in sadness. We walked back to our car and sat for an hour, watching the waves and the sea. We were sharing our sorrow. Then Carolyn suggested we go for a coffee, so we drove to a nearby pub and ordered some refreshments.

We talked, gossiped and joked with the waiter. There was a delicate love between us, like a sweet perfume. Then we hugged, bid each other goodbye, climbed into our separate cars and left for our respective cities. Nothing had been resolved. We had no agreement. But our love for one another had grown.

I found it difficult to contemplate trying for a child, because I was doubtful if I would have the energy to raise a child, because of my disability. I was also concerned that I had no income because at that time I was living on government disability benefit. We carried on with our relationship, trusting our mutual commitment to finding creative solutions that we could both embrace would carry us through the difficulties. Instead of focusing on the problem, we began to focus on strengthening our commitment and nurturing our love. I began spending more time living with Carolyn in Dublin. We were beginning to find true intimacy and to really trust one another.

During the time we were apart I had decided to change from using my first Christian name, Robert, to using my other Christian name, Wallace. Being called Wallace instead of Robert was separating me from my painful past, which I associated with my first name. My friends in Belfast had co-operated with this change; but Carolyn found it very difficult to call me Wallace. As a result all her friends and family called me Robert in Dublin.

That spring we were discussing the issue of having children and Carolyn offered to get married without trying for a child. I accepted her offer, but still could not bring myself to ask for her hand in marriage. My mother and sisters were telling me of the importance of children as an essential part of a marriage for most women. I knew Carolyn loved children dearly and that it would be very difficult for her to enter into a marriage without the prospects of raising a family. In May I invited Carolyn to Belfast for the weekend. I had planned to ask her to marry me and had everything arranged to make it a memorable weekend. Before I asked for her hand in marriage, I wanted to talk once more about having a marriage without children.

I invited her for a long walk along the Lagan towpath. When I asked if she would accept a marriage without children, she said she would. We walked on admiring the fresh green of leaves in early spring, coming eventually to a pedestrian bridge where a swan was floating motionless on the water. We turned and walked back along the river. As we sauntered towards the car I knew I had to get to the bottom of this issue. I had to use my insight to fully understand the issue that separated us. As soon as our walk was finished I planned to initiate our special weekend and become engaged. Once we were engaged our prospective marriage would be based on everything we had agreed together in our years of courtship. After we had become engaged I knew it would be difficult and painful to change what we had agreed prior to our engagement.

UNFOLDING YOUR WINGS

Often issues that are unsuccessfully resolved during courtship undermine the subsequent marriage for years to come. Courtship is a very precious time to develop intimacy and trust. By developing intimacy and trust in the smaller details of living, we are empowered to address larger contentious issues sensitively and creatively. Through this conflict resolving process we are preparing for engagement. It is wise to become engaged only after all outstanding issues have been talked through and resolved to the satisfaction of both people. An engagement based on a sound shared vision of your life together, will greatly increase the prospects of a successful married life.

This was a critical moment and I was being prompted by my intuition to explore further. Carolyn was telling me she would accept a marriage without children—but would this work? I asked Carolyn a further question. "Could you accept a marriage without the prospect of children in your heart?" She replied that she could accept a marriage without the prospects of children in her head but not in her heart. I knew then that I could not go ahead with the planned engagement that weekend. We needed more time.

Then when the summer came Carolyn suggested we remain together during the three months she was on holiday from her teaching post. We enjoyed the summer together, laughing, playing squash, seeing mutual friends, and dining out. We felt very united. During this time I saw the love Carolyn had for young children. Recalling the conversations with my sisters and mother, I realised it would be very difficult for Carolyn to accept a marriage without the prospects of children. She also told me that although I had a disability she did not see why as a couple we wouldn't be strong enough to raise a child.

I took time to contemplate this. As we enjoyed our summer together I began to sense our creative power. This feeling of being in a united, capable partnership twenty-four hours a day was new and exciting. Was I being too cautious? Carolyn was challenging my belief that I would not have the strength and stamina to raise a child. Could I rise to this challenge? Could I change this long held belief? I was having my dreams fulfilled in our relationship. If I could rise to Carolyn's challenge and change my belief, then she could have her dreams fulfilled as well. During this time together I dreamt that Carolyn's love was entering into me and driving out all negativity. I took this dream to be a sign that I was right to reconsider my position. I saw that we were blocked because we were both resisting each other's needs. I was resisting Carolyn's need for a child and she was resisting my need to be called by my new name. If we could both stretch our love so that we met one another's needs then there would be nothing preventing us from becoming engaged.

These thoughts were becoming clearer. I was beginning to find peace with these thoughts. I began to sense this could be the way forward.

Through my insight I saw this as the positive path leading to a more abundant and fulfilling life for both of us. Inner guidance was supporting this move.

 ## UNFOLDING YOUR WINGS

I f you are in a relationship, try making a vow with your partner that you will keep your heart open to one another. Even though you may be discussing difficult and contentious issues hold on to the feeling that you are in this together. Do not allow yourself to feel separate from your partner. By stubbornly nurturing this sense of unity you will be keeping your love alive. Then by searching for creative solutions where you can both win and that expand your aspirations, you will be empowered to find agreement. Through such agreements your life together will grow in love, unity and abundance.

I wondered how I could find the courage to suggest these changes in our relationship. Sometimes life has the knack of lending a helping hand. That summer we began to look at houses. I saw an attractive house advertised in the newspaper. It seemed like a potential dream home. We decided to visit it. As we drove up to the gates of the house, set in the Wicklow Mountains, I turned to Carolyn and said, "What will we do if we both fall in love with this place?" We did! When we arrived back home in Dublin we looked at one another. Nothing was said but we both knew what we were thinking. "How can we place a bid for this property if we haven't made a commitment to one another?"

The next morning I suggested to Carolyn that we both stop blocking the progress of our relationship by meeting our respective needs. I would offer to try for a child with Carolyn, and she would do her best to call me Wallace. She agreed. That night in a quaint French restaurant in Dublin, I asked Carolyn to marry me. She said she would love to. Our bid for the dream property was unsuccessful, but we created a dream of another kind. We were married in a small, blue, country church on a beautiful sunny day in November.

A partnership is born out of the fire of stubborn determination, child-like creativity, exquisite sensitivity and high aspiration. This is how we are inspired by our radiant inner swan to find new heights of love and union in our relationships.

Envoi

My partner is annoyed.
I am annoyed.
Because I have made a vow
I take time to reflect.
I take time to listen within.

The call shows me where I am going wrong.
The call helps me understand my needs
And those of my partner.
The call guides me in how to communicate in loving ways,

Empowering my determination,
Challenging my creativity,
Expanding my aspirations,

Shaping me into the best that I can be.

I return to my partner.
Our communication is full of love and understanding.
And my broken relationship is healed.

Seagulls saunter serenely across dank green grass. A flock of small brown birds arrive and land together. The seagulls flap into flight. They rise together, circle two nearby trees and glide to the ground gracefully. The small brown birds continue pecking. The seagulls saunter in a circle. Disturbed, the small brown birds rise en masse and leave.

Your Healing From Meaningless And Pointless Existence

When we are lonely, depressed and full of buried emotional pain, we can feel as if no one wants to know us. Life seems meaningless and pointless. This is because we are cut off from our true selves—the still lake where the radiant inner swan glides, which is always there but which we only experience when we are in love with the whole of life and are at peace.

I was lonely and depressed for a number of years. I suffered such inner turmoil that I desperately wanted to find a quick way to escape this pain. Committing suicide seemed the quickest method of escape. As a result, for two years, thoughts of suicide and methods of suicide were predominant. I imagined taking my own life many times and in many ways. If I were walking across a bridge I would imagine throwing myself into the river. If I were holding a kitchen knife I would fantasise about using it to harm myself. Once I even set everything in place to attempt suicide but could not go through with it. The pain I felt was so great I would consider doing anything for a quick release. Those were dark days. It is painful to remember them.

We all want a quick cure for our pain. The more we are in pain the faster we want the cure. The actual cure—listening to our calling and embracing our potential, can appear dauntingly difficult to commit to, and achingly slow in its ability to release us from our pain. That is why I refused to listen to my calling for two years. For those two years I lay on a couch most of the day with my head full of negative, destructive thoughts and limiting beliefs about my own ability and potential. I believed that because I could no longer manage a nine to five job, I could not work. I then believed that because I could not work I would be unable to marry and have children. I had become a slave to my own negativity.

UNFOLDING YOUR WINGS

Be careful about the limiting beliefs you hold for your life. These beliefs will work away in your subconscious like an invisible prison without bars, keeping you enslaved. Try to become aware of any limiting beliefs that you hold and, when you are ready, gently let them go by replacing them with new, more expansive beliefs brought to you by inner guidance.

I could not face what seemed like a daunting uphill journey that had to be travelled to escape from my depression. I was alone with the healing call but refused to see it. After two years lying on the couch with my face to the wall and suicide my predominant dark, menacing thought, I knew I had to turn and face the light of the world. It was then, at that precise moment, that I saw my calling, gleaming like a beautiful radiant swan, and I began to follow it. As a result I made a commitment to work in an Oxfam shop. (See Your Healing From Adversity, page 179). This was my first difficult and tentative step towards release. Other steps followed. (See Your Healing From Fear, Anger And Grief, page 223 and Your Healing From Loneliness, page 199). These steps gradually led me away from despair towards inner peace and boundless love.

The early stages of this journey were a very difficult part of my life. I felt that my life had become meaningful and hopeful no matter how steep the hill I was climbing appeared, and this feeling of meaning and hope helped shake off the suicidal and despairing thoughts. Meaning and hope had entered into my life because I had set out on the healing path.

UNFOLDING YOUR WINGS

If you are in despair and are feeling suicidal, you have my sympathy. Try hanging on to the light, no matter how dark your life may seem. In the midst of the darkness, endeavour to remember that although your life seems unbearable at present, this does not mean it will always be so dark and forbidding. This too will pass. See if you can sense a positive action you can take that will bring a small measure of relief. Taking even one small step is enormously helpful because it rekindles hope. You may find that once you have taken one small positive step the next step will be easier.

Today I am very thankful that I turned to the call and followed it. It has guided me every step of the way into a pre-eminent quality of life.

Envoi

I am in great pain.
My life seems empty and pointless.
Destructive thoughts of quick escape
Hover close by, compounding the despair.

Deep inside I know there is another way.
Deep inside I know about the call.

The call is always there.
It is present as an ever-loving friend,
Even when all others have deserted me.

The call loves me more than I can imagine.
No friend ever loved me thus.

Slowly, slowly the call guides me to the healing path.
I commit to my potential, freedom and release,
And I am healed of my meaningless and pointless existence.

Dark brown waters move with serene steadiness. Rippling reflections of banked trees, blue sky and white cloud shimmer silently. Leaves and grass float past with silken smoothness. Water gently laps the grassy bank. All around traffic passes oblivious of the river's great depth.

Your Healing From Fear, Anger And Grief

Our emotional life is to be found in the depths of our heart. There are only two core emotions—love and fear. Associated with fear are a host of other emotions like anger and grief. It is by feeling and expressing these difficult fear-related emotions that the fear in us is transformed to love and its associated emotions of joy and peace. As we explore our potential we become emotional alchemists; instead of changing lead into gold, we change fear into love.

My first encounter with fear—I mean real terror, not a minor fear and anxiety—was when I lost my job because I had a disability and could not cope. This was different from previous situations when I had lost my job, because this time I could not get another one. My schizophrenia was sufficiently disabling to make it impossible for me to cope with any job. I remember the day I came home from my interview with the psychiatrist. I sat in a big easy chair in my parents' lounge. Suddenly I chose to accept the belief that I could not work again. I felt a terror I had never known.

In that moment I chose to give up my dreams as a young man of having a career, earning money, getting married and raising a family. I was terrified and I was angry. These negative thoughts made me very angry. I was angry at being cheated of the life I had planned for myself and the life I had worked so hard to help achieve.

I did not know how to cope with the feeling of rage that was surging through my veins. In Glencraig I had a friend who worked in woodlands, so I asked if I could work with him chopping wood. He was felling large trees at the time and was glad of the help, so I joined him. I think he was utterly amazed at how an "Office Johnnie," as he saw me, could chop up so many logs vigorously in such a short space of time. Enormous amounts of energy were being spent chopping wood, because I was trying to work the anger I was feeling out of my system.

I stuck at this for a few days but try as I might I could not come to terms with the anger I felt. Eventually panic feelings overtook me and I had to be taken into hospital. When in hospital the panic left me and severe depression took over. I didn't know it then, but I had just locked all those intense feelings I was experiencing deep inside.

The fear, anger and grief remained locked away for the next two years. These were the worst two years of my life. This was the devil's chair. This was how I was choosing to torture and enslave myself in the years ahead. I simply survived those two years lost in a black depression caused by the limiting beliefs I had about myself. I had become a slave to these beliefs and could see no hope of escape. After two years I began to listen to inner guidance. My intuition led me to experiment with feeling the emotions I had locked away. At first feeling these emotions was difficult. They were shut away as if behind a wall.

I slowly began to experiment with letting them out. I did this privately in my home. (See Your Calling Is Elevated Through The Release Of Pain, page 66). I would lie on a couch and let the terror take over. Anger came out along with the terror. I expressed the anger by thumping cushions, kicking and shouting. Behind the anger there was often grief, which I expressed by crying and sobbing. At the end of a period of emotional catharsis I would lie exhausted on the couch, cover myself with a blanket and find comfort.

This practice went on for years. Initially the fear, anger and grief that I uncovered were loud, raw emotion. Gradually the rawness of the emotion eased and to my surprise, while I was releasing emotion, I began to have memories of early childhood traumas and eventually even of birth experiences. These memories were more of a sensed inner feeling than distinct events remembered visually. I realised that by this process of emotional catharsis, I was shedding decades of fear, anger and grief that had somehow become stuck in my body, mind and heart. I knew when to engage this emotional catharsis and how best to express the emotion by listening to and following my intuition's gentle inner promptings.

As the process of emotional catharsis continued I began to receive insights. I saw that the feelings that had surfaced were due to an unhealthy and rigid adherence to my life plan. As my catharsis proceeded, I learned a new way of relating to life. I became more flexible and less determined that my life should work out in a certain pre-ordained way. By becoming more sensitive I learned to depend on inner guidance.

I lost my materialistic tendencies with all the associated dreams of owning an airplane, big house and fancy car. I found abundance in the little that I had because in reality I had all I needed. I didn't long for the career I had lost. That career was of interest because of what it could do for me. Instead I learnt to serve others simply and directly. As long as my goal was to serve, I realised that I would always find sufficient activity to engage my talents, despite having a disability. I learnt that having a family was not the panacea it was often held up to be, and became a contented single person. Through realising that I was being protected, an inner calmness developed. I could sense that everything was going to work out.

I also lost the fear of trying new challenges. If I felt fear associated with a challenge I knew I could release it as inner pain. I dropped my limiting belief that I could not work again and began to take on new challenges like organising and managing a rock concert for Africa and starting a management consultancy practice part-time. By trying different things I discovered that although I could not work in a nine to five job, if I accepted my limitations and worked within them there was plenty of work that I could do. I discovered real power in this approach and began to unfold my wings and fly.

UNFOLDING YOUR WINGS

If you feel imprisoned by a situation you cannot change, try to simply accept these limitations and not fight against them. By accepting what you cannot change and focusing all your attention creatively on what you can do and on the resources you have available, then by taking a simple step toward your goal every day, you can accomplish the seemingly impossible.

I have learned to live with my disability, to accept it and work with it. This has challenged me to become more creative and to have new and exciting beliefs. Today I believe I am being called to support others in transforming their lives and am responding accordingly.

By expressing my locked in fear, anger and grief I became healed of a cripplingly severe depression and gained many spiritual insights and healings. Listening to my calling and following it saved me from the devil's chair and took me to a previously unknown place where I am blessed with feelings of love, peace and joy.

Envoi

Inside I am depressed.
I have shut down and I am cut off from my feelings.
They are locked away inside.

My calling gently prompts me to explore these feelings.

As I explore I feel my fear.
As I explore I release my anger.
As I explore I express my grief.

Slowly, slowly I am carried out of the jaws of hell
Up to the gates of heaven,
And I am healed of my fear, anger and grief.

Five ancient oak trees grow alone in the meadow. Each oak reaches for the sky with a huge canopy of leaves sprouting from an ancient twisting trunk. These oaks are rooted in the level grass carpet. Dark green reeds and clumps of yellow wild flowers decorate the ground. Dense woodland embraces this soft lush loam, wrapping the meadow in a semi-circle. The outermost tips of the oaks bob and vibrate in the gentle breeze, accompanied by delicate birdsong flowing from the surrounding wood. On the edge of the meadow an ancient oak has split asunder. Its empty branches lie like a giant white skeleton.

Your Healing From Fear Of Death

A few years ago I learned that dad was seriously ill. I came back from holiday with my girlfriend, Carolyn, to be told that he had been taken to hospital as an emergency case. He was in hospital for seven weeks, undergoing a series of investigations to determine the cause of his problem. During this period I visited him nearly every day.

Although these tests had not revealed the cause of his ill health, I sensed that dad might be coming near the end of his life. Carolyn encouraged me to tell him that I loved him. This was not easy because all his life dad had found it difficult to receive such comments, brushing them aside with a sharp rebuff. As a result I felt nervous about revealing how much I loved him. I had never told dad that I loved him. Carolyn advised me to tell him and keep telling him even if he did try and brush me aside. My inner guidance agreed with her suggestion. I knew it was the right action to take.

Choosing a moment when we were alone I proceeded to tell dad how much I loved him. To my surprise he did not brush me aside but listened. Encouraged I went on to talk about our life together, remembering and thanking him for many of the great sacrifices he had made to raise me as his son. He said nothing but I could tell he was listening intently. I talked to dad in this way whenever we were alone. During our time together he said very little, but sometimes we cried as we recalled evocative shared memories. These shared tears said much more than words.

Then after seven weeks the doctors discovered the problem, he had a large cancerous tumour next to his bowel. It was not immediately life threatening, but they would have to do a small investigative operation to discover the type of tumour, so that they would know how to treat it.

The family visited dad the night before his operation. I was last in and when I appeared he held his hand out in a spontaneous welcoming gesture that I had rarely seen before. The others disappeared and we were left alone. I only stayed a few minutes, because he was tired, but in those few minutes I detected a peace surrounding him that was not of this world.

The following morning loud banging on my front door wakened me. It was my sister. Surprised I invited her in. She simply said, "I'm sorry."

I knew instantly that dad had died.

Death can approach like a king in a snowstorm who has come to capture us. But we can escape. We can use its pervasive presence to galvanise us to action. Death has much to teach us, especially about life. So what is beyond death?

Immortality is:

The great presence in the heart of our pain
The great letting go in the heart of our control
The great sacrifice at the heart of our selfishness
The great mystery in the heart of our reasoning
The great radiance in the heart of our ill health
The great perfection in the heart of our flawed existence
The great trust in the heart of our despair
The great eternity in the heart of our time
The great oneness in the heart of our aloneness
The great silence in the heart of our noise
The great stillness in the heart of our activity
The great nowhere and everywhere in the heart of our world
The great peace in the heart of our fear

What can we learn from a phenomenon as monumentally significant as this?

The great presence in the heart of our pain
As we throw off our pain and open our heart we become aware of a presence that starts to walk with us. That presence is our own immortal-

ity. As we are healed of our pain immortality comes very close. It follows us around like a beautiful radiant swan that wants to enter fully into us but cannot because we are not yet perfect. As immortality approaches and lives in us, we notice a powerful surge in our creativity and in our love of life. The beauty of the radiant inner swan inspires our whole being. Living with immortality is so freeing. We no longer need to be impatient. We are enveloped by the timeless and the eternal and develop a deep patience that is able to overcome every problem. As the eternal enters more fully into us we yield increasingly to the call and live a highly spontaneous radical life.

The great letting go at the heart of our control

As we age immortality closes in. At the point of death itself, we must surrender our control completely. Yet all our lives many of us act as if we can control our life, pitting our will against immortality and the call, which comes from the great beyond within. If we have lived like this then immortality will come as a great psychological shock, a devouring monster that has come to separate us from all we hold dear. If we learn instead to embrace immortality while still alive, by letting go and listening to and following the call, we will be dying to our past and opening fully to the possibilities of the present moment. To live fully and totally in the present moment awakens an awareness of immortality. Then we are reborn as children of radiant Being, leading lives inspired by the beauty of the graceful inner swan.

The great sacrifice at the heart of our selfishness

Perhaps the most important question we need to answer before we die is "Who am I?" To answer this question we must travel from selfishness to unselfishness. We must change from experiencing our own true self as this person and this body, to all people and everybody. As we respond to the inner call to offer more love to more people, we die to all jealousy, greed, vanity, anger, boredom, hate, and sorrow. Through sharing ourselves with the world, the pain we feel inside is transformed into love. We are able to live in this love with complete faith, in the amazing knowledge that what we need will come to us precisely when we need it. We become an ever-expanding vessel where love flows both in and out, wearing away all traces of selfishness and egotism.

The great mystery in the heart of our reasoning

Death is an encounter with the unknown. You cannot reason it out.
You cannot intellectualise it. You cannot escape it. Immortality is the
great inescapable climax of life. Many of us live as if we know everything, our arrogance permeating every facet of our life. Yet much more
is unknown than is known. How often have we heard someone say, "I
don't know"?

We love to reason out everything, endlessly turning topics over in our
mind. We like to know. I went on a nature walk a few years ago. The
guide was well educated. He had studied the trees, the plants and the
animals that lived in the woods. Yet his delivery was dry and technical.
Although he worked in the woods and had studied the flora and fauna,
he was oblivious to the mystery of the woods. He could not convey to his
audience the wonder of a woodland walk. He was not acquainted with
immortality. He was trapped in the known.

The great radiance in the heart of our ill health

As we age the death urge makes its presence felt. We develop the
aches, pains and disabilities associated with the approach of our death.
Yet to many of us the rising presence of our death wound comes as a
bitter pill. I suffered an awful shock when in my mid twenties I was diagnosed as having schizophrenia. I could not understand. I had imagined
I would have perfect health. For years I could not accept this disability
into my life. This wound exposed my vulnerability and taught me more
about life and living than anything that has happened before or since.
Today I am learning from my wound how to reach that place beyond
pain and suffering, the immortal place where bliss prevails.

The great perfection in the heart of our flawed existence

We painstakingly construct our life to suit our imagined needs and
requirements. Many of us, especially those of us who regard ourselves
as materially successful, are proud of the life we have so carefully built.
We surround ourselves with comfort and luxury as we strive to create the
perfect existence. Yet our carefully constructed life, so manicured, so perfect, has a flaw. That flaw is death. It can strike at any moment. When
death strikes, our carefully manicured lawns, neatly clipped hedges and
beautifully decorated rooms lose their significance. Immortality, the

great leveller, has come to take us, or our loved one, home. The beautiful lawns, hedges and rooms fail to attract our interest as we grapple with the approach of the unknown. Instead, if we learn to Be, we can discover true perfection, the immortal place, known only by childlike people working to heal a world in need and pain.

The great trust in the heart of our despair

Death, loss and grief can throw us into despair. Yet we often have to reach the bottom of our despair to find the ability to trust anew. Time and again people facing death also face despair only to find, as the appointed hour of their passing approaches, despair gives way to a kind of complete trusting. They no longer worry about the future. Soon the past will be no more. They discover Being. Immortal living is an expression of complete faith and total surrender to Being. As we learn to trust Being, the beautiful radiant swan within, we can discover immortality while still alive!

The great eternity in the heart of our time

Eternity is that point where the loving presence surfaces in the full embrace of the present moment. To those of us who live close to immortality, it is a great open space at the centre of our lives. To feel eternity we need to draw close to immortality. The extent to which we experience eternity is dependent on our own ability to accept and then transcend our death urge. We do not need to be actually dying physically to experience this. Opening our heart and surrendering our pain will take us there. When we do this, we enter into eternity's great inner space. We find we have room to breathe where others are struggling. Now we are no longer crowded by deadlines, schedules and timetables. We may still operate in this world, but are not cramped by it.

The great oneness in the heart of our aloneness

We are alone. We may have a marriage partner, friends, family and work colleagues as part of our lives, but we remain unitary. We are one, not two. We enter the world alone and we leave it alone. In our aloneness many of us feel separate. We feel both alone and separate. This separation is an illusion born of the fear of death. As we embrace immortality and release our grief and pain, its light enters into us and our ego shell dissolves. We are still alone, but our separation has been replaced by childlike oneness. We are surprised to find that we are the world.

The great silence in the heart of our noise

I was walking along a remote beach in the west of Ireland one summer when I heard two teenagers complain, "There's nothing happening. It's dead around here."

By dying to our pain and entering into immortality we embrace the emptiness and silence from where all conversation, music and creativity emanate. To build a relationship with silence is to build a relationship with immortality. But how many of us fill our lives with noise? It is clear that for many, silence, immortality's container, is simply too much to bear. So we busy ourselves with a hundred different distractions—but we do not transcend pain to face the joy of our silent inner essence. By cultivating and valuing extended periods of silence in our lives, we open to our pain. We grieve, we grow and we allow immortality's presence to enter into us in the spontaneity of the present moment.

The great stillness in the heart of our activity

I overheard a mother say to her child, " Don't just sit there, do something."

From an early age we are indoctrinated with the idea that "doing something" is good and "just sitting" is bad. In our school days and later in our working life we are cajoled into "doing." So much so that "just sitting" becomes something alien. We develop frantic lives in the mistaken notion that we are "living life to the full." I remember, as a young man, getting lost in a remote area of Donegal in the west of Ireland. I knocked at the door of a small white cottage at the side of the road.

"Come in," I was told.

I entered to find an elderly couple sitting quietly in a room with no noise whatever except the restful tick of an old grandfather clock. At that time in my life this was an alien experience. I nearly always had noise present in the background. Here were a couple that were completely content without such distractions. I could sense the peace and the love in that room. Where peace and love are, stillness and immortality are also.

The great nowhere and everywhere in the heart of our world

Before we are born we come from nowhere and when we die we simply disappear back to the everywhere from whence we came. This nowhere-everywhere is a wonderful place filled with beings of light and celestial music. It permeates our world of space and time and it exists within our own hearts. We cannot see it and we cannot hear it, so we pretend it does not exist. We busy ourselves with the affairs of the world and are cut off from our true home, the great wonderland within and beyond. By spending time in stillness and silence we can come to know this world beyond space and time. As we die to all our hurt, negativity, sorrow, grief and pain, we restore some balance into our lives by becoming acquainted with immortality. It is important that we come to know the childlike inner world. It is the essential part of our nature and our reality.

The great peace in the heart of our fear

Ultimately, all fear stems from a fear of death. As we heed the call, which comes from inner stillness, we are taken on a life of adventure away from the secure and the conventional, the tried and the tested, into an unknown future. This journey takes us into our fear. This journey is the method the call uses to exorcise our fear. If we want to progress spiritually great gains can be had from the contemplation and awareness of our own birth trauma, vulnerability and pain. To face our traumatic beginning and our impending ending is to face our deepest fear. By exorcising this fear we awaken Being...the timeless, immortal, childlike, place where the radiant swan dwells.

 UNFOLDING
YOUR WINGS

If you want to experience the beauty, sensitivity, and joy of life, remind yourself each day of its delicacy. Being grateful for the precious gift that is life brings many abundant rewards.

Our experience of immortality is greatly nurtured if, as well as dying to all our pain anger and grief, we also believe in an afterlife in this silent, eternal, nowhere-everywhere, immortal place. By its very nature the existence of this afterlife cannot be scientifically proven. Its existence has to be taken on faith or experienced by direct perception. Personally I know with every fibre of my being that there is such an afterlife and that I will be happy to make my home there when I have passed over. I know I am a spirit having a bodily experience.

Envoi

My own immortality,

You are the light that follows my every step.
From the day I was born
Across the years to the present moment,
You accompany me.
As I learn to die to all sorrow, pain and negativity,
And live more fully in the here and now,
You enter into me
Like a beautiful, radiant swan,
Who brings me peace, love, joy and immortality,
And I am healed of the fear of death.

A small copse of oak grows among green grass. Dappled sunlight shines through dripping branches. An adjacent pond catches drips from trees. Each drop creates ripples that roll across the pond's still, shiny surface. Glimmers of light sparkle on the surface of each radiating ripple. Birds sing together from branches overhead.

Your Healing From Separation

Divinity can be experienced in everyday life. This part of the book has covered the healing of a number of undesirable tendencies. When these undesirable tendencies are evident in our lives we are separate. As we heal these tendencies we begin to merge.

By slowly merging the divine qualities of love, peace and joy prevail. Life takes on a new transcendent quality. We experience the pain of others as our own, because we feel the oneness of life. We perceive the exquisite sensitivity of nature. There is a newfound innocence, wonder and simplicity. In a strange way we remember this state from long ago. It is similar to how we experienced life in early childhood. This childlike state has returned but to a fully mature adult, who is acting responsibly to help heal a world community in need and pain. This everyday world of pain, trauma and stress is taken by most to be the real world, but to the healed person it seems more like a dream world.

I remember being in a supermarket recently. I was helping my mother with her shopping. I pushed the trolley around the supermarket. Other trolleys whizzed past pushed by frantic shoppers, their faces full of stress. Glitter and bright garish colours were everywhere. Insipid canned music was playing in the background. As I stood at the checkout watching these busy shoppers being processed, I felt that I was in a world that belonged to me, but that had no hold over me. It actually felt like a dream world.

This is the sense in which the healed person can feel he is in the world, but not of it. By healing our preoccupations with wealth, sex, violence and other obsessive tendencies, we cease to be caught in the drama of life. Yet this dramatic world, fuelled by materialism, lust and anger is our world. We are joined to it by our compassion. We are hurt when people behave insensitively or even violently, enslaving others or damaging the planet, for we are all One.

The healing of our separation is realised when we are able to escape from our world of pain, anger and grief to the still lake and unite with the beautiful radiant swan that lives within.

Envoi

The Wholeness of Life,
Everyday I long to merge with you.

The ocean wave is your heartbeat.
The wind in the trees is your music.
The frost on the grass is your jewellery.

I have great wealth of which others know little.
I have great joy of which others know less.
I have great peace, which others do not know.

To be fully merged is to be fully free,
And I am healed of my separation.

Wind blasts through the trees, bending branches. A flurry of leaves loosens and drips drop with each passing gust. The ground is scattered with spent leaves, their yellow, gold, russet and brown blending with green grass. Branches sway and leaves sing with each icy blast. All around are the sound of drips from spent rain. The cold gale heralds the onset of winter.

Your Healing Gives Special Rewards

As we listen to our calling and explore our potential we receive healing. By persisting with the journey we are eventually healed of many of the undesirable tendencies that trouble our hearts and agitate our minds. We commune with our radiant inner swans and our hearts begin to sing again, just as they did in early childhood, and in our minds we experience stillness and peace.

As we continue to listen intuitively, following our potential, we slowly discover that we are being abundantly rewarded for having undertaken and persisted with the journey. We notice that our character is developing. The undesirable tendencies are being replaced by desirable qualities. These are the rewards from our inner healing. These are the qualities to which Christ alluded, when he encouraged people to store up their riches in heaven and not on earth where they would rust and decay.

These rewards are spiritual in their nature. They act inwardly in our hearts and minds to improve our character, give us glimpses of immortality, nurture a childlike innocence and expand the quality of our lives. Through these rewards we become who we really are, a person with a simple dignity, integrity and wisdom. We find increasingly that we can help others by sharing and serving openly and honestly. Days are spent in simple dedicated service, until a day dawns when we are delighted to have discovered the power to fulfil our life's mission. Once we have discovered this power the bonds break and we are free.

Throughout history this experience of rising inner power has been recorded and explained in myth and legend.

Envoi

I am full of joy.
Healing has bestowed newfound wisdom, integrity and peace.
Life has become simple once more.

In that simplicity lies daily fulfilment.
In that simplicity lies monthly progress.
In that simplicity lies yearly celebration,

As with each passing year my inner rewards grow and multiply.

Would you like help in developing your inner guidance?
If so, visit *www.alifediscovered.org*

- Receive one to one coaching by email from the author on how to develop inner guidance.
- Discover how to solve your problems by tuning into inner guidance on an online tutorial.
- Find out about opportunities for personal development.
- Discuss your calling with other readers.

Your Pass Code is **star**

Visit the home page at *www.alifediscovered.org*. Then, enter through the archway in the home page.

Full details about the website on page 292.

Part Four

Your Rewards

Your Rewards communicates the benefits that await those who embark on the healing path. It is written in the form of a myth, set in ancient Celtic Ireland. This myth effectively encapsulates the book's teachings by bringing them to life. By identifying with this symbolic story, you will be able to trust that your personal difficulties will eventually lead to a new life filled with joy, purpose and meaning.

"To the illumined mind
The whole world burns and sparkles with light."
—Ralph Waldo Emerson

Dusk

There is an occasional vibrant chirping from across the river. Now there is complete stillness.

Dusk is settling.

The swan floats motionless, preening herself in the centre of the lake.
A solitary tall man in red and blue stops for a moment to watch and then moves on.

The swan is absolutely alone... her graceful, pristine white body mirrored in the still water.

The lake is dark and mysterious. There is only the gentlest of breezes. Colours are fading to browns and greys. In the far distance a cacophony of sound erupts from where the crows are nesting and drifts downriver on the gentle breeze.

The path around the lake is empty. The swan is floating motionless. She watches the lake-shore...she watches the water...she watches the sky.

The crows are calling again in a great symphony of sound. It is the call of eternity. Then complete silence.

The swan has drifted into darkness.
There is aloneness.

Peace penetrates.

Awareness awakens.

Oneness opens.

Love blossoms at the close of another day.

Winter Tales

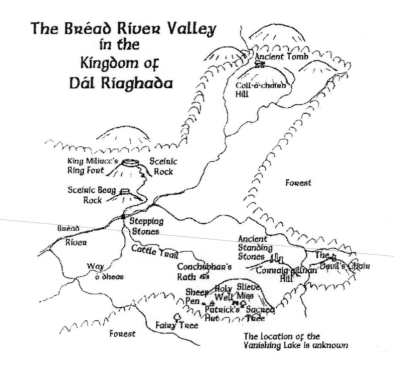

**The Bréað River Valley
in the
Kingdom of
Dál Riaghaða**

Ancient Tomb

Coll-á-chaiah
Hill

King Miliucc's
Ring Fort

Sceinic
Rock

Sceinic Beag
Rock

Forest

Bréað
River

Stepping
Stones

Cattle Trail

Ancient
Standing
Stones

The
Devil's Chain

Way
ó ðheas

Conchúbhan's
Rath

Connaig Hill

Sheep
Pen

Holy
Well

Slieve
Miss

Patrick's
Hut

Sacred
Tree

Fairy Tree

Forest

The location of the
Vanishing Lake is unknown

The Myth Of The Sacred Swan

The purple heather-coated mountains rise majestically forming a natural tree lined amphitheatre. Bright morning sun sends shadows across the hill- sides. At the heart of the amphitheatre the lake is completely still, dark and mysterious. A thin transparent layer of white mist hovers above the silent water. A solitary swan appears from the mist, making small ripples that fan outward on either side of her pure white body.

Rising Above The Heartbreak Of Enslavement

Out from between the trees, along the lakeland path, walks a boy, whistling a joyful early morning tune. His fine woollen tunic and close-fitting leather sandals reveal his privileged background in the village of

Bannavem Taberniae. The sight of a large smooth rock on the lakeshore delights the youth. He pauses to rest, taking in the tranquil scene. He sits in contemplative mood, watching the swan glide back and forth across the still water.

"You are so serene and peaceful," he thinks to himself. "Why are you here all alone? Perhaps you are on your way to some far off distant land."

The swan glides serenely across the lake, turns and draws close to the youth. As the swan draws near the youth feels inspired. His contemplation takes a new more introspective turn that reveals a hunger deep in his heart.

"I wonder where my life is leading? Sometimes I feel a great destiny ahead of me, but I don't know what it is, or where I am heading, but when I think of it I feel full of hope and longing."

This early stirring of his deep inner call causes the youth to sense feelings that are entirely new.

" I am sure I have important work to do, some vital mission to undertake. How am I to know what my mission is?"

The youth is lost within his new-found feelings and does not hear bushes close to the rock rustle and, between the leaves, the glint of sunlight off metal.

"There's another one. Get him."

Following the command three warriors emerge from behind the bush and sprint down the path towards the young boy sitting dreaming on the rock by the side of the lake.

As the youth rises from the rock one of the warriors grabs him by the neck while the other snarls, "If you don't stop struggling I'll stick my sword in your stomach." To emphasise the point he pokes the sharp end of his short, sharp sword into the youth's tunic.

"That hurts."

"It'll hurt a lot more if you don't keep still. Put the chains on him and we'll march him to the boat."

One of the warriors, a large burly man with a broken nose and blackened teeth, chains the boy's legs together, sticks the point of his sword into the youth's back and marches him round the lake and through the town, where thousands of others are being herded onto boats.

"Sit on the deck and keep silent," the warrior growls, "I want no trouble during the voyage."

The youth sits and shivers with cold and fear as the boat casts off and sails out to sea.

Once beyond the bay the wind rises dramatically, catching the large white sails. The rigging creaks ominously. A warrior walks between the captives with a writing slate.

"What's your name?" he barks.

"Patrick."

"You are number seventeen." He attaches the cloth number to the front of Patrick's tunic.

As they head out to sea, the waves begin to swell and crash against the side of the boat, making the entire ship vibrate and shake. Looking skyward Patrick can see gulls gliding into wind just above the mast. Lowering his gaze he sees the fixed stare of people in shock and rivers of puke that run back and forth over the ship's decking. "I can't believe this is happening to me," he murmurs.

The ship sails all day and into the night. The howling wind blows the ship westwards until on the morning of the next day the captives sight land. The ship docks and the captives are led ashore.

"Welcome to Dál Riaghada," laughs the warrior with the black teeth. "There's no escape from here."

The captives shuffle ashore walking as best they can in the heavy chains that bind their legs.

"Line up. Line up," the warrior shouts.

Patrick, along with the other captives, stands in a line along the dockside. A seething mass of people gathers to stare at the long row of captives. Then the bidding starts.

"What am I bid for number one, a fine young women. There's plenty of work in her. Who'll give me five pieces of gold?"

It dawns on Patrick as he watches the bidding that he is to be sold into slavery. He waits for his number to come up.

"Number seventeen. He is a fit looking young lad. Who'll give me three gold pieces?"

Patrick watches as the bidders vie to buy him.

"Sold to King Miliucc for six gold pieces."

Patrick is sold into slavery for a handful of gold and is marched, hungry and naked, to Slieve Miss where he is assigned as a shepherd to

Conchubhar, a local farmer. His heart is broken by the experience and he is emotionally traumatised. He begins to wonder what will become of him. For a time he sinks into a black hole of deep despair. Despite his troubles, he remains hopeful. As time progresses he strengthens his connection to his calling, continues to believe in his destiny, nurtures his healing from the trauma of being captured and develops tremendous strength of character...

Envoi

Although my wounded heart is assailed by troubles
And plagued by doubt,
I continue to listen to my calling,
To believe in my destiny,
To nurture my healing,
And develop my character.

As I embark on my journey,
Who knows what great mission is waiting to be revealed.

A blustery west wind is blowing in from the North Atlantic. Clouds roll across the Bréad Valley thick with moisture and smother the top of Slieve Miss in a dewy mist. Rain lashes against the rocks that cover the mountain's steep upper slopes. The rock's surface is alive with dancing drops. Even amidst the melee of wind and rain the sound of bleating sheep still echoes across the hillside.

Learning Forgiveness From A Mountain

"Here sheep, this way. This way, you stupid animal. Tóir, go get that sheep. No Tóir, over there."

In the early months of learning to herd sheep Patrick is very angry with both the sheep and his sheepdog, Tóir. He still feels bitter and resentful about the deep injustice at being captured, taken across the sea and enslaved. He vents his anger on the animals in his care.

Winter gives way to spring, summer, autumn and then winter comes round once again. Six years pass. Slowly, imperceptibly, the majesty and beauty of the mountain begins to exert its healing power on Patrick. He rises early to care for the sheep and walks with them for miles across the mountain's rock strewn slopes. As he walks he talks, up to a hundred times a day, to the highest most elevated part of himself. While he talks he listens to the springs as they gurgle out from between rocks wrapped in grass. He watches the golden eagle as he circles above the mountain's steep slopes. He smells the advent of rain as it whistles in on westerly winds. In the evening he leads the sheep around to the mountain's westerly slope. Sitting with his dog he watches the clouds change from white to fiery pink and then to purple, as the sun sets over the hills on the far side of the Bréad Valley.

Sometimes as he sits and contemplates the sunset he sobs the heartfelt cry known only by those who have had their hopes quashed. Rivers of tears flow from his cheeks onto the rocks beneath.

At night, with the help of Tóir, he herds his sheep into a fold. Patrick then retires to a small thatched hut beside the pen, where he falls asleep with Tóir to help keep him warm. Occasionally he pens his sheep early, and goes into the woods at the foot of Slieve Miss to play with local children. As the seasons change and the years go by, through communicating with the most elevated part of himself, he feels a deep inner call to accept his life as a slave and develop a special sensitivity to the animals in his care.

With the passage of time, aided by the mountain's majestic beauty and his deep inner call, his heart opens enough for him to forgive his captors and all others who have hurt him. He also forgives himself for treating the animals in his care so badly. During these six years Patrick learns to see that he deserved to be captured since he had led a life far removed from the truth. As his grieving slowly subsides a beautiful, sensitive love is born deep within his being. He feels The Spirit glowing within. This love, moulded from the mountain's rain, mist, rock and sheep dung, and from heartfelt forgiveness, solitude and the perception of truth, is strong enough to see value in being a slave and to withstand, without complaint, the rigors of his daily life. He still feels the pull of his great destiny deep within, but acknowledges that this is not the time for his mission to become clear.

Envoi

I have become bitter and resentful.
I feel enslaved.
I am undervalued.
My hopes are quashed.
At times I fell frustrated.
At times I feel angry.

As the seasons come and go,
And the years pass,
I learn to see value in service
And a deeper meaning in living.
I am learning the art of forgiveness.

A cool west wind rustles the grass. Dense woodland, the trees bare and grey, grows along the valley floor, disguising the Bréad River as it secretly drains water from tree-covered earth. This woodland runs all the way down the valley where it joins the great forest around Lough Neagh and up the valley where it shelters a small rath of round thatched huts, enclosed by a circular earthen dyke.

Confusion Around The Log Fire

"It is mid-week. I must bring the flock down to Conchubhar to be checked."

Wind blows across the hillside and raindrops dance on the rocks as Patrick and Tóir carefully guide the flock down the mountain through the opening in the dyke, and into the rath. Patrick leaves the flock with Tóir and goes to find Conchubhar.

"It is Midweek, Conchubhar, and I have brought your sheep."

"I will be with you directly."

Patrick decides to return to the flock and wait for Conchubhar to arrive. There are five huts in the hamlet, each one belonging to a different family. Each hut is circular with a honey coloured thatched roof that extends out well beyond the mud walls. The earthen dyke embraces all five huts and provides a safe haven where animals are kept. Patrick senses the intimacy offered by the enclosure. The views of woods and hills with which he is so familiar are absent, except for Slieve Miss which Patrick can see rising majestically above the surrounding dyke to the south.

"Shall we count the sheep, Pat? One, two three...forty one, forty two. Yes they are all there, as usual. Have you had any trouble with them?"

"I lost one last week. For some reason she decided to wander off on her own, but Tóir and I found her bleating behind a rock. She was a little anxious and was glad to see us. She had come to no harm so we took her back to the flock."

"When you pen the sheep at night, Pat, could you sleep with the door of your hut slightly ajar? That way you will be able to hear if the sheep are being troubled by wolves," says Conchubhar.

"That's no problem, I'll gladly do that. I've had a good look at the sheep and they seem in excellent condition," Patrick replies.

"Have you had any lame ones?" asks Conchubhar.

"None were lame last week. I've memorised the parts of the mountain where the sheep find it difficult to clamber over the rocks and I keep them away from those areas. That way they are less likely to damage their legs."

Conchubhar is delighted with the care Patrick takes with his flock.

"That's excellent, Pat. I'm pleased with your progress since you took over the flock. There's no-one at home, so would you like to come in for some sheep's milk before heading up the mountain?"

Patrick agrees and enters Conchubhar's home for the first time. The inside of the hut has the heavy smell of wood smoke. Patrick notices why. A log fire is burning in the centre of the large single room. The acrid smoke fills the room making it difficult to see clearly. The wood-smoke is blinding Conchubhar, making his eyes water slightly.

"Please be seated, Pat."

Patrick and Conchubhar sit on the floor by the fire and drink some warm sheep's milk. Patrick finds this very welcome after many cold days out on the mountain.

"You know Pat, you're not like the other slaves I've had helping me. You seem to care more about your work. This is good—very good. I've never had a slave who cared about his work as you do. Are you from an educated family?" asks Conchubhar.

Patrick nods.

"Did you like poetry?" asks Conchubhar curiously.

"My parents used to recite poetry to me when I was a child."

"I'd like to recite one of my poems Pat, I think you might appreciate it."

Conchubhar draws a deep breath, composes himself and begins to recite a long poem. Patrick is entranced.

The poem tells the story of a place where everything begins and ends, a secret Vanishing Lake, deep in the forest that, the myth says, will disappear the day a youth becomes a king on its shores.

"It's a lovely poem," Patrick comments. "Has anyone ever seen this lake?"

"I've searched for it with other men from the rath, but we've never found it," replies Conchubhar. "Nobody is sure if it really exists."

Conchubhar can feel himself drawn to trust Patrick and he decides to take a risk.

"Pat, have you ever met King Miliucc, the ruler of Dál Riaghada?"

"I think he was the man who bought me. I only saw him briefly."

"King Miliucc is a brutal man, Pat. He owns all the slaves in this area. We have to pay him tithes each year and it's impossible to keep up these payments. If we don't pay we are publicly flogged and our children taken into slavery. Sometimes I lie awake at night wondering how I am going to meet this year's payments."

Patrick listens sympathetically.

Conchubhar continues, "Whether there is a lake where kings are crowned is irrelevant, Pat, because I intend to become king by force of arms. I lead a secret band of warriors and I am inviting you to join us and fight against King Miliucc."

Patrick is shocked and surprised.

"If you join with us then when I take over the kingdom, I will free you from slavery, give you gold and your own fiefdom."

Patrick thinks deeply. "No Conchubhar," he replies with conviction.

"Are you sure?"

"Yes, but your secret is safe with me."

At this comment Conchubhar flies into a temper.

"You're a fool, Pat. You're only a slave. Look at what I am offering you to fight for me."

"That may be, Conchubhar, but I still won't do it," replies Patrick strongly.

"Then return to the mountain where you belong," and with pointed finger Conchubhar directs Patrick to the door.

Patrick knows he must escape from slavery if he is to find and fulfil his mission, but he also knows that Conchubhar's offer does not rest comfortably in his heart. He returns to his sheep and to the mountain, trusting that by continuing to listen to his calling someday his mission will become clear.

Envoi

Though others abuse me,
And offer the arrogance of power and wealth
Gathered from corrupt ventures,

I know I must remain true to my calling,
Content to serve simply and joyfully
Until my mission becomes clear
And I can humbly serve.

Wind blows blasts of air along the hillside. Driving rain is howling in from the west. Overhead swirling dark cloud masks the mountaintop. Rivers of water run between rocks. Puddles form in hollows between boulders. In these puddles the rain dances and sings.

Entering The Ring Fort

Through the wind and rain Patrick thinks he hears someone's voice. He listens more intently. Then drifting through the storm he hears his name being called,

"Patrick. Patrick."

He recognises Conchubhar's voice.

"I'm over here, Conchubhar."

A figure appears in the distance emerging from the mist and rain. Conchubhar is out of breath.

"I've come to tell you that King Miliucc has summoned all the slaves in the kingdom to his ring fort. I've been directed to gather the slaves together and take them there. Can you pen the sheep immediately and come down to my home?"

Later that morning, Patrick walks into the rath where Conchubhar lives and finds about twenty slaves gathered outside his hut. He joins them and soon Conchubhar emerges and addresses the gathering.

"You have all been summoned to see King Miliucc. We are going to walk across the Bréad Valley to his ring fort crossing the Bréad River on the way. I want you to walk together in a group. There's to be no misbehaving."

With that Conchubhar walks out through the gates of the rath with its circular earthen bank and sets off downhill towards the Bréad River. The slaves follow behind.

They follow a muddy cattle path and pass between small green fertile fields. In the distance beyond the valley they can see the rounded tree covered hills of Dál Riaghada. On one of the hills smoke is seen billowing skyward. "That's the Druids celebrating the winter solstice," Conchubhar explains.

Below the Bréad River, its surface rippled by the strong wind, creates a silvery band that winds through the green fields. Beyond the river stone walled fields lead up to Sceiric Beag, a small knoll with a rath sheltering the farmers on this side of the valley. Beyond Sceiric Beag is Sceiric Rock, home to King Miliucc's ring fort with its circular stone walls.

Conchubhar looks back to check the slaves and notices that they are all walking with their heads bowed looking at the ground or at their feet, except for Patrick, who has his head held high and seems to be inspired by the beauty of the natural scenery. Conchubhar notices his attitude and invites Patrick forward to walk with him.

"Isn't the scenery in this part of the valley an inspiration, Pat?"

Patrick nods his head and gives a wide smile of agreement.

"It's at times like this that I feel like composing some poetry."

"When do you compose, Conchubhar?" Patrick enquires.

"Oh, usually late at night by the fire. We sit up and tell each other stories of times past, then in the dead of night, when the others have gone to bed I sometimes have an idea for a poem."

They walk on silently, both men admiring the scenery.

"Do you remember King Miliucc from the time when he bought you as a slave?" Conchubhar continues.

"Vaguely," replies Patrick.

"As I told you he's an evil man, Pat. He wants everyone in the king-dom to be at his command and will stop at nothing to achieve that. Sometimes people who disobey him are whipped and tortured. That is why I think you should join my secret band of warriors to resist this cru-elty. You are not like the other slaves. You have spirit. You would make an excellent warrior. Would you not you like to see King Miliucc burned at the stake?"

Patrick says nothing. He continues to take in the scenery.

"Your silence annoys me. Do you not agree that King Miliucc needs to be killed?"

"We all have our faults," Patrick replies, and turns to join the band of slaves walking behind.

Conchubhar continues to lead the group towards the ring fort, but feels frustrated.

The cattle trail leads down to the river. Each member of the group takes it in turn to wade through the deep mud and balance carefully on the stepping stones that provide a safe crossing point to the far bank, and to the trail up to Sceiric Rock. Patrick crosses the river and sets out with the other slaves to walk uphill. He can feel the cold sticky mud squeeze between his toes. As he climbs the wet, muddy path he sees the rock cliffs and imposing stone walls of King Miluicc's ring fort come into view through the swirling mist. Conchubhar leads the band of slaves round the foot of the cliff to the entrance gates.

Patrick wonders how they will be able to enter. Conchubhar sees a warrior standing looking over the stone wall.

"Ahoy there, I am Conchubhar and am leading the slaves from the other side of the Bréad Valley to meet King Miliucc as he has ordered."

His voice is barely audible above the wind as it howls and roars around the hilltop. Patrick hears a rough creaking sound and the large wooden gate swings open. The slaves and their minders walk through the gap in the defences into the bowels of the ring fort.

Two warriors with leather strapping and armed with spears march the slaves and their minders towards the huge, circular wooden building in the centre of the ring fort. The slaves stand together in a group, listening to the sound of wooden planks being removed followed by creaking, and the doors open to reveal a large banqueting hall filled with lords and noblemen eating beef and drinking beer.

Patrick surveys the scene as Conchubhar goes to talk to King Miliucc. The hardened mud floor is covered in dried grass. Wooden posts form an inner circle that support the sloping thatched roof, some distance in from the wall. Within this circle the noblemen of Dál Riaghada sit on the floor. In the centre of the ring of seated noblemen sits King Miliucc on a large, solid wooden throne. The strong, heavy smell of earth and grass fills the room.

Hunting dogs are running from table to table eating scraps dropped by the noblemen. Servant women scurry about outside the circle of seated men, supplying all their needs. Conchubhar finishes talking to King Miliucc, who then stands up and orders the slaves to come forward one by one into the centre of the circle and swear lifelong allegiance to him.

Each of the slaves is called forward and without hesitating each swears allegiance to King Miliucc. Finally it is Patrick's turn. As he approaches the king's throne, ringed with noblemen, he knows that he cannot swear allegiance to King Miliucc; he knows there is a greater power to which he has already surrendered his life. He steps forward to do what he knows he must, with trust and with faith. When ordered to swear allegiance, he refuses.

Enraged, King Miliucc reaches to strike Patrick, but Conchubhar steps forward to defend him saying, "Patrick is no ordinary slave, your majesty. He is an excellent worker and does everything that I ask of him. I beg you to spare him."

There is a tense silence. No slave has ever refused to swear allegiance until now. Everyone in the hall waits to see what will happen.

King Miliucc puts his hands on the arms of his throne then reaches over saying in a hiss, through clenched teeth, "An excellent worker, eh! Well if this excellent worker disobeys me again he will be tied to a stake at the foot of the cliff, and left for the crows to peck out his eyes."

With that he drops back into his large oak chair and roars with laughter. The noblemen in the hall laugh with him. Patrick returns to the band of slaves and they are led out of the fort.

As they walk home Conchubhar is once again critical of King Miliucc, and says he is looking forward to burning him at the stake. Patrick sighs in response.

Envoi

Others may lust for fame, power and money,
And in that lusting,
Though others abuse me, I do not flinch,
Though others humiliate me, I do not cower,
Though others reach to strike me, I do not yield,

I do not answer to others.

I answer only to this prompting deep within my heart.
I remain true to this prompting and do not fear,
I remain true to this prompting and do not worry,
I remain true to this prompting and do not tremble,
For I know I am protected.
And feel compassion for my abuser.

The wavy waters whisper as they wander through the glade. The river is swollen to a torrent. Dark water winds its way between the river's brown banks. Under hanging trees, just before the bend, recently formed rapids bubble in the morning sunlight. The little, wooden, slatted bridge presents the only safe crossing. Its still presence contrasts with the fast flowing waters.

Learning To Love

Patrick has penned his sheep to protect them from the storm and is wandering along the banks of the swollen Bréad River into the woods when, in the distance, from behind some hawthorn bushes, he hears sobbing. He walks ahead to investigate. As he rounds the bushes he sees a young girl kneeling at the edge of the riverbank crying. He gently approaches the girl to comfort her.

"Why are you crying, little one?" he says softly.

The girl stops sobbing and looks up. Her freckled face is stained with tears.

"My uncle, who looks after me, has chased me from the house. I accidentally dropped his meal and he spurned me, saying that all young women are stupid." The young girl bursts into tears once more as she recalls the painful moment. She looks again at Patrick, her pale face searching for words of comfort and reassurance.

"I don't think you are stupid," says Patrick. "I think you are very beautiful."

"Do you really think so?" she enquires, her face softening as she senses Patrick's willingness to acknowledge her own deep need to be assured of her attractiveness.

"Of course I do," he replies.

"Then why can my uncle not see it?" she questions with a playful huffiness.

"Far away across the sea I have an uncle like that," Patrick affirms. "Do you know in all the years I knew him he never had a kind word for me."

"Why was that?" the girl enquired.

"I don't know. For years I thought I was stupid, then one day I realised that my uncle was like that with everyone he met and that there was nothing wrong with me."

"I think my uncle might be like yours," she replies. "Families can be difficult."

"Indeed they can," replies Patrick. "But they can be a refuge of love and understanding as well—but unfortunately I've lost my family."

"How can you lose your family?" she asked.

"My father, Calpernius, was a Briton and a deacon. My mother, Concess, was a Frank and a close relative of Saint Martin of Tours. I suspect that my parents and sister were killed when I was captured. I was taken to Dál Riaghada on a ship and sold as a slave to King Miliucc. I work as a shepherd on Slieve Miss looking after Conchubhar's herd of sheep."

"Oh, you poor thing." the young girl sighs, "I am sorry to hear that." She then hesitates and introduces herself. "I am called Maebh," she says, and she gives Patrick an attractive open smile.

"Look," Patrick changes the subject, "I bet I could beat you in a leaf race down river." Patrick and Maebh each pick up a leaf from the forest floor and throw it into the fast flowing waters, then both of them run down river to see whose leaf will reach the bend first.

"I won, I won," shouts Maebh as her leaf is carried around the bend ahead of Patrick's.

"Just good fortune," murmurs Patrick as he leans against a tree. "Where does the Bréad River come from Maebh?" he enquires after recovering his breath.

"I'll show you," she exclaims with a glint in her eye. "Follow me," and she spins round and walks upriver into the forest.

Together Maebh and Patrick follow the river higher and higher into the hills. As they climb, the river turns into a stream and then into a gurgling brook. Just as Patrick is beginning to feel as if he has climbed far enough, he hears Maebh say, "Shush, listen."

Patrick stops. As he listens he can hear the sound of a small waterfall ahead.

"We're nearly there," says Maebh, and she runs ahead to where the waterfall flows.

Patrick passes her and scrambles up the steep slope to discover a serene silent lake, enfolded in soft willow trees. The lake is so still and silent that it feels sacred.

"This is the secret Vanishing Lake," Maebh whispers.

Patrick is surprised and recalls Conchubhar's mythical poem.

"Is this the lake where everything begins and ends, the place where a youth will one day be crowned king?" he whispers.

"Yes," she replies reverently.

They stare at the still blue water and watch the clouds reflect in the smooth surface. Then silently, smoothly a pure white swan glides out from behind a willow tree. As Patrick watches the swan he is overcome with a feeling of peace and wonder. He begins to sense the pull of his destiny and starts to cry.

"What's the matter, Patrick?" Maebh asks gently.

"I feel I have a great mission to accomplish but I don't know what it is or how to start," he sobs. "I do not know how I can have these feelings when I am living the life of a slave with no way of seeing how I can attain my freedom." Patrick breaks down completely, sits on the lakeshore and cries bitterly.

"Do you hate your captors?" Maebh asks gently.

Before he answers the swan glides closer to the lakeshore where he sits. "No," he says, "I don't hate my captors—but sometimes I wonder if my life is ever going to change and my mission become true. I know I must learn to love my captors and to trust that my dreams will come to pass, but it is hard, very hard."

Maebh sits down beside Patrick, puts her arms around him and whispers,

"You need to speak to Mythendical the Druid."

Envoi

I learn to trust.
As I trust all prejudice melts away,
And I am blessed with an openness of spirit.
Into that openness comes love.
Into that openness comes support.
Into that openness comes joy.
I am relieved of my need to hate and despise,
And am open to friendship.

Mid-afternoon sunshine is casting strong shadows from rocks. Out on the horizon the hills are dark and sombre while above grey blue clouds lie in streaks. Between the clouds the sky shines with a soft translucent blue. Then, without warning, the silver sun glides behind a cloud and the shadows disappear. A sombre feeling spreads across the mountain.

A Shepherd's Devotion

Patrick is still feeling the dark effects of yesterday's grief. As he whistles instructions to Tóir, his spirits slowly lift.

"Here Tóir, here boy."

Patrick and Tóir slowly guide the sheep safely down the slopes of Slieve Miss towards the sheep pen. As he nears the pen he sees Conchubhar standing close by.

"Hello Conchubhar! What brings you up the mountain?"

"I've come to count the sheep."

Conchubhar watches as Patrick directs Tóir to guide the sheep into the pen. He is amazed at the close working relationship between Patrick and his dog.

"I have a lame sheep here, Conchubhar. I think I will separate her from the flock and see what the problem is."

Tóir is skilfully guided to send the flock into the pen while at the same time keeping the lame sheep out so that she can be examined.

"Could you give me a hand here, Conchubhar?"

Patrick and Conchubhar catch the lame sheep and turn her over on her back. Patrick examines the lame hoof, finds a stone and removes it with a sharp stone. The two men then guide the sheep by hand into the pen.

"That's great, Pat, I will just count the sheep now. One, two, three...forty one, forty two. Yes they are all here. Pat, I am much pleased at the care you have for my sheep. Would you like to walk home with me and come into the house for a meal?"

"That would be wonderful, Conchubhar."

The two men walk down the slope of Slieve Miss and see the hills of Dál Riaghada spread out before them. As they walk, Conchubhar shares his appreciation of the work Patrick is doing for him.

"You know, Pat, you have become an excellent shepherd. You are very diligent and attentive and you work hard."

"I wasn't always a hard worker, Conchubhar." Patrick replies, smirking.

"You weren't?"

"No. When I was living at home I was often asked by my parents to help with the chores and I was always looking for ways to avoid doing my duties."

The two men laugh.

"Well, Pat, my previous slave didn't work anything like as hard as you do. I always felt he didn't really care. I lost a lot of sheep because of his slothfulness. Those were worrying times, Pat, worrying times."

Patrick notices Conchubhar look into the far distance with a faint pained expression that hints at an unknown and troubled past. Then Conchubhar slowly returns his awareness to the conversation.

"I need to tell you Pat, my family and I have come to depend on you. I feel we would be lost without you."

A reflective silence descends on the poet warrior and the shepherd as each recognises how they are mutually dependant. Then Conchubhar breaks the silence. "The meal won't be ready for sometime, lets walk to the standing stones on Corraig-gillnán Hill and look at the view."

The two men climb the next hill together. At the ancient standing stones they silently look across the moor reflecting on the generations of people who have herded sheep on these hills.

They stand still and quiet, the comfortable silence expressing a well-established fellowship carved in sheep dung and Slieve Miss's mighty presence, a bond of love between them that transcends master and slave. Then, with the whistling icy wind in their ears, Patrick feels this calling deep in his heart, turns to Conchubhar and says, "Conchubhar, I want you to know that your family can depend on my support and loyalty."

Envoi

Through work I serve others.
Through work I express caring and love.
Through work I build relationships.

Though others may view work with distaste,
I know it is my duty to do my best
At whatever I am given to do.
Choosing to labour with love,
I know the joy of service.

The bleating of sheep reverberates around the mountain. The early morning sky is dark and forbidding. A dense blanket of rain hides the distant horizon. Water runs in rivulets between boulders, soaking heather and grass. At the foot of the mountain, beside the sheep pen, sits a small, damp thatched hut.

Meeting A Wise Old Man

Patrick rolls over in his bed of straw, reluctant to get up on such a damp wet day. He lies in bed reflecting on the previous day's conversation.

"I was right to make that promise to Conchubhar, but I can't see how I am ever going to achieve my mission," he ponders despondently. Patrick feels confused and frustrated. "I wish I had someone to talk to," he sighs. "But there is no one."

Eventually, with the demands of the day prominent in his mind, he rises, picks up his sheepskin bag, throws on his cloak and heads out to collect some fresh drinking water from the Holy Well.

Emerging from his hut he briefly gazes up the slope into the dense grey mist that is clothing Slieve Miss in a thick blanket of fog and rain.

"Such a damp day," he sighs, and sets off around the mountain to the Holy Well.

As he walks he can feel the cold rain run down his neck and water rise through the sodden earth to squelch between his toes.

"My life is so full of adversity how can I possibly find and achieve my mission?" he thinks.

Eventually Patrick sees the Holy Well emerging from the mist and rain. Marking the site of the well is the mysterious Sacred Tree—the only tree able to grow on this windswept mountainside. Patrick decides to shelter from the rain under its overarching branches. As he approaches he sees someone sitting with his back to the trunk in what appears to be a Druid's cloak.

"May I sit with you out of the rain?" Patrick asks.

The stranger pulls back his hood, gazes lovingly towards Patrick and says in a deep resonant voice, "Certainly, sit on this stone beside me."

The two men sit in silence gazing across the mountainside at the mist

and rain. Patrick senses a deep love radiate from the wizened, old man.
As the two strangers begin to talk he feels drawn to tell his life story, while
the old man sits and listens patiently.

"So you see," says Patrick concluding his tale, "I feel this strong sense
of mission, but it appears so out of reach."

The old man feels Patrick's frustration.

"You need to remember," he says, "that it is not possible to do great
things, it is only possible to do small things with great love every day.
Continue with your promise to your master and his family. For the present try and be content to serve faithfully with a good heart. Time brings
many changes. If you continue to serve faithfully and loyally, opportunities will be revealed."

Patrick sits in silence. As he contemplates these words of wisdom, the
rain stops. The sun breaks through from behind grey cloud and lights
up the whole mountain. The rocks and grass glisten and shimmer in the
strong sunlight. Patrick and the old man rise, bid each other farewell,
and go their separate ways.

As Patrick is walking back to his hut carrying his bag of fresh water, he
remembers the comment Maebh whispered on the shore of the Vanishing Lake and thinks excitedly, "That must be Mythendical the Druid!"

Envoi

Even though I am burdened with adversity,
I can learn to trust
And share with others who care,
Living each day
Doing the small things to the best of my ability.
By taking these small daily steps to fulfil my potential,
Each day brings growth and new opportunities.

The swollen stream flows partially underground, the water tinkling as it bubbles over rocks. A large ivy-encrusted trunk lies across the stream's flow. Gentle sounds of gurgling fill the air. The stream is being sheltered by the evergreen leaves of a holly bush. Each time there is a gust of wind a flurry of drops pat the wet earth.

Dancing Around The Fairy Tree

"That was a lot of rain yesterday, Pat," says Conchubhar as he greets Patrick in the forest. "Are you on your way back to Slieve Miss?"

"Yes I have come into the forest to cut myself a new staff from one of the trees." With that Patrick grabs a low-lying branch, bends it and cuts it off the trunk. The two men talk as Patrick trims the branch into a shepherd's crook.

Now that they are surrounded by the privacy of the forest, Conchubhar returns to his favourite topic of conversation.

"Do you realise, Pat, that the day I become king I can have any of the most beautiful women in Dál Riaghada share my bed? It's a pity you won't join me. As a nobleman, you could also pick women of your choice."

Patrick is silent.

The two men continue to walk through the dark sodden forest until they come across an open grass space with a small hawthorn tree, lit by a ray of sunshine shining through a gap in the cloud.

"Look, I think that is a fairy tree," says Patrick. "Is it not a wonderful sight?"

Then, just as he finishes speaking, he hears laughing voices coming from the surrounding forest. The voices grow louder and Patrick is surprised to see Maebh run out into the clearing followed by her friends.

The children start to hold hands and dance in a circle round and round the fairy tree in the bright sunlight. Maebh dances beautifully, her long skirt billowing in the wind. Patrick turns to share her beauty with Conchubhar, but sees his eyes narrow as he looks lustfully in her direction, so he declines. As the children dance Patrick notices deer, rabbits and a fox stand on the edge of the clearing watching the joyful scene.

Patrick feels a calling to dance with the children and he asks Conchubhar to join in. Conchubhar freezes.

"That is not something a warrior does," and he refuses to share in the fun.

To Conchubhar's amazement, Patrick runs across the clearing and joins the dance around the fairy tree with the children.

Envoi

By following my calling
I learn to feel the love of a child in my heart.
Through that love I open to the wonder of the world.
I come to leave behind all harsh sexual desires
And rejoice in innocence.

The sky is grey and overcast. In the distance ponds of light brighten the forest where sunbeams break through cloud. Then, without warning, clouds part and a bright ray of sunlight descends on the slope of Slieve Miss. The rocks sparkle and the grasses dance in the brightness. Some distance away there is persistent bleating.

The Gift Of Hidden Treasure

Patrick hears bleating and clambers over the sunlit rocks to find one of his sheep trapped, her hoof stuck in a crevice. Patrick bends down to release the sheep and as he does so he sees the corner of an old leather bag, its brown weathered surface picked out by strong sunshine. Curious, he reaches to pull the bag out from the crevice. As he pulls the corner rips and spills gold coins and jewellery over the rocks. Patrick is astounded. He gathers up the treasure and thinks how pleased Conchubhar will be when he gives it to him. As soon as he has gathered up the jewellery, the sunlight disappears and the mountain reverts to its dark, sombre, winter presence.

He calls Tóir and together they guide the sheep down off the mountain. The sky is dull and brooding. All sunshine has left the land. He can smell the presence of rain. Looking west he sees rain clouds gather over the Bréad Valley. The wind is gaining force and the grass starts to wave back and forth tracing the flow of gusts across the face of the mountain. Patrick and Tóir herd the sheep into the open pen. He closes the pen and heads off down the mountain to tell Conchubhar the good news.

As he nears Conchubhar's farming settlement he feels a great excitement grow in his breast. He imagines how delighted Conchubhar will be at the sight of the buried treasure. His enthusiasm rises. He starts to run and continues to run until he reaches Conchubhar's home. As he nears the raft rain starts to fall, driven on by the wind. He sees lightening flash and hears the crack of thunder. Inside Fionnula is quietly making a tunic for one of her children, when the door bursts open, startling her.

"Pat it's you," she exclaims in a surprised tone.

Fionnula's mother is shocked and rounds on Patrick, who is standing wet through in the doorway.

"How dare you burst into our home without even knocking. You needn't expect any more meals in our house."

Patrick apologises.

"I'm so excited that I forgot to knock. I've found this!" and he thrusts the open bag with all the coins and jewellery into Fionnula's hands. "I found it on your farm. It's for Conchubhar."

Fionnula bursts into tears and appears grief stricken. Patrick, thinking she would be pleased, is very confused.

"Why are you so upset?" he asks gently.

"Conchubhar has been killed by King Miliucc in a rebellion," she sobs.

Patrick is deeply shocked and distressed. They sit and talk. The sound of thunder rumbles outside.

"He led a raid on the ring fort with his band of armed warriors. They managed to storm the fort and get inside but they were all killed. It was King Miliucc himself who killed Conchubhar in a sword fight. I can't bear the pain and loneliness."

The two embrace and sob.

After grieving together for a while, they separate. Fionnula shares her fears. "How I am ever going to look after the farm and feed the children?" she sobs.

Patrick reassures her.

"This buried treasure I found will keep your family for life. Please, take it."

Fionnula takes out the gold coins and the jewellery and sets them on the floor. They sparkle in the light from the fire.

"You are right, Pat, these are very valuable. I am deeply grateful."

She reaches across the floor, picks up a beautiful gold brooch encrusted with gemstones and hands it to Patrick.

"I want you to have this," she says, smiling.

Patrick is delighted, thanks her for her generosity and leaves to let the family grieve in private.

Fionnula turns to her mother. "Pat doesn't know it, but I have just given him the Brooch of Loughinra—the king's brooch."

Envoi

Though others display meanness,
I offer generosity.
Through generosity I give, share and enrich friendships.
I know that all that I give, I give to myself
And that my needs are amply provided
In surprising and delightful ways.

The bare trees are picked out by the low slanting, winter sunshine. Bird-song fills the air. A gentle river gurgles between brown banks. Large green ferns waver in the soft breeze. The woodland path follows the gurgling river higher into the hills.

The First Hint Of Freedom

Patrick is thinking of Conchubhar's death and the failed rebellion as he follows the path higher and higher. A duck darts out from the river-bank and scoots across the water as he nears an old blown-down tree.

"Conchubhar failed. His rebellion failed," he muses. "There must be a better way."

As he reflects on Conchubhar's death, his mind turns to the Vanishing Lake and the pure, graceful, white swan. He feels drawn, as if by an invisible hand, back to the lake.

He decides to visit the lake by continuing up the Bréad River by the path that Maebh had taken. As he climbs, the river becomes smaller and smaller until it is only a small bubbling stream, then as he clambers up the bank by the waterfall, he is in rapture at the still presence of the lake's calm water. There, floating in the centre of the still lake, is the swan.

Patrick sits on the banks of the lake and tries to relax. Much he tries he finds his mind troubled and stressed by the death of Conchubhar and his feelings of bondage and slavery.

"Now that Conchubhar is dead, I feel more trapped than ever," he muses. As he sits in this stressed and perplexed state, the swan glides over close to the bank where he sits.

"Why do this lake and the swan feel so significant?" he ponders.

Then Patrick hears a rustling in the trees behind him and out skips Maebh and some of the children he recognises from the time he danced with them around the fairy thorn. They form a circle around Patrick and dance round and round laughing, singing and playing jokes. Eventually the children sit in a group in front of Patrick with Maebh in the middle.

"Why are you feeling so morose, Pat?" she asks.

The swan draws closer to where Patrick sits. He feels this calling to confide in the children. He tells them of his despair at being a slave, his grief at the death of Conchubhar, how he found the treasure and was given the brooch and of his great calling, which seems so out of reach. The children listen sympathetically. Then Maebh says, "Pat, I feel you can now release yourself from your commitment to Conchubhar's family. Their needs are now met by the buried treasure."

"Yes, and you don't have to stick with Lord Meliucc because you never swore allegiance to him," Amergin adds.

Patrick is surprised. "I never looked at it like that," he replies. "But how can I break away?"

" Why don't we return to the Vanishing Lake, and we'll create an escape plan," Maebh suggests.

Then the children rise, run into the forest laughing and singing, and disappear. Patrick sits quietly. He feels a deep sense of relaxation as he rests by the lake in the presence of the swan. He watches her glide gracefully across the lake, her pristine white body reflecting in the still blue water.

"Why are you here?" he ponders. "Why do you never fly?"

Envoi

I feel stressed.
I am worried, confused and perplexed.
By trusting my calling,
I share these worries openly and honestly
With others who care,
Gaining greater understanding
And reaching new depths of relaxation

*There is the slight hint of a path, a wandering line of flattened ivy, trod-
den underfoot. A space opens in the forest canopy where an ancient tree has
fallen. In this space young saplings and brambles grow, each hunting hun-
grily for light. The fallen tree lies covered in the ivy and brambles. The path
wends its way around the edge of this opening and runs along the banks of
the Bréad River.*

The Dark Shadow Of Loneliness

Patrick follows this path along the river through the forest on his way
back to Slieve Miss. He reflects on his friendship with Conchubhar, his
decision to escape and his great mission, which is yet to materialise. He
decides that the next day he will visit Conchubhar's grave.

The following afternoon is bright and clear. Low slanting sunlight
is casting long shadows from the posts that support the sheep pen. Patrick pens his sheep, and sets out to find Conchubhar's grave. He walks
around the lower sun bathed slopes of Slieve Miss to the far side. As
he rounds the end of Slieve Miss and walks onto the eastern slope, he
enters a dark shadow cast by the mountain. In this shadow the birds have
stopped singing. He walks on into the gloom. Then ahead lying on the
ground he sees a small circular furrow. He walks up to the circle, stands,
and reflects: "Here lies Conchubhar, The Poet Warrior."

For a moment Patrick is stunned. He realises that below this circular
furrow lies the body of his master and friend with whom he had so many
good times. Tears of sadness and grief begin to well up in his eyes. He
becomes aware of pain and a sense of loss deep in his heart.

He reflects on their time together. As he reflects he senses the loneliness of Conchubhar's life and that he was probably the only close friend
Conchubhar ever had. He feels that he is now able to rescind his commitment to serve Conchubhar's family and find his own path. Patrick is
moved to speak into the dark shadow.

"You had a desire to bring justice and freedom from bondage and
chose to play out that desire in battle. I too have the same desire but my
destiny points to an alternative path. I will choose differently."

He turns and walks out of the darkness into the light.

Envoi

I offer friendship to all.
I befriend the sad, the confused, the lonely and the violent.
To many I am their close companion,
To most I am the only friend who understands,
To all I offer to share my life,
And I am deeply enriched.

The winter sun hovers motionless above the horizon. The sky is clear and blue. High in the sky the moon reflects the sun's gentle rays. Birds are singing and there is a developing crispness in the air.

White Wings In The Distance

Patrick is wandering aimlessly down the mountain feeling lost, insecure and worried.

"My time here is coming to an end. I can sense it. But where do I go to now? How am I to know my mission?" he worries to himself.

He continues down the mountain, lost in thought. As he wanders, not knowing what to do or where to turn, he hears the chant of the Druid coming from the direction of the Holy Well. This chant is carried around the mountain and out over the vast empty space of the Bréad Valley. Its ancient tones resonate deep within him, evoking the sacred. Patrick follows these sounds. They grow louder as he is inexorably drawn back to the Holy Well, where he sees Mythendical, meditating at the foot of the Sacred Tree.

Patrick takes a drink from the well's pure water, sits beside the Druid and gazes out across the sunlit valley. Mythendical senses his presence and, emerging from his meditation, smiles sweetly at Patrick. Then after looking lovingly into Patrick's eyes the old Druid slowly turns his head and gazes across the valley.

"Something's troubling you, Pat, I can tell," he says gently.

Patrick feels comfortable confiding in the old man. He tells Mythendical about Conchubhar's death, the insecurity this has engendered, his feeling that the time has come to find his own path and to discover his mission. Mythendical turns his head slowly back from the sunlit valley, re-engages Patrick's eyes and gently says, "Trust the passion of your calling and your mission will reveal itself."

Then after suggesting that Patrick ask for guidance, he disappears down the mountain and into the woods.

Patrick sits alone, the gentle sunshine warming his bare face and hands, as he gazes out across the valley. Each leafless tree is picked out by soft sunlight. He can just make out the wandering line running through the fields, where the Bréad River flows. He feels still and calm as he contemplates the Druid's wise words, and asks within how he can discover his mission.

Then, in the distance, he sees shining white wings beating gracefully above the river. The wings come closer and closer until Patrick sees the long graceful neck and head of...the swan! She passes above him, her white plumage radiant against the clear blue of the sky. As he talks to the highest part of himself, he feels intimacy with the swan. Remembering the Druid's wise words, he asks for his mission to be revealed, while watching the swan climb higher and higher in the vastness of the empty, blue sky. He senses the flow of cool winter air over her plumage, feels the wind vibrating her outstretched wingtip feathers and hears the swish of air through her wings as they beat in a slow powerful rhythm, lifting the great bird higher and higher in the sky's immense emptiness.

Then in that instant he discovers freedom. The exquisite beauty of the swan moves him to tears. Everything is clear. The moment passes and he is a slave once again sitting on the slope of Slieve Miss.

Something of that moment stays with Patrick. His insecurity is gone, replaced by a security he has never known. Rising from the grassy bank at the foot of the Sacred Tree he turns to walk back to the sheep pen and his slave's hut, but he is different. He feels the pull of his mission stronger than ever and resolves to return to the Vanishing Lake once again.

Envoi

I feel insecure.
Fearfully turning worries over in my mind
Will not give me security.
To find security I turn within,
To my calling, to my mission
And to communion with the highest part of myself.
Then in an instant I feel intimacy
With all that was, is and will be,
Exquisite sensitivity is released,
Because I am the other.
In my otherness I know total security.

Sensuous, curving willow branches stretch over the lake. Green leaved shrubs soften the water's edge. Straight reeds with black tips grow along the lakeshore causing tiny ripples in the water's still, smooth surface. Coloured stones decorate the lakebed.

An Inspiring Escape Plan

Patrick sits on the bank, occasionally dipping his toe into the water, to feel the chill of the water and watch ripples from his foot spread out across the perfectly still surface. He gently and lovingly contemplates his future as he plays with the lake's calm water.

"Will I escape? If I were to decide to escape, how could I possibly manage it?"

Patrick sits with these questions, letting them gently come and go in his mind, as he rests in the place where everything begins and ends.

Then in the distance he sees movement. Looking up, he watches as the pure white swan glides from behind a reed bed across the lake's calm surface. He watches the swan drift into the centre of the lake where she floats motionless. The swan watches Patrick from a distance. Her beauty captivates Patrick. As he gazes on the pure white body reflected in the still water, he senses that it is right for him to escape. He feels a steely resolve.

As he accepts and embraces this resolve, he hears voices coming from the forest. Out from behind the trees run the children laughing and singing. They dance around him, teasing him with little rhymes, "Pat. Pat. Where's your hat. You haven't got one, because your head's too flat."

Patrick smiles and playfully picks a large leaf, and puts it on his head pretending it's a hat. The children fall about laughing and gather at his feet.

"Have you thought any further about escaping?" asks Maebh.

"I've given the matter some thought and I've decided to create an escape plan," Patrick replies.

The children all cheer, except for Ossian who sits brooding to one side.

"Will you help me?" Pat asks.

"Of course we will," they reply.

Ossian is not happy.

"I think it's impossible to escape. The roads are all patrolled by warriors, the woods are too dense to walk through, you would be cut by brambles and, you would be killed if the warriors caught you. It's not worth trying."

"Steady on Ossian, let's just try and see if we can create an escape plan. If we all pool our ideas you never know what we might come up with," replies Patrick. "Why don't we all sit silently and see if anyone has a good idea."

As the group sits in silence the swan glides over to be near the riverbank where they are gathered. The swan stops and floats motionlessly beside the children. Everyone is still and quiet. Suddenly one of the boys suggests, "Why don't you walk along the Way Ó Dheas out of Dál Riaghada? If you wear your golden brooch nobody will suspect you are a slave."

Another boy adds, "We'll follow you. If any warriors appear we'll dash into the woods. Then when they challenge you we'll fire stones at them."

"And then they will chase us into the woods and we will run, leading them further into the forest."

A girl joins in, "That'll give you a chance to get past the patrol."

The children are delighted with their ideas. They jump up and down excitedly and cry, "What do you think, Pat? What do you think?"

Patrick ponders for a moment and replies, "I think it's a great plan...I need time to think it over."

Envoi

What we need to achieve, we can achieve.
Though some are unable to solve their problems,
I am not deterred.
I stop and sense the silence, for I know,
That in silence there is great beauty, great love
And great leaps of imagination.
In that silence lies my calling
And the answers to all my problems.
My creativity knows no bounds.

Sheep leave trails in the green, dew soaked, lowland pasture. A dense thicket of oak encloses the grazing on one side. On the edge of the thicket a deer stands watching, his great antlers forking like the branches of a tree. The path winds along the edge of the thicket, dips into a hollow and then climbs toward the brow of a hill.

The Tomb At Coll-á-chairn

Patrick is walking north to collect some sheep for Conchubhar's brother, Aenghus. Aenghus has taken over Conchubhar's flock and intends to add it to his own. Not content with this, he wants to increase the number of his sheep still further, and has sent Patrick on a long journey to the north coast to bring a flock of sheep back to Slieve Miss. Patrick contemplates the conversation he had with Aenghus. He is lost in thought.

"I really don't understand why he wants to keep adding and adding to the flock on Slieve Miss. There isn't enough grass. I explained this to him but he just goes on adding more and more sheep. When all the grass is eaten these sheep will starve."

Although Patrick had conveyed his doubts, Aenghus was adamant.

When he arrives at the brow of the hill, Patrick sees that the path north curves away from the thicket into a dip past the Tomb of Coll-á-chairn. He had often heard of this place, a burial tomb built by ancient peoples. The tomb is so old that no one can remember where these people came from, who they were or where they had gone. As he nears the tomb he can see the standing stones shrouded in white mist that has gathered in the hollow.

"This is a good place to stop and have something to eat," he muses as the stones of the tomb come closer into view. He stops and sits on the grass bank to one side of the tomb, unties his leather bag where he keeps his food and begins to eat. The low slanting rays from the winter sun cast long deep shadows across the face of the tombstones. At the foot of the stones the mist forms a gently moving carpet of white. The gentle sound of sheep bleating drifts across the pasture.

These stones evoke in Patrick a time so old, so far away, that he cannot imagine it. He falls into a reverie. In the mistiness of his mind he feels the preoccupations and concerns of the day slip away, replaced by the timeless and the eternal.

"What are the preoccupations of today when set against eternity?" he thinks to himself.

For a brief moment he tries to imagine his whole life as a shepherd on Slieve Miss. This image does not rest easy in his heart and he feels more strongly than ever that he must escape. As he drifts in this ocean of timelessness he dreams of a great mystical bird that will help him, and of a ship setting sail across the sea with him on board.

When he emerges from his reverie he decides to go ahead with the escape plan. Patrick resolves to return to the Vanishing Lake and meet once again with the children of the forest. He lies back against the grass bank and feels deep contentment rise within.

Envoi

As I learn to see my day within the timeless and eternal,
All compulsions and preoccupations fall away.
By sensing the great span of time
Into the past and into the future,
The urgency of time disappears,
Replaced by deep contentment.
In that contentment I know what I must do.

Grey mistiness covers the sky. The air is turning colder and sharper. Each tree is completely still. Not even the smallest branches are moving. Every tree is reflected perfectly in the lake's mirrored surface. Beyond these reflections, the swan glides effortlessly. The crisp, still air and misty cloud suggest the imminence of snow.

The Vow Of Love

Patrick is sitting contemplating the swan. The reflections of her long, elegant neck and white body in the lake's still water captivate him. As Patrick watches, the swan glides into the centre of the lake and floats motionless watching, not even the tiniest ripple emanating from her body.

Patrick turns once again to his decision to escape. He wonders how he will tell the children. As he observes the swan, a presence descends. The lake seems more real than ever. Then he hears a sweet melody drift across the lake. It is the voice of a young boy singing.

> "I am a stag: of seven tines,
> I am a flood: across a plain,
> I am a wind: on a deep lake,
> I am a tear: the sun let fall,
> I am a hawk: above the cliff,
> I am a thorn: beneath the nail,
> I am a wonder: among the flowers."

Patrick is entranced. "Where does this singing come from?" he wonders.

He looks across the lake to the source and sees a large ancient standing stone. He rises to investigate. As he walks around the lake he sees the children gathered around the stone and Amergin singing. Patrick continues around the lake to greet the children.

When he approaches, the singing stops.

"We have been waiting for you," says Maebh. "Have you thought any more about the escape plan?"

Patrick stops and observes the gathering. Each young face is looking eagerly and expectantly up at him. He is aware of the sacrifice each of them will be making if he says yes and they decide to support him in his escape plan. They are waiting for an answer.

"I've decided to go ahead with the plan."

Maebh stands up and announces, "I'm right with you, Pat." The others follow suit. "We're all right with you, Pat," Maebh confirms.

"But you are risking your life by joining this plan!" exclaims Patrick.

"We are happy to do it for you, Pat," Maebh replies.

The others nod in agreement.

Maebh points to the ancient standing stone. It has a hole in the centre just big enough to put a hand through.

"This is the holestone," she comments. "In ancient times members of a clan who made a solemn agreement shook hands through the hole in this stone. I suggest we do the same."

So as the Song of Amergin is sung, each of the children step forward, shake Patrick's hand and swear allegiance to him and to his plan.

This simple ceremony continues until all but one of the children has sworn allegiance.   Then, after hesitating for a moment, Ossian steps up to the holestone and takes Patrick firmly by the hand.

"You too, Ossian! You too!"

After taking Ossian's hand and hearing him swear allegiance, Patrick is overcome with emotion. The children gather around him lovingly.

"We know how you feel," they say gently.

Envoi

Love heals and inspires.
We are inspired to sacrifice ourselves for the other's benefit.
We willingly put ourselves forward so the other will gain.
We offer ourselves willingly in service to the other.
Through that offering our broken relationships are healed
And we are bathed in the beauty of companionship.

Daylight is disappearing. Colours are blending into shades of grey. The water of the lake is still and peaceful. The swan glides gracefully across the still water, making ripples that fan on either side. Her white body stands out against the grey water. The moon emerges from behind cloud and then disappears.

Alone With The Swan

The children have left and Patrick sits alone on the shore of the Vanishing Lake. In this place, where everything begins and ends, he watches the moon appear and disappear as it is reflected in the lake's calm water. He is intrigued at the prospect of escaping to a new and different future.

"What will my future hold? Where will it take me?" he ponders.

His mind gradually turns from contemplating his future to remembering his past—the years he spent herding sheep on Slieve Miss. He remembers his capture, the rough boat trip and his enslavement.

"Those were tough times," he thinks. "My life appeared meaningless then."

He reflects on his life as a slave and feels it was an interesting life with many happy memories, the friendship with Conchubhar and his family, meeting the Druid, finding the buried treasure and the many good times he had with the forest children and his dog Tóir.

Lifting his eyes he gazes at the swan floating silently in the centre of the lake. The moon comes into view and in the increased brightness he thinks he glimpses light emanating from the swan. Then the moon disappears and the moment is gone.

"It cannot be," he thinks to himself. "I must be imagining things."

As Patrick observes, the swan glides closer to the bank where he sits. He senses a familiar question.

"Why are you here?" A deep longing follows this question. "I would love to know what it feels like to fly the way you do."

As he observes the swan he is drawn to think once more about the very different future that awaits. He wonders what it will be like. Patrick makes a decision.

"Whatever my future holds, I promise to love others who suffer and to help release them from bondage."

The swan draws nearer. Suddenly his heart opens and he is filled with joy. The joy is so great and so strong that he cannot contain it. He is overcome with a passionate desire to share this joy that has arisen in his breast. He wonders what can he do? How can he start?

Then the joy slowly subsides like a glimpse into another world—a world of passion, freedom and love. He rises to leave the Vanishing Lake and join Meabh at the Bréad River, but he leaves knowing that the time for his mission is at hand.

Envoi

Though my life may have seemed meaningless and pointless,
Love has rescued me.
By reaching out, by expressing love,
By expanding and extending love,
I have been led to the place where joy resides.
Now I am ready to give even more abundantly
With joy in my heart.

The outline of the hills can just be seen against the night sky. Invisible trees, stirred by a fresh breeze, rustle in the distance. Underfoot the long grass is soft and damp. The glow of distant flame lights a nearby hilltop.

The Devil's Chair

"What's that glow in the distance, Maebh?"

Patrick is walking over the hills as he returns to Slieve Miss from the Vanishing Lake.

"It must be a clan meeting. That's where King Miliucc has his throne; the Devil's Chair."

"Let's go and investigate, Maebh," says Patrick.

"Oh, should we? It'll be very dangerous to spy on them."

"Come on, Maebh. Let's see what they are up to."

Patrick and Maebh climb the hill in darkness. When they reach the hilltop, they see a meeting of the lords and noblemen of Dál Riaghada.

"Quick Meabh, let's crouch down behind this rock."

As they gaze out over the rock into the darkness, they see King Miliucc sitting in a hollow the shape of a chair cut out of bare rock.

"That's the Devil's Chair," whispers Maebh.

King Miliucc is giving a speech to the assembled gathering. Behind King Miliucc stand a line of warriors, each holding a yellow torch flame that flickers in the freezing wind. The gold on the noblemen's cloaks is sparkling in the yellow torchlight. Hunting dogs crouch at the noblemen's feet, their eyes picked out by the shimmering flame.

Patrick and Maebh listen in silence to King Miliucc's speech.

"Some slaves do not realise how lucky they are to have such a lenient Master. They have defied me. They do not work hard. They do not show respect. One even refused to swear allegiance to me."

"That's you, Pat," whispers Maebh.

"From now on, we are going to show these slaves who their real master is," King Miliucc continues. "I am making a decree that from today, if any slave is found away from the farm where he works, he will be killed instantly. There will be no exceptions. Do I make myself understood?"

The noblemen all nod in agreement. Patrick and Maebh look at one another in disbelief, then turn and creep down the hillside.

Both Maebh and Patrick continue on their way to Slieve Miss, a solemn silence between them. Then Meabh breaks the quiet, her voice trembling with fear,

"I'm really angry at King Miliucc. He's a real brute. Now all the slaves have virtually no freedoms left, and what about you, Pat? It's going to be even more difficult to escape."

Patrick eases Maebh's nervousness. He has a tone to his voice that surprises and reassures.

"Everything will work out, Maebh."

She notices that Patrick exudes a deep peace she had never seen in anyone else. This is because despite the dangers, Patrick feels a strong sense of protection. As they walk they feel the wind grow colder and colder. They decide to ask the children to help Patrick escape the next day.

Envoi

While others may fear threats
And respond with angry vilification.
I retain my integrity and my courage.
The compassion I feel for my abuser
Opens peace in my heart.
A peace that is present even in my direst moments.
A peace that comes because I know I am connected
To my destiny and my mission.
Feeling this connection I sense my personal power.

The trees bend and flex as the gale howls and roars. The road and wood-
land are one white carpet woven by driven snow. Even the sides of the trees
facing the wind are covered. Everything is a blur in this howling mael-
strom.

Escaping From King Miliucc

Patrick is battling his way through the winter gale along the Way Ó
Dheas that leads out of Dál Riaghada. The forest children are following
behind. The group have managed to travel almost to the border of the
kingdom without being challenged. The brooch is acting as a good disguise and none of the people they are meeting in the cold and snow suspect he is a slave. Now they are nearing the edge of Dál Riaghada and
Patrick's heart is starting to sing with the thought of freedom.

Then in the distance, through the howling blizzard, Patrick hears the
approach of horse's hooves. Maebh signals to the children and they run
to either side of the road and hide among the trees. Patrick is left to face
the horsemen alone. The sound of the horses increase until round the
bend come three warriors on horseback, one of whom Patrick recognises
as King Miliucc. King Miliucc also recognises him, despite his disguise.

"Slave. What are you doing leagues distance from your farm and why
are you wearing the Brooch of Loughinra, my king's brooch?"

Before Patrick can answer, a hail of stones comes flying out of the
woods and strike the two warriors accompanying King Miliucc. They
break left and right into the forest to Tóir and the children. Patrick
stands alone, facing the man who sat on the Devil's Chair. They both
look directly into each other's eyes.

"You defied me once, slave, but you will never defy me again," shouts
King Miliucc above the howling wind and snow and, balancing on his
horse, he reaches down and draws his long, twin bladed sword.

He holds the sword high above his head and prepares to strike.

The two men stand eyeball to eyeball. King Miliucc hesitates. He
notices that Patrick's eyes show no fear and are full of steely determination.

"Don't you realise slave, I can cut your head off and never blink an
eye."

Patrick replies with calm but determined resolution, "Don't you realise, King Miliucc, that I can have my head cut off and never blink an eye." King Miliucc hesitates further. He has never met a man who did not fear death.

Then a large stone comes spinning out of the trees and strikes King Miliucc on his helmet. He is momentarily dazed and drops his guard.

"Run, Pat, run," cry voices from the forest.

Patrick dodges past King Miliucc and sprints into the woods jinking between trees. As he runs he can hear King Miliucc turn and come after him on his horse. Patrick runs faster but sees he is leaving tell tale footprints in the snow. His mind begins to race as he thinks of ways of shaking off King Miliucc on his horse.

He runs on at speed deep into the dense forest where he weaves between closely spaced tree trunks that give him an advantage over the larger horse and rider. In the distance he sees a shallow river. He has an idea.

"If I run up the river I will no longer be leaving a trail in the snow."

Patrick sprints up the river, comes to a fork in the stream and goes left, later, at another fork, he breaks right and runs on further. Stopping for breath he listens for the sound of horses' hooves but hears only the wind in the trees. He realises he has shaken off King Miliucc and his two warriors and is relieved. He decides to follow the river through the dense woods to freedom and a new life.

Envoi

I do not fear death,
Therefore I fear no man.
Without fear no one can hold me.
No one can keep me in bondage.
By not fearing I am free to make my own way,
Despite setback's and despite challenges,
To a fresh start and a new beginning.

In the star studded sky, soft light from the full moon is casting shadows across the forest floor. The air is crisp and clear. Only the sound of running water disturbs the quiet as the dark stream flows and spills around boulders.

Life's Mission Revealed

Patrick is trudging through the snow alongside the stream that had disguised his escape. He has mixed feelings, lost and alone at having left his friends, and joy at having broken free. His mind turns to the forest children, who had risked their lives to help him and he wonders where they are now. Full of gratitude and admiration for their bravery in distracting the warriors, he asks that they will be protected.

His thoughts turn toward his destiny.

"I am free—but how can I realise my mission?" he ponders.

Patrick continues to follow the stream's twisting path higher into the depths of the woods. On he journeys, deeper and deeper into the dark, snow-covered forest. Then, just as he is feeling totally lost, he climbs a bank and there before him is the Vanishing Lake. This place, where everything begins and ends, is sparkling in moonlight. Immediately he is filled with a deep sense of security.

Tired, he rests against the trunk of an old, gnarled oak tree. He recalls his time with Conchubhar and his family. Memories emerge of the period he spent herding sheep, visiting King Miliucc's ring fort, dancing around the Fairy Tree, meeting Mythendical The Druid, making the vow of love with the children and finding buried treasure. Looking down at the gold glinting on his tunic, a gentle smile crosses Patrick's face as he reflects on how he, a mere slave, came to be wearing the king's brooch. Leaning back against the tree, he wonders where his life will lead now.

He gazes across the lake's still, dark water to the opposite bank, where shadows from the moon's gentle light follow the undulations of the forest floor. Even the twigs of each tree are visible. Overhead the stars twinkle in the black night sky. Patrick dips his hands in the still lake and drinks the pure clear water.

As he drinks his fill while gazing at this enchanted scene, he becomes lighter and lighter. Slowly he feels his awareness transcend the confines of his body. Suddenly the snow-covered scene becomes alive with enchantment. He sees moonlight glinting in icicles that hang from the trees. The snow sparkles like a forest of diamonds, as the moon reflects off its pure white surface. A gentle puff of wind touches his cheek. He follows the breeze as it creates a faint ripple on the lake's calm water. The lake, the trees, the snow and the moonlight create a delicate beauty that is almost painful.

His mind is pure and clear like the water in the lake. Walking around the shore, Patrick moves with the flowing grace of a swan on water. Time stands still in this blossoming of eternal presence. Sitting on the bank, he rests his back against the holestone where he made the vow of love with the children. Unperturbed by the snow's icy coldness, he lets his legs dangle over the bank.

"So I am not my body," he whispers, a curious wonder held within that question. "Who am I?" he asks, his delicate, softly spoken words drifting across the still, empty lake.

As he asks this question, Patrick hears the call of the slaves who are starting their day's toil in the far distance. These mournful, anguished cries penetrate to the very depths of his heart causing him to wince with pain.

Suddenly Patrick notices wet stones sparkling on the lakeshore. He realises that water is beginning to drain from the lake. Then from behind rushes, the swan glides elegantly into the still water. Patrick is fascinated by her smooth passage.

"Why are you here?" he asks once again. "I'd love to know what it feels like to fly the way you do," he ponders, offering his thoughts into the lake's serene silence.

He waits silently, as if expecting a response.

In the clear, soft moonlight, he notices that the swan is surrounded by ethereal pink light that extends to fill the lake and then, looking upwards, he sees blue light beyond the pink, reaching to fill the entire horizon. Patrick watches in amazement as the swan draws close to the bank where he is sitting, and glides right up to him. They gaze lovingly into each other's eyes. In that gaze Patrick senses that the swan knows both his past and his future. A great love bursts forth in his heart.

Immersed in that love he feels completely at One. Patrick hears a delicate melody reverberating around the lake. Turning his head toward the horizon he sees lines of mauve radiate from a shining silver sun. Clouds are being touched by fiery pink, amid this wind of light. The emerging fiery pink heralds the days might, revealing the brown, green and white of the snow filled forest.

"I have become the world," he gasps.

The swan speaks:

> "I am the light of the world, whoever follows me will have the light of life and will never walk in darkness. No one can enter the Kingdom of God unless he is born of water and the Spirit. Believe in God and believe also in me. I am the way, the truth, and the life; no one goes to the Father except by me. Remain united to me, and I will remain united to you. If you remain in me and my words remain in you, then you will ask for anything you wish, and you shall have it. I will love you just as my father loves me; remain in my love. Take care of my sheep."[2]

As the Swan unfolds her wings and flaps in preparation for flight Patrick feels each wing beat inside his breast. Overwhelmed with joy he remembers the call of the slaves, and, raising his hands in exaltation, cries, "I want to give myself to the world!"

The Swan turns and speaks once more.

"Your ship is waiting."

NOTES

1. From The Song of Amergin http://www.klammeraffe.org/~brandy/hexen/amergin.html

2. Christ's words from the Gospel According To John

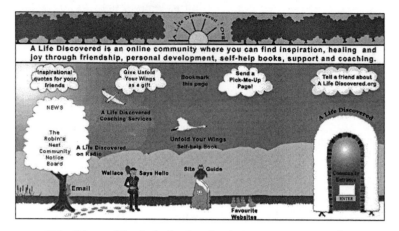

A Life Discovered is an online community where you can find inspiration, healing and joy through friendship, personal development, self-help books, support and coaching.

Inspirational quotes for your friends

Give Unfold Your Wings as a gift

Bookmark this page

Send a Pick-Me-Up Page!

Tell a friend about A Life Discovered.org

NEWS

A Life Discovered Coaching Services

The Robin's Nest Community Notice Board

A Life Discovered on Radio

Unfold Your Wings Self-help Book

A Life Discovered

Wallace Says Hello

Site Guide

Community Entrance

ENTER

Email

Favourite Websites

Would you like help in developing your inner guidance?

If so, visit *www.alifediscovered.org*
Membership is free to anyone who has bought
Unfold Your Wings and Watch Life Take Off

This online healing community offers you:

• A Confidential Coaching Room
Where you can receive one to one coaching by email from the author. He will give you personal instruction in using inner guidance to solve your problems.

• A Coaching Facility
Where you can teach yourself how to tune into inner guidance by using a tutorial that responds to your needs.

• Sharing Your Inner Guidance
Where you can share what you are learning with a close personal friend.

• The Unfold Your Wings Book Club
Where you can share your understanding of inner guidance with a group of friends.

• The Unfold Your Wings Workshop
Where you can learn how to give evening classes on inner guidance
to your local woman's group, church group, or community centre.

• The New Horizons Social Club
Where you can download a manual that shows you how to
start a social club for people interested in personal development.

• The Unfold Your Wings Discussion Forum
Where you can exchange views, receive support
and make friends with other readers worldwide.

• Book Ordering Service
Where you can order additional copies of
Unfold Your Wings and Watch Life Take Off for your friends.

Your Pass Code is **star**

Enter through the archway in the home page.
Visit the home page at *www.alifediscovered.org*
Perhaps I'll meet you there!

Kind Regards,
Wallace

To Order More Copies of
Unfold Your Wings and Watch Life Take Off

Individual Customers
Visit the book's supporting website at *www.alifediscovered.org*
    Or
Order by phone from Booksurge.
Ring 001 if outside the USA then 866 308 6235 (this number is toll free within the USA)
Ring 001 if outside the USA then 843-579-0000 (this number is not toll free)
    Or
Type the title, author or ISBN 1-59457-582-7
into the search facility of the following websites
www.booksurge.com
www.amazon.com
www.barnesandnoble.com
www.alibris.com
www.booksinprint.com
www.globalbooksinprint.com
www.bruna.nl

Wholesalers, Distributors, Shops and Libraries
You can set up a wholesale account for international orders at
www.booksurgedirect.com
RR Bowker's www.booksinprint.com
www.globalbooksinprint.com
www.whitaker.co.uk for UK orders
Baker and Taylor www.btol.com for USA orders

"Life is a challenge, meet it.
Life is a dream, realise it.
Life is a game, play it
Life is love, enjoy it"
—Sri Sathya Sai Baba

I wish to thank my teacher, mentor and guide, Sri Sathya Sai Baba, whose teachings and life of self-less service have inspired me to write this book and create the "A Life Discovered" website.

Suggested Reading

Sai Baba, The Embodiment of Love
Peggy Mason and Ron Laing

Life, Death and Liberation
Sai Baba

Meditation, Man Perfection in God Satisfaction
Sri Chinmoy